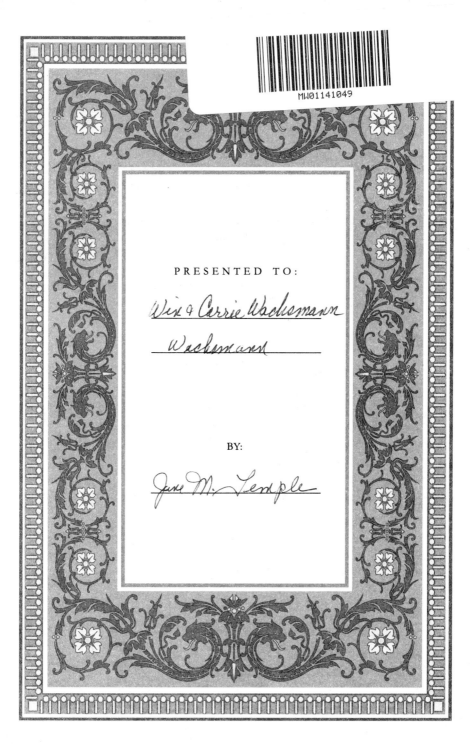

PRESENTED TO:

Wix & Carrie Wachsmann

Wachsmann

BY:

Jane M. Temple

O Come, Let Us Adore Him !

Dr. June M. Temple

Shandal Publishers, Sankt-Petersburg, Russia

O COME, LET US ADORE HIM!

Published by Shandal Publishing,
P.O. Box 614, St. Petersburg, 197198, Russia
e-mail: julia@shandal.ru

Designed by Zhury Svetlana

Compiled by Dr. June M. Temple
C325 1909 Salton Rd.
Abbotsford, B.C. V2S 5B6
e-mail jmt@rapidnet.net

ISBN: 5-93925-058-0

Printed in Russia

CONTENTS

With Thankfulness in my heart
to my brothers in Christ,
Gene Parkins and Win Wachsmann,
for the hours they have spent
to make the publication
of this yearly Devotional possible.

COME LET US ADORE HIM!

Do you feel something is missing in your prayer life? If so, have you taken the time to ADORE God?

What is the meaning of ADORE?

Webster claims the noun ADORATION, or the verb ADORE means to worship with profound reverence, or the act of paying honor to the Divine Being; the worship paid to God with exalted thoughts, with prayer and with thanksgiving.

One method of ADORING God, and the method employed in this book, is to contemplate and meditate on Bible verses and other material dealing with who God is. Then praise the Almighty for what you learned about Him. After the ADORATION go on with Confession, Thanksgiving and Supplication.

January

THE GOD OF BEAUTY

BEAUTY — A gathering of perfection by which an object appears pleasing to the eye. Any particular thing which is beautiful and pleasing. (Webster)

*O*ne thing I have desired of the Lord, that will I seek: That I may dwell in the house of the Lord all the days of my life, to behold the BEAUTY of the Lord, and to inquire in His temple.

Psalm 27:4 (New American Standard)

*G*ive to the Lord the glory due His name; bring an offering, and come before Him. Oh, worship the Lord in the BEAUTY of holiness.

1 Chronicles 16:29 (New King James)

*M*y God, how wonderful Thou art,
Thy majesty how bright,
How BEAUTIFUL Thy mercy seat,
In depths of burning light.

How wonderful, how BEAUTIFUL
The sight of Thee must be
Thine endless wisdom, boundless power
And awesome purity.

(by Frederick William Faber)

Begin your prayer time with adoration and praising God for His BEAUTY.

THE GOD OF BEAUTY

BEAUTY Synonyms — BEAUTIFUL (Webster) Loveliness, grace, fairness, fine, handsome, elegant, seemliness, picturesqueness.

The Mighty One, God, the Lord, speaks and summons the earth from the rising of the sun to the place where it sets. From Zion, perfect in BEAUTY, God shines forth.

Psalm 50:1 & 2 (NIV)

Give unto the Lord the glory due unto his name; bring an offering, and come into His courts. O worship the Lord in the BEAUTY of holiness; fear before Him, all the earth.

Psalm 96:8 & 9 (King James)

> Majestic sweetness sits enthroned
> Upon the Savior's brow;
> His head with radiant glories crowned
> His lips with grace o'erflow
>
> No mortal can with Him compare,
> Among the sons of men;
> FAIRER is He than all the fair
> Who fill the heavenly train
>
> *(by Samuel Stennett)*

Begin your prayer time with adoration and praises to God for His BEAUTY.

THE GOD OF BEAUTY

FAIR — Used in the Bible to mean "good", unspotted, attractive or beautiful, making a fine display. (Today's Dictionary of the Bible)

Great is the Eternal, loudly to be praised within the city of our God, upon His sacred hill. High and FAIR on the northern slope, the joy of all the world, the hill of Sion lies, the city of the great King.

Psalm 48:1 & 2 (Moffatt)

Great is the Lord, and greatly to be praised; He is to be feared above all Gods. For the idols of the peoples are idols; but the Lord made the heavens. Honor and majesty are before Him; strength and BEAUTY are in his sanctuary.

Psalm 96:4 & 6 (Revised Standard Version)

> FAIREST Lord Jesus! Ruler of all nature
> O Thou of God and man the Son!
> Thee will I cherish, Thee will I honor,
> Thou my soul's glory, joy and crown
>
> FAIR are the meadows, FAIRER still the woodlands,
> Robed in the blooming garb of spring:
> Jesus is FAIRER, Jesus is purer,
> Who makes the woeful heart to sing.
>
> *(from Munster Gesangbuch)*

Begin your prayer time with adoration and praises to God for His BEAUTY.

THE GOD OF BEAUTY

*A*nd when he had consulted with the people, he appointed those who should sing to the Lord, and who should praise the BEAUTY of holiness, as they went out before the army and were saying: "Praise the Lord, For His mercy endures forever."

2 Chronicles 20 (NKJ)

*G*ive unto the Lord the glory due his name; worship the Lord in the BEAUTY of holiness.

Psalm 29:2 (KJ)

*H*onor and majesty are before Him strength and BEAUTY are in His sanctuary.

Psalm 96:6 (RSV)

*I*n that day the Lord Almighty will be a glorious crown, a BEAUTIFUL wreath for the remnant of His people. He will be a Spirit of justice to him who sits in judgment, a source of strength to those who turn back the battle at the gate.

Isaiah 28:5 & 6 (NIV)

*B*EAUTIFUL Saviour!
Lord of the nations
Son of God and Son of Man!
Glory and honor,
Praise and adoration
Now and forever more be Thine!

(Author unknown)

Begin your prayer time with adoration and praises to God for His BEAUTY.

THE GOD OF BEAUTY
WHO PROVIDES BEAUTIFUL THINGS FOR US TO SEE

*W*hat does the worker gain from his toil? I have seen the burden God has laid on men. He has made everything BEAUTIFUL in its time. He has also put eternity in the hearts of men.

Ecclesiastics 3:9-11a (NIV)

*I*n that day shall the branch of the Lord be BEAUTIFUL and glorious, and the fruit of the earth shall be excellent and comely for them that are escaped of Israel.

Isaiah 4:2 (KJ)

*H*ow LOVELY is your tabernacle. O Lord of hosts My soul longs, yes, even faints for the courts of the Lord; my heart and my flesh cry out for the living God.

Psalm 84:1 (NKJ)

> *F*AIREST of all the earth beside,
> Chiefest of all unto Thy bride,
> Fullness Divine in Thee I see,
> BEAUTIFUL Man of Calvary!
> That man of Calvary has won my heart from me,
> And died to set me free, blest Man of Calvary!
>
> *(by M. P. Ferguson)*

Begin your prayer time with adoring the God of BEAUTY and thanking Him for the beauty He provides around us.

THE GOD OF BEAUTY
WHO PROVIDES BEAUTIFUL THINGS FOR US TO SEE

Think about the stars, the moon, the sunshine, the lakes and seas.

God said, "Let there be light," and there was light. God saw that the light was good, and He separated the light from the darkness.

Genesis 1:3 & 4 (Moffatt)

Then God said, "Let the earth sprout vegetation, plants yielding seed, and fruit trees bearing fruit after their own kind, with seed in them, on the earth: and it was so."

Genesis 1:11 (NAS)

God created great sea serpents and every kind of living creature with which the waters team, and every kind of winged creature. God saw that it was good.

Genesis 1:21 (NJB)

And God said, "Let the land produce living creatures according to their kinds: livestock, creatures that move along the ground, and wild animals, each according to its kind. And it was so. God made the wild animals according to their kinds, the livestock according to their kinds, and all the creatures that move along the ground according to their kinds. And God saw that it was good.

Genesis 1:24 & 25 (NIV)

For the BEAUTY of the earth, for the glory of the skies,
For the love which from our birth over and around us lies:
Christ our God to Thee we raise this our song of grateful praise.
For the wonder of each hour of the day and of the night,
Hill and vale and tree and flower, sun and moon and stars of light,
Christ our God to Thee we raise this our song of grateful praise.

(by Folliott S. Pierpoint)

Begin your prayer time with adoration of the God of BEAUTY and thanking Him for the BEAUTY He provides around us.

January 7

THE GOD OF ABUNDANCE

ABUNDANCE — Great plenty; an overflowing quantity; ample sufficiency; fullness; overflowing; fully sufficient. (Webster)

I know that You are a gracious and merciful God, slow to anger and ABUNDANT in lovingkindness, One who relents from doing harm.

Jonah 4:2b (NKJ)

*B*ut Thou, O Lord, art a God merciful and gracious, slow to anger and ABUNDANT in lovingkindness and truth.

Psalm 86:15 (NAS)

*A*nd the grace of our Lord was exceedingly ABUNDANT, with faith and love which are in Christ Jesus.

1 Timothy 1:14 (NKJ)

> *N*ow thank we all our God
> With hearts and hands and voices,
> Who wondrous things hath done,
> In whom this world rejoices;
> Who from our mothers' arms
> Hath blessed us on our way
> With COUNTLESS gifts of love,
> And still is ours today.
>
> *(by Martin Rinkart)*

Begin your prayer time adoring God for His ABUNDANCE.

THE GOD OF ABUNDANCE

ABUNDANCE synonyms—plenteousness, plenty, riches, affluence, copiousness, wealth, ample. (Webster)

*B*ehold, I will bring to it health and healing, and I will heal them and reveal to them ABUNDANCE of prosperity and security.

Jeremiah 33:6 (RSV)

A little longer, and the godless will be gone; look in his haunts, and he is there no more! The land will be left to the humble, to enjoy PLENTEOUS PROSPERITY.

Psalm 37:10 & 11 (Moffatt)

*C*ome, all you who are thirsty, come to the waters; and you who have no money, come, buy and eat! Come buy wine and milk without money or cost. Why spend money on that which is not bread, and your labor on what does not satisfy? Listen to Me, and eat what is good, and your soul will delight on the RICHEST of fare.

Isaiah 55:1 & 2 (NIV)

*F*rom war's alarms, from deadly pestilence,
Be Thy strong arm our ever sure defense;
Thy true religion in our hearts increase,
Thy BOUNTEOUS goodness, nourish us in peace.

Refresh Thy people on their toil-some way,
Lead us from night to never ending day;
Fill all our lives with love and grace divine,
And glory, laud, and praise be ever Thine.

(by Daniel C. Roberts)

Begin your prayer time adoring God for His ABUNDANCE.

THE GOD OF ABUNDANCE

*Y*ours, O Lord, is the greatness and the power and the glory and the majesty and the splendor, for everything in heaven and earth is yours. Yours, O Lord, is the kingdom; which You are exalted as head over all. WEALTH and honor come from You; You are the ruler of all things. In Your hands are strength and power to exalt and give strength to all.

1 Chronicles 29:11 & 12 (NIV)

*T*he reward of humility and the reverent and worshipful fear of the Lord is RICHES and honor and life.

Proverbs 22:4 (Amplified Version)

*H*e called on the name of Yahweh. Yahweh passed before him and proclaimed, Yahweh, Yahweh, a God of tenderness and compassion, slow to anger, RICH in kindness and faithfulness.

Exodus 46:6 (JB)

> *W*hen all Thy mercies, O my God,
> My rising soul surveys,
> Transported with the view,
> I'm lost in wonder, love and praise
>
> UNNUMBERED comforts to my soul
> Thy tender care bestowed,
> Before my infant heart conceived
> From whom those comforts flowed
>
> *(by Joseph Addison)*

Begin your prayer time adoring God for His ABUNDANCE.

THE GOD OF ABUNDANCE

*T*he thief cometh not, but for to steal, and to kill, and to destroy: I am come that they might have life, and that they might have it more ABUNDANTLY.

John 10:10 (KJ)

*D*ear friends, God the Father chose you long ago and knew you would become His children. And the Holy Spirit has been at work in your hearts, cleansing you with the blood of Jesus Christ and making you to please Him. May God bless you RICHLY and grant you increasing freedom from all anxiety and fear.

1 Peter 1:2 & 3 (LB)

*N*ow to Him, who is able with the power that works within us, to do everything IMMEASURABLY far beyond what we pray or think of, to Him be glory in the church and in Christ Jesus through all generations for ever and ever.

Ephesians 3:20 & 21 (Berkeley Version)

*N*ot a burden we bear,
Not a sorrow we share
But our toil He doth RICHLY repay;
Not a grief nor a loss

Not a frown nor a cross
But is blest if we trust and obey.
Trust and obey, for there's no other way
To be happy in Jesus but to trust and obey.

(by John H. Sammis)

Begin your prayer time adoring God for His ABUNDANCE.

THE GOD OF ABUNDANCE

For if, because of one man's trespass (lapse, offense) death reigned through that one, much more surely will those who receive (God's) OVERFLOWING grace (unmerited favor) and the free gift of righteousness (putting them into right standing with Himself) reign as kings in life through the One, Jesus Christ, The Messiah, the Anointed One.

Romans 5:17 (Amplified)

Thus God, determining to show more ABUNDANTLY to the heirs of promise the immutability of His counsel, confirmed it by an oath, that by two immutable things in which it is impossible for God to lie, we might have strong consolation, who have fled for refuge to lay hold of the hope set before us.

Hebrews 6:17 & 18 (NKJ)

To me, who am less than the least of all God's people, He has granted of His grace the privilege of proclaiming to the Gentiles the good news of the unfathomable RICHES of Christ.

Ephesians 3:8 (New English Bible)

> Gracious God, we worship thee,
> Reverently we bow the knee;
> Jesus Christ our only plea:
> Father we adore Thee.
>
> Vast the love—how deep, how wide
> In the gift of Him who died;
> Great the RICHES of Thy grace:
> Father we adore Thee.
>
> *(by S. Trevor Francis)*

Begin your prayer time adoring God for His ABUNDANCE.

THE GOD OF ABUNDANCE

*B*ut God's mercy is so RICH, and His love for us is so great, that while we were spiritually dead in our disobedience he brought us to life in Christ; it is by God's grace that you have been saved. And in union with Christ Jesus He raised us up to rule with Him in the heavenly world. He did this to demonstrate for all time to come the ABUNDANT RICHES of His grace in the love He showed us in Christ Jesus. For it is by God's grace that you have been saved through faith.

Ephesians 2:4-9 (Good News)

*A*nd I saw, and I heard a voice of many angels who encircled the throne and a voice of the living beings and of the elders and their number was ten thousand times ten thousand and thousands of thousands—saying with a great voice, Worthy is the Lamb who has been slain to receive power and RICHES and wisdom and might and honor and glory and eulogy.

Revelation 5:11 & 12 (Wuest)

*W*hat RICH eternal bursts of praise
Shall fill your courts through endless days,
When time shall cease to be!
Around that throne the notes shall swell,
As each redeemed one joins to tell
Thy love so vast and free

Our joy unhindered then with Thee,
Our eyes undimmed Thy glory see,
Whilst worthy praise we give
Through that eternal cloudless day,
Our burning Hearts with rapture say,
He died that we might live.

(by G. W. Frazer)

Begin your prayer time adoring God for His ABUNDANCE.

THE GOD OF ABUNDANCE

*M*oreover, brethren, we make known to you the grace of God bestowed on the churches of Macedonia: that in a great ABUNDANCE of their joy and their deep poverty abounded in the RICHES of their liberality.

2 Corinthians 8:1 & 2 (NKJ)

*H*ow excellent is Thy lovingkindness, O God! Therefore the children of men put their trust under the shadow of Thy wings. They shall be ABUNDANTLY satisfied with the FATNESS of Thy house; and Thou shalt make them drink of the river of Thy pleasures.

Psalm 36:7 & 8 (KJ)

*W*hen the kindness and generosity of God our Saviour dawned upon the world, then, not for any good deeds of our own, but because he was merciful, he saved us through the water of rebirth and the renewing power of the Holy Spirit. For he sent down the Spirit upon us PLENTIFULLY through Jesus Christ our Saviour, so that, justified by his grace, we might in hope become heirs to eternal life. These are words you may trust.

Titus 3:3-8 (NEB)

*T*hy love divine hath lead us in the past,
In this free land by Thee our lot is cast;
Be Thou our Ruler, Guardian, Guide and Stay,
Thy Word our law, Thy paths our chosen way.

From wars alarms, from deadly pestilence,
Be Thy strong arm our ever sure defense;
Thy true religion in our hearts increase,
Thy BOUNTEOUS goodness nourish us in peace.

(by Daniel C. Roberts)

Begin your prayer time adoring God for His ABUNDANCE.

THE ABIDING GOD

ABIDE—To rest, or dwell. To tarry or stay. To remain; to continue. To wait for. (Webster)

O Lord, who may ABIDE in Thy tent?
Who may DWELL on Thy holy Hill?
He who walks with integrity,
and works righteousness, and speaks truth in his heart.
He does not slander with his tongue,
nor does evil to his neighbor,
nor takes up a reproach against his friend;
in whose eyes a reprobate is despised,
but who honors those who fear the Lord;
he swears to his own hurt,
and does not change;
he does not put out money at interest,
nor does he take a bribe against the innocent.
He who does these things will never be shaken.

Psalm 15 (NAS)

He who DWELLS in the secret place of the Most High shall ABIDE under the shadow of the Almighty.

Psalm 91:1 (NKJ)

So Jesus addressed the Jews who had believed him, saying, "If you ABIDE by what I say, you are really disciples of mine: you will understand the truth, and the truth will set you free."

John 8:31 & 32 (Moffatt)

Walk in the light! So shalt thou know that fellowship of love
His Spirit only can bestow who reigns in light above.
Walk in the light! And thou shalt find thy heart made truly His,
Who DWELLS in cloudless light enshrined, in whom no darkness is.

Walk in the Light! And thou shalt own thy darkness passed away,
Because that light hath on thee shone in which is perfect day.
Walk in the light! Thy path shall be a path, though thorny, bright;
For God, by grace, shall DWELL in thee, and God Himself is light.

(by Bernard Barton)

Begin your prayer time adoring the God who ABIDES in heaven and on earth.

THE GOD WHO ABIDES

ABIDE synonyms—inhabit, dwell, live, lodge, remain, rest, sojourn, stay, tarry, wait.

*H*e shall ABIDE before God forever: O prepare mercy and truth, which may preserve him.

Psalm 61:7 (KJ)

*R*EMAIN in me, and I will REMAIN in you. A branch cannot produce fruit alone but must REMAIN in the vine. In the same way, you cannot produce fruit alone, but must REMAIN in me.

John 15:4 (New Century Bible)

*A*nd now these three REMAIN: faith, hope and love. But the greatest of these is love.

1 Corinthians 13:13 (NIV)

*A*BIDE with me—fast falls the eventide,
The darkness deepens—Lord with me ABIDE;
When other helpers fail and comforts flee,
Help of the helpless, O ABIDE with me!

Swift to its close ebbs out life's little day,
Earth's joys grow dim, its glories pass away;
Change and decay in all around I see,
O Thou who changest not, ABIDE with me!

(by John Newton)

Begin you prayer time adoring the God who ABIDES with you.

THE ABIDING GOD

If you love me, obey me; and I will ask the Father and He will give you another Comforter, and he will NEVER LEAVE you.

John 14:15 & 16 (Living Bible)

And a slave does not ABIDE in the house forever, but a son ABIDES forever.

John 8:35 (NKJ)

If you REMAIN in me and my words REMAIN in you, you may ask what you will and you shall get it.

John 15:7 (NJB)

I love you just as the Father loves me; REMAIN in my love.

John 15:9 (Good News)

I need Thy presence every passing hour
What but Thy grace can foil the tempters power?
Who like Thyself my guide and stay can be?
Through cloud and sunshine, O ABIDE with me.

Hold Thou Thy word before my closing eyes,
Shine through the gloom and point me to the skies;
Heaven's morning breaks and earth's vain shadows flee
In life, in death, O Lord, ABIDE with me

(by John Newton)

Begin your prayer time adoring and glorifying the God who ABIDES.

THE ABIDING GOD

*W*hoever possesses the world's resources and notices that his brother suffers need and then locks his deep sympathies away from him, how is the love of God LODGING in him?

1 John 3:17 (Berkeley)

*N*o man has at any time (yet) seen God. But if we love one another, God ABIDES (LIVES and REMAINS) in us and His love (that love which is essentially His) is brought to completion—to its full maturity, runs its full course, is perfected—in us! By this we come to know (perceive, recognize and understand) that we ABIDE (LIVE and REMAIN) in Him and He in us; because He has given (imparted) to us of His (Holy) Spirit.

1 John 4:12 & 13 (Amplified)

*T*hose who trust in the Lord are as Mount Zion, which cannot be moved, but ABIDES forever.

Psalm 125:1 (NAS)

*Y*ou have been born anew, not of mortal parentage but of immortal, through the living and ENDURING word of God. For (as Scripture says) "All mortals are like grass; All their splendor like the flower of the field; The grass withers, the flower falls; but the word of God ENDURES for evermore."

1 Peter 1:23-25 (NEB)

*S*un of my soul, Thou Saviour dear,
It is not night if Thou be near;
O may no earth-born cloud arise
To hide Thee from Thy servant's eyes.

ABIDE with me from morn till eve,
For without Thee I cannot live;
ABIDE with me when night is nigh
For without Thee I dare not die.

(by John Keble)

Begin you prayer time adoring the ABIDING God.

THE ABIDING GOD

*A*nd the world is being caused to pass away, and its passionate desire. But the one who keeps on habitually doing the will of God ABIDES forever.

1 John 2:17 (Wuest)

*W*e know we have crossed the frontier from death to life because we love our brothers. The man without love for his brother is living in death already. The man who actively hates his brother is a potential murderer, and you will readily see that the eternal life of God cannot LIVE in the heart of a murderer.

1 John 5:14 & 15 (Phillips)

I will lie down and sleep in peace, for you alone, O Lord make me DWELL in safety.

Psalm 4:8 (NIV)

*A*ll nations he has created from a common origin to DWELL all over the earth, fixing their allotted periods and the boundaries of the ABODES, meaning them to seek for God on the chance they find him as the grope for him. Though indeed he is close to each one of us, for it is in him that we LIVE and move and exist

Acts 17:26-28a (Moffatt)

*C*ome, ye thankful people, come—Raise the song of harvest home:
All is safely gathered in ere the winter storms begin.
God, our Maker, doth provide for our wants to be supplied:
Come, ye thankful people, come—raise the song of harvest home.

Even so, Lord, quickly come to Thy final harvest home:
Gather Thou Thy people in, free from sorrow, free from sin;
There, forever purified, in Thy presence to ABIDE:
Come, with all Thine angels, come—raise the glorious harvest home.

(by Henry Alford)

Begin your prayer time with adoration and praises to the ABIDING God.

THE ABIDING GOD

*O*ne thing I have desired of the Lord, That will I seek: That I may DWELL in the house of the Lord all the days of my life, To behold the beauty of the Lord, And to inquire in His temple.

Psalm 27:4 (NKJ)

*Y*ou, however, are controlled not by the sinful nature but by the Spirit, if the Spirit of God LIVES in you. And if anyone does not have the Spirit of Christ, he does not belong to Christ. But if Christ is in you, your body is dead because of sin, yet your spirit is alive because of righteousness. And if the Spirit of him who raised Jesus from the dead is LIVING in you, he who raised Christ from the dead will also give life to your mortal bodies through his Spirit, who LIVES in you.

Romans 8:9-11 (NIV)

I ask God, from the wealth of his glory, to give you power through his Spirit to be strong in your inner selves, and that Christ will make his HOME in your hearts.

Ephesians 6:16 & 17 (Good News)

*T*hen I saw a new heaven and a new earth. The first heaven and the first earth had disappeared, and there was no sea anymore. And I saw the holy city, the new Jerusalem, coming down out of heaven from God. It was prepared like a bride dressed for her husband. And I heard a loud voice from the throne, saying, "Now God's presence is with people, and he will LIVE with them, and they will be his people. God himself will be with them and will be their God.

Revelation 21:1-3 (New Century Version)

O Jesus, Friend unfailing, how dear Thou art to me!
Are cares or fears assailing? I find my strength in Thee.
Why should my feet grow weary of this my pilgrim way?
Rough though the path and dreary, it ends in perfect day.

O worldly pomp and glory, your charms are spread in vain!
I've heard a sweeter story, I've found a truer gain.
Where Christ a place prepareth, there is my loved ABODE;
There shall I gaze on Jesus: There shall I DWELL with God.

(by Samuel Kuster)

Adore God for ABIDING in us and allowing us to ABIDE in Him.

THE GOD OF AUTHORITY

AUTHORITY—Legal power, or a right to command or to act (Webster)

When Jesus finished his speech, the crowds were astounded at his teaching; for he taught them like an AUTHORITY, not like their own scribes.

Matthew 7:28 & 29 (Moffatt)

As Jesus approached them, He said, All AUTHORITY in heaven and on earth has been given Me.

Matthew 28:18 (Berkeley)

For even as the Father has life in Himself and is self-existent, so He has given to the Son to have life in Himself and be self-existent. And He has given Him AUTHORITY and granted Him power to execute (exercise, practice) judgment, because He is a son of man (very man).

John 5:26 & 27 (Amplified)

I sing the mighty POWER of God that made the mountains rise,
That spread the flowing seas abroad and built the lofty skies.
I sing the wisdom that ordained the sun to rule the day;
The moon shines full at His command, and all the stars obey.

There's not a plant of flower below but makes Thy glories known;
And clouds arise and tempests blow by order from Thy throne;
While all that borrows life from Thee Is ever in Thy care,
And everywhere that man can be, Thou, God, art present there.

(by Isaac Watts)

Begin your prayer time adoring God for His AUTHORITY.

THE GOD OF AUTHORITY

■ AUTHORITY synonyms—Ascendancy, dominion, rule, influence, force, power, command, sovereign, sway, control. (Webster)

Thy right hand, O Lord, is majestic in POWER, Thy right hand, O Lord shatters the enemy.

Exodus 15:6 (NAS)

God is my strength and POWER: and he maketh my way perfect.

2 Samuel 22:33 (KJ)

After these words Jesus looked up to heaven and said: "Father, the hour has come. Glorify thy Son, that the son may glorify thee. For thou hast made him SOVEREIGN over all mankind, to give eternal life to all whom thou hast given him.

John 17:1 & 2 (NEB)

All hail the POWER of Jesus name! Let angels prostrate fall;
Bring forth the royal diadem, and crown Him Lord of all

Ye chosen seed of Israel's race, ye ransomed from the fall,
Hail Him who saves you by His grace, and crown Him Lord of all.

Let every kindred, every tribe, on this terrestrial ball,
To Him all majesty ascribe, and crown Him Lord of all.

O that with yonder sacred throng we at his feet may fall!
We'll join the everlasting song, and crown Him Lord of all.

(by Edward Perronet)

Begin you prayer time adoring God for His AUTHORITY.

THE GOD OF AUTHORITY

*A*ccept our praise, O Lord, for all your glorious POWER. We will write songs to celebrate your mighty acts.

Psalm 21:13 (Paraphrased)

*B*ut I will sing of Your mighty strength and POWER; yes, I will sing aloud of Your mercy and loving-kindness in the morning; for You have been to me a defense—a fortress and a high tower—and a refuge in the day of distress.

Psalm 59:16 (Amplified)

*J*esus said to them, "The Father is the only One who has the AUTHORITY to decide dates and times. These things are not for you to know. But when the Holy Spirit comes to you, you will receive POWER. You will be my witnesses in Jerusalem, in all Judea, in Samaria, and in every part of the world.

Acts 1:7 & 8 (NCV)

*E*very Christian ought to obey the civil authorities, for all legitimate authority is derived from God's AUTHORITY, and the existing authority is appointed under God.

Romans 13:1 (Phillips)

*B*reak forth and sing the song of "Glory to the Lamb!"
Wake every heart and every tongue, to praise the Saviour's name.
Sing of His dying love; sing of His rising POWER;
Sing how He intercedes above for those whose sins He bore.

Soon shall we hear Him say, "ye ransomed pilgrims come;"
Soon will He call us hence away, and take us to His home.
Then shall each raptured tongue, His fullest praise proclaim;
And sweeter voices wake the song Of "Glory to the Lamb!"

Begin your prayer time praising the God of AUTHORITY.

THE GOD OF AUTHORITY

*B*ut God draws the mighty away with His POWER; He rises up, but no man is sure of life. DOMINION and fear belong to Him; He makes peace in His high places.

Job 24:22 & Job 25:2 (NKJ)

*Y*our kingdom is an everlasting kingdom, and your DOMINION endures through all generations. The Lord is faithful to all his promises and loving toward all he has made.

Psalm 145:13 (NIV)

*A*nd the God of all grace, who called you into his eternal glory in Christ, will himself, after your brief suffering, restore, establish, and strengthen you on a firm foundation. He holds DOMINION for ever and ever.

1 Peter 5:10 & 11 (NEB)

*T*o Him who loves us and has freed us from our sins by His own blood, and has made us into royalty, into priests of God, even His Father, to Him be the majesty and the DOMINION for ever and ever. Amen.

Revelation 1:6 (Berkeley)

*C*onquering now and still to conquer, Jesus, Thou RULER of all,
Thrones and their scepters all shall perish, crowns and their splendor shall fall,
Yet shall the armies Thou leadest, faithful and true to the last,
Find in Thy mansions eternal rest, when their warfare is past.
Not to the strong is the battle, not to the swift is the race,
Yet to the true and the faithful victory is promised through grace.

(by Fanny J. Crosby)

Begin your prayer time adoring God for His AUTHORITY.

THE GOD ABOVE

⬛ ABOVE—Literally, higher in place. Figuratively, superior in any respect. (Webster)

*T*herefore be sure of this, remind yourselves, that it is the Eternal who is God in heaven ABOVE and on the earth beneath, the only God.

Deuteronomy 4:39 (Moffatt)

*A*nd he (Jacob) has a dream, and behold, a ladder was set on the earth with its top reaching to heaven; and behold, the angels of God were ascending and descending on it. And behold, the Lord stood ABOVE it and said, "I am the Lord, the God of your father Abraham and the God of Isaac."

Genesis 28:12 & 13a (NAS)

*H*e who comes from ABOVE is greater than all; he who is from the earth belongs to the earth and speaks about earthly matters. He who comes from heaven is ABOVE all.

John 3:31 (Good News)

*A*nd He was saying to them, As for you, from beneath you are. As for myself, from ABOVE I am. As for you, of this world you are. As for myself, I am not of this world.

John 8:23 (Wuest)

*T*he God of Abraham praise, Who reigns enthroned ABOVE;
Ancient of everlasting days, and God of love.
Jehovah, great I AM, by earth and heaven confessed;
I bow and bless the sacred Name, forever blest.

The whole triumphant host Give thanks to God on high;
"Hail, Father, Son, and Holy Ghost!" They ever cry.
Hail, Abram's God and mine! I join the heavenly lays;
All might and majesty are Thine, and endless praise.

(by Daniel ben Judah)

Begin your prayer time adoring the God who is ABOVE all.

THE GOD WHO IS ABOVE

I know that the Eternal has given you this country, and how the terror of you has fallen upon us, till all the natives are quivering before you. For we have heard how the Eternal dried up the water of the Reed Sea before you, when you left Egypt, and how you treated the two Amorite kings on the east of the Jordan, Sihon and Og, whom you wiped off the earth. As soon as we heard it, our hearts quivered and everyone became utterly dispirited because of you, for the Eternal you God is God in heaven ABOVE and on the earth below.

Joshua 2:9-11 (Moffatt)

O Lord our Lord, how excellent is thy name in all the earth! Who has set thy glory ABOVE the heavens.

Psalm 8:1 (KJ)

*B*earing the human likeness, revealed in human shape, he humbled himself, and in obedience accepted even death—death on a cross. Therefore God raised him to THE HEIGHTS and bestowed on him the name ABOVE all names,

Philippians 2:8 & 9 (NEB)

*B*ut every good endowment that we possess and every complete gift that we have received must come from ABOVE, from the Father of all lights, with whom there is never the slightest variation or shadow of inconsistency.

James 1:17 (Phillips)

*J*esus, wondrous Saviour! Christ, of kings the king!
Angels fall before Thee, prostrate, worshipping
Fairest they confess Thee in the heaven ABOVE,
We would sing Thee fairest here in hymns of love.

All earth's flowing pleasures were a wintry sea:
Heaven itself without Thee dark as night would be.
Lamb of God! Thy glory is the light ABOVE.
Lamb of God Thy glory is Thy deathless love.

(by D. A. McGregor)

Begin your prayer time adoring the God who reigns ABOVE.

THE GOD ABOVE

*L*ord, be exalted ABOVE the highest heaven! Show your glory high ABOVE the earth.

Psalm 57:5 (Paraphrased)

*F*or You, Lord, are high ABOVE all the earth; You are exalted far ABOVE all gods.

Psalm 97:9 (Amplified)

*M*ay the God of our Lord Jesus Christ, the Father of glory, give you a spirit and perception of what is revealed, to bring you to full knowledge of him. May he enlighten the eyes of your mind so that you can see what hope his call holds for you, what rich glories he has promised the saints will inherit and how infinitely great is the power that he has exercised for us believers. This you can tell from the strength of his power at work in Christ, when he used it to raise him from the dead and to make him sit at his right hand, in heaven, far ABOVE every Sovereignty, Authority, Power, or Domination, or any other name that can be named, not only in this age but also in the age to come.

Ephesians 1:17-22 (NJB)

*B*ut the wisdom that is from ABOVE is first pure, then peaceable, gentle, willing to yield, full of mercy and good fruits, without partiality and without hypocrisy.

James 3:17 (NKJ)

> *B*ehold the Lamb, with glory crowned,
> To Him all power is given:
> No place to high for Him is found,
> No place too high in heaven.
>
> To Him whom men despise and slight,
> To Him be glory given;
> The crown is His, and His by right
> The HIGHEST place in heaven.
>
> *(by Thomas Kelly)*

Begin your prayer time adoring and praising the God who is ABOVE.

THE GOD ABOVE

Then Solomon stood facing the Lord's altar, and all the Israelites were standing behind him. He spread out his hands toward the sky and said: "Lord, God of Israel, there is no god like you in heaven ABOVE or on earth below. You keep your agreement of love with your servants who truly follow you."

1 Kings 8:22 & 23 (NCV)

Be exalted, O God, ABOVE the heavens, and let your glory be over all the earth.

Psalm 108:5 (NIV)

The Lord is high ABOVE all the nations; His glory is ABOVE the heavens. Who is like the Lord our God, Who is enthroned on HIGH.

Psalm 113:4 & 5 (NAS)

(There is) one body and one spirit, just as there is one hope (that belongs) to the calling you received. (There is) one Lord, one faith, one baptism, One God and Father of (us) all, Who is ABOVE all (Sovereign over all) pervading all and (living) in us all.

Ephesians 4:4-6 (Amplified)

Here we have a firm foundation,
Here the refuge of the lost;
Christ's the Rock of our salvation,
Paid our debt at such a cost.

Lamb of God, for sinners wounded,
Seated now in heaven ABOVE;
All our foes He has confounded,
He now saves for He is love.

(by Thomas Kelly)

Begin your prayer time glorifying the God ABOVE.

THE GOD WHO SAID, "ASK"

▣ ASK—To request; to seek to obtain by words; to petition. (Webster)

(The words of Jesus)—"And I say to you, ASK, and it will be given to you; seek, and you will find; knock and it will be opened unto you. For every one who ASKS receives, and he who seeks finds, and to him who knocks it will be opened."

Luke 11:9 (NKJ)

And Judah gathered themselves together, to ASK help of the Lord: even out of all the cities of Judah they came to seek the Lord.

2 Chronicles 20:4 (KJ)

"Well, then," they said, "ASK God whether or not our trip will be successful."

Judges 18:5 (Paraphrased)

A ruler once came to Jesus by night
To ASK Him the way of salvation and light;
The Master made answer in words true and plain,
"Ye must be born again."
I verily say unto thee, Ye must be born again.

O ye who would enter that glorious rest,
And sing with the ransomed the song of the blest;
The life everlasting if ye would obtain,
"Ye must be born again."
I verily, verily say unto thee, Ye must be born again.

(by William T. Sleeper)

Begin you prayer time adoring the God who is willing to listen to our PETITIONS.

THE GOD WHO SAID, "ASK"

ASK Synonyms—entreat, inquire, request, beg, petition, beseech.

ASK of Me, and I will surely give the nations as thine inheritance, and the very ends of thy earth as thy possessions.

Psalms 2:8 (NAS)

ASK the Lord for rain in the springtime; it is the Lord who makes the storm clouds. He gives showers of rain to men, and plants of the field to everyone.

Zechariah 10:1 (NIV)

Indeed anything you ASK in my name I will do, so that the Father may be glorified in the Son. If you ASK anything in my name I will do it.

John 14:13 & 14 (NEB)

Truly I assure you, whatever you ASK the Father, He will grant you in My name. Thus far you have ASKED nothing in My name. ASK and you will receive, so that your joy may be complete.

John 16:23b & 24 (Berkeley)

The hymn "Guide us, O Thou great Jehovah" is a PETITION hymn

> GUIDE US, O Thou great Jehovah
> Pilgrims through this barren land;
> We are weak, but Thou at mighty;
> HOLD US by Thy powerful hand;
> Bread of heaven, FEED US now and evermore.
>
> While we tread this vale of sorrow,
> May we in Thy love abide;
> KEEP US, O our gracious Saviour!
> Cleaving closely to Thy side:
> Still relying on out Father's changeless love.
>
> *(by William Williams)*

Begin your prayer time adoring the God who listens to our PETITIONS.

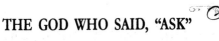

THE GOD WHO SAID, "ASK"

*N*ow, Yahweh my God, you have made your servant king in succession to David my father. But I am a very young man, unskilled in leadership. Your servant finds himself in the midst of this people of yours that you have chosen, a people so many its number cannot be counted or reckoned. GIVE your servant a heart to understand how to discern between good and evil, for who could govern this people of yours that is so great? It pleased Yahweh that Solomon should have ASKED for this, "since you have ASKED for this" Yahweh said, "and not asked for long life for yourself or riches or the lives of your enemies, but have ASKED for a discerning judgment for yourself, here and now I do what you ASK. I give you a heart wise and shrewd as none before you has had and none will have after you. What you have not asked I shall give you too: such riches and glory as no other king ever had. And I give you a long life, if you follow my ways, keeping my laws and commandments, as your father David followed them."

1 Kings 3:7-13 (NJB)

*A*nd if, in the process, any of you does not know how to meet any particular problem he has only to ASK God—who gives generously to all men without making them feel foolish or guilty—and he may be quite sure that the necessary wisdom will be given him.

James 1:5 & 6 (Phillips)

*K*eep on ASKING for something to be given and it shall be given you. Keep on seeking, and you shall find. Keep on reverently knocking, and it shall be opened to you. For everyone who keeps on ASKING for something to be given, keeps on receiving.

Matthew 7:7 & 8a (Wuest)

Draw Me Nearer is a PETITION hymn

I am Thine, O Lord, I have heard Thy voice, and it told Thy love to me:
But I long to rise in the arms of faith, and be closer drawn to Thee.
DRAW ME nearer, nearer, blessed Lord, to the cross where Thou hast died;
DRAW ME nearer, nearer, nearer, blessed Lord, to Thyself now glorified.

Consecrate me now to Thy service Lord, by the power of grace divine;
Let my soul look up with a steadfast hope, and my will be lost in Thine.
DRAW ME nearer, nearer, blessed Lord, To the cross where Thou hast died;
DRAW ME nearer, nearer, nearer, blessed Lord, To Thyself now glorified.

(Fanny J. Crosby)

Begin your prayer time adoring the God who hears our PETITIONS.

THE GOD OF THE AFFLICTED

AFFLICT—To give (the body or mind) pain which is continued or of some permanence; to trouble, grieve or distress: (Webster)

*A*nd the Angel of the Lord said to her: "Behold, you are with child, And you shall bear a son. You shall call his name Ishmael, Because the Lord has heard your AFFLICTION.

Genesis 16:11 (NAS)

*F*or You deliver an AFFLICTED and humble people, but will bring down haughty looks.

Psalm 18:27 (Amplified)

*F*or the Lord saw the AFFLICTION of Israel, which was very bitter: for there was neither bond nor free, nor was there any helper for Israel.

2 Kings 14:26 (NKJ)

> *I* need Thee every hour, Most gracious Lord;
> No tender voice like Thine can peace afford.
> I need Thee, O I need Thee; Every hour I need Thee;
> O bless me now, my Saviour, I come to Thee.
>
> I need Thee every hour, in joy or PAIN;
> Come quickly and abide, Or life is vain.
> I need Thee, O I need Thee; Every hour I need Thee;
> O bless me now, my Saviour, I come to Thee.
>
> *(by Annie S. Hawks)*

Begin your prayer time adoring God because He cares about our AFFLICTION.

February

THE GOD OF THE AFFLICTED

Synonyms for AFFLICTION—Trouble, distress, sorrow, adversity, misfortune, grief, regret, sadness, suffering, tribulation, trial. (Webster)

*Y*ou saw the SUFFERING of our forefathers in Egypt; you heard their cry at the Red sea. You sent miraculous signs and wonders against Pharaoh, against all his officials and all the people of the land, for you knew how arrogantly the Egyptians treated them.

Nehemiah 9:9 & 10 (NIV)

*M*any a time he (God) rescued them; but they would take their own rebellious way, till evildoing wasted them away. Yet, he regarded their DISTRESS, when he heard them wailing; he remembered for their sake his compact, in his great goodness he relented.

Psalm 106:43 & 45 (Moffatt)

*I*s any among you AFFLICTED-ILL-TREATED, SUFFERING evil? He should pray. Is any one glad at heart? He should sing praise to (God).

James 5:13 (Amplified)

> *I*n shady, green pastures, so rich and so sweet,
> God leads His dear children along;
> Where the water's cool flow bathes the weary ones feet,
> God leads His dear children along.
>
> Though SORROWS befall us and Satan oppose,
> God leads His dear children along
> Through grace we can conquer, defeat all our foes,
> God leads his dear children along.
>
> Some through the waters, some through the flood,
> Some through the fire, but all through the blood;
> Some Through great SORROW, but God gives a song,
> In the night season and all the day long.
>
> *(by G. A. Young)*

Begin your prayer time adoring the God who listens to AFFLICTION.

THE GOD OF THE AFFLICTED,
BUT WHO ALSO USES AFFLICTION

*T*hen Moses heard the people weep throughout their families, every man in the door of his tent: and the anger of the Lord was kindled greatly; Moses also was displeased. And Moses said unto the Lord, Wherefore hast thou AFFLICTED thy servant? And wherefore have I not found favor in thy sight, that thou layest the burden of all this people upon me?

NUMBERS 11:10 & 11 (KJ)

*S*ome sat in darkness and in the shadow of death, being bound in AFFLICTION and in irons, Because they rebelled against the words of God, and spurned the counsel of the Most High.

Psalm 107:10 & 11 (Amplified)

*W*ho could believe what we have heard, and to whom has the power of Yahweh been revealed? Like a sapling he grew up in front of us, like a root in arid ground. Without beauty, without majesty (we saw him), no looks to attract our eyes; a thing despised and rejected by men, a man of SORROWS and familiar with SUFFERING, a man to make people screen their faces; he was despised and we took no account of him. And yet ours were the SUFFERINGS he bore, ours were the SORROWS he carried.

Isaiah 53:1-3 (NJB)

"*M*an of SORROWS," what a name for the Son of God who came
Ruined sinners to reclaim! Hallelujah! What a Saviour!
Bearing shame and scoffing rude, In my place condemned He stood;
Sealed my pardon with His blood; Hallelujah! What a Saviour!

Guilty, vile and helpless we; Spotless Lamb of God was He;
Full atonement can it be? Hallelujah! What a Saviour!
Lifted up was He to die, "It is finished," was His cry
Now in heaven exalted high; Hallelujah! What a Saviour!

(by Philip P. Bliss)

Begin your prayer time adoring the God who uses AFFLICTION.

THE GOD WHO CONSOLES THE AFFLICTED

*A*t that time I will punish all those who HARMED you. I will save my people who CANNOT WALK and gather my people who have been THROWN OUT. I will give them praise and honor in every place where they were SHAMED.

Zephaniah 3:9 (NCV)

*T*hese little TROUBLES (which are really so transitory) are winning for us a permanent, glorious and solid reward out of all proportion to our PAIN.

2 Corinthians 4:17 (Phillips)

*I*f you want a pattern of patience under ILL-TREATMENT, take the prophets who spoke in the name of the Lord; remember: "We count those happy who stood firm." You have all heard how Job stood firm, and you have seen how the Lord treated him in the end. For the Lord is full of pity and compassion.

James 5:10 & 11 (NEB)

*B*e firm in your faith and resist him (Satan), for you know that your fellow believers in all the world are going through the same kind of SUFFERINGS. But after you have SUFFERED for a little while, the God of all grace, who calls you to share his eternal glory in union with Christ, will himself perfect you, and give you firmness, strength, and a sure foundation.

1 Peter 5:9 & 10 (Good News)

*C*all Jehovah thy salvation, rest beneath the Almighty shade,
In his secret habitation dwell and never be DISMAYED:
There no TUMULT shall alarm thee, thou shalt DREAD no hidden snare;
GUILE nor VIOLENCE can harm thee, In eternal safeguard there.

Since with pure and firm affection, thou on God hast set thy love,
With the wings of His protection He will shield thee from above:
Thou shalt call on Him in TROUBLE, He will hearken, He will save;
Here for GRIEF reward thee double, Crown with life beyond the grave.

(translated by James Montgomery)

Begin your prayer time adoring the God who comforts AFFLICTION.

THE GOD WHO CONSOLES THE AFFLICTED

In BITTERNESS of soul Hannah wept much and prayed to the Lord. And she made a vow, saying, "O Lord Almighty, if you will only look upon your servants MISERY and remember me, and not forget your servant but give her a son, then I will give him to the Lord for all the days of his life, and no razor will ever be used on his head." ...So in the course of time Hannah conceived and gave birth to a son. She named him Samuel, saying, "Because I asked the Lord for him."

Samuel 1:10 & 11:20 (NIV)

Never forget your promises to me your servant, for they are my only hope. They give me strength in all my TROUBLES; how they refresh and revive me!

Psalm 119:49 & 50 (Amplified)

For he said, Surely they are my people, children that will not lie; so he was their Saviour. In all their AFFLICTION, he was AFFLICTED, and the angel of his presence saved them: in his love he redeemed them; and he bare them, and carried them all the days of old.

Isaiah 63:8 & 9 (KJ)

No wonder we do not lose heart! Though our outward humanity is in DECAY, yet day by day we are inwardly renewed. Our TROUBLES are slight and short-lived; and their outcome an eternal glory which outweighs them far.

2 Corinthians 4:16 & 17 (NEB)

What a Friend we have in Jesus, all our sins and GRIEFS to bear!
What a privilege to carry everything to God in prayer!
O what peace we often forfeit, O what needless PAIN we bear,
All because we do not carry everything to God in prayer!

Have we TRIALS and temptations? Is there TROUBLE anywhere?
We should never be DISCOURAGED, take it to the Lord in prayer.
Can we find a friend so faithful who will all our SORROWS share?
Jesus knows our every WEAKNESS, take it to the Lord in prayer.

(by Joseph Scriven)

Begin your prayer time adoring the God who consoles the AFFLICTED.

GOD'S ALTAR

🔲 ALTAR—The ALTARS in Jewish culture consist of the ALTARS of incense, of burnt offering, and of showbread; all of shittim wood, and covered with gold or brass. (Webster)

Then Noah built an ALTAR to the Lord, and taking some of all the clean animals and clean birds, he sacrificed burnt offerings on it.

Genesis 8:20 (NIV)

Then the Lord said to Moses, Give Aaron and his sons these regulations concerning the burnt offering. "The burnt offering shall be left upon the ALTAR all night, with the ALTAR fire kept burning."

Leviticus 6:8 & 9 (Paraphrased)

And the Lord spake unto Moses saying, For the life of the flesh is in the blood: and I have given it to you upon the ALTAR to make an atonement for your souls: for it is the blood that maketh an atonement for the soul.

Leviticus 17:1 & 11 (KJ)

> *You have longed for sweet peace and for faith to increase,*
> And have earnestly, fervently prayed;
> But you cannot have rest or be perfectly blest
> Until all on the ALTAR is laid.
>
> Is your all on the ALTAR of sacrifice laid?
> Your heart does the Spirit control?
> You can only be blest and have peace and sweet rest
> As you yield Him your body and soul.
>
> *(by Elisha A. Hoffman)*

Begin you prayer time adoring the God who provides an ALTAR.

GOD'S ALTAR

■ ALTAR—In Christian Churches, the communion table; and figuratively, a church; a place of worship. (Webster)

*A*nd the sons of Reuben and the sons of Gad called the ALTAR Witness; "For," they said, "it is a witness between us that the Lord is God."

Joshua 22:34 (NAS)

*N*ow Gideon perceived that He was the Angel of the Lord. So Gideon said, "Alas, O Lord God! For I have seen the Angel of the Lord face to face." Then the Lord said to him, "Peace be with you; do not fear, you shall not die." So Gideon built an ALTAR there to the Lord, and called it The Lord-Shalom.

Judges 6: 22-24b (NKJ)

*S*o if, when you are offering your gift at the ALTAR you there remember that your brother has any grievance against you, leave your gift at the ALTAR and go; first make peace with your brother, and then come back and present your gift.

Matthew 5:23 & 24 (Amplified)

*W*ould you walk with the Lord in the light of His Word,
And have peace and contentment alway?
You must do His sweet will to be free from all ill
On the ALTAR your all you must lay.

O we never can know what the Lord will bestow
Of the blessings for which we have prayed,
Till our body and soul He doth fully control,
And our all on the ALTAR is laid.

(by Elisha A. Hoffman)

Begin your prayer time adoring the God who provides an ALTAR.

GOD'S ALTAR

🔲 ALTAR—In the Tabernacle it was a hallow square, five cubits in length and breadth and three cubits high, and was made with shittim wood, overlaid with brass. The corners terminated in horns. The ALTAR had a grating, which projected through openings on two sides, and had four rings fastened to it for the poles with which the ALTAR was carried. (Unger's Bible Dictionary)

*T*hen shall there be an ALTAR to the Eternal in the heart of the land of Egypt, and a pillar to the Eternal on the frontier.

Isaiah 19:19 (Moffatt)

*N*ow Araunah looked, and saw the king and his servants coming toward him. So Araunah went out and bowed before the king with his face to the ground. Then Araunah said, "Why has my king come to his servant?" And David said, "To buy the threshing floor from you, to build an ALTAR to the Lord, that the plague may be withdrawn from the people."

2 Samuel 24:21 & 22 (NKJ)

*S*urely you know that those who work in the Temple get their food from the Temple, and those who serve at the ALTAR get part of what is offered at the ALTAR. In the same way, the Lord has commanded that those who tell the Good News should get their living from this work.

1 Corinthians 9:13 & 14 (NCV)

*W*ho can tell all the love He will send from above,
And how happy our hearts will be made,
Of the fellowship sweet we shall share at His feet
When our all on the ALTAR is laid.

Is your all on the ALTAR of sacrifice laid?
Your heart does the Spirit control?
You can only be blest and have peace and sweet rest
As you yield Him your body and soul.

(by Elisha A. Hoffman)

Begin your prayer time with adoration to the God who provides an ALTAR.

GOD'S ALTAR

ALTAR—(Hebrew, mizbe'ah, from a word meaning "to slay") any structure of earth, or unwrought stone on which sacrifices were offered. (Today's Dictionary of the Bible.)

*H*ow I love your palace, Yahweh Sabaoth! How my soul yearns and pines for Yahweh's courts! My heart and my flesh sing for joy to the living God. The sparrow has found a nest for its young, Your ALTARS, Yahweh Sabaoth, my king and my God.

Psalm 84:1-3 (NJB)

*S*o Paul standing in the center of the Areopagus (Mars Hill auditorium) said: Men of Athens, I perceive in every way—on every hand and with every turn I make—that you are most religious (very reverent to demons). For as I passed along and carefully observed your objects of worship, I came also upon an ALTAR with this inscription, To the unknown God. Now what you are already worshipping as unknown, this I set forth to you.

Acts 17:22 & 23 (Amplified)

*A*nd when he opened the seventh seal there came a silence in heaven for about half an hour. And I saw the seven angels who had taken a stand before God and who were standing there. And there was given to them seven trumpets. And another angel came and stood over the ALTAR, holding a golden censer. And there was given to him much incense in order that he might add it to the prayers of all the saints upon the golden ALTAR which is before the throne.

Revelation 8:1-4 (Wuest)

*W*hen we walk with the Lord
In the light of His Word
What a glory He sheds on our way!
While we do His good will
He abides with us still,
And with all who will trust and obey.

But we never can prove
The delights of His love
Until all on the ALTAR we lay;
For the favor He shows,
And the joy He bestows
Are for them who will trust and obey.

(by John H. Sammis)

Begin your prayer time adoring the God who provides an ALTAR.

THE GOD WHO SAID "BELIEVE"

▦ To BELIEVE-IN; to trust; to have the utmost confidence in the existence of; to trust implicitly in the ability of. (Webster)

*A*nd they rose early in the morning, and went forth into the wilderness of Tekoa: and as they went forth, Jehoshaphat stood and said, Hear me, O Judah, and ye inhabitants of Jerusalem; BELIEVE IN the Lord your God, so shall ye be established; BELIEVE in his prophets, so shall ye prosper.

2 Chronicles 20:20 (KJ)

I would have despaired unless I had BELIEVED that I would see the goodness of the Lord in the land of the living.

Psalm 27:13 (NAS)

*W*hen Jesus heard what had happened, he found the man and said, "Do you BELIEVE in the Messiah?" The man answered, "Who is he, sir, for I want to." "You have seen him," Jesus said, "and he is speaking to you!" "Yes, Lord," the man said, "I" BELIEVE!" and he worshipped Jesus.

John 9:35-38 (Paraphrased)

> *T*here's a story ever new,
> It is wonderful and true,
> And the best thing you can do,
> Is BELIEVE it;
>
> It will calm your troubled breast,
> And will give you peace and rest
> It's of all the news the best,
> Oh, BELIEVE it.
>
> Christ has died upon the tree,
> That from sin you might be free;
> Jesus died for you and me,
> Oh, BELIEVE it.
>
> *(by John Ferguson)*

Begin your prayer time adoring the God who can be BELIEVED.

THE GOD WHO SAID "BELIEVE"

BELIEVE—In theology, to assent to anything; to yield the will and affections, accompanied with humble reliance on Christ for salvation. (Webster)

He (God) took him (Abram) outside and said, "Look up at the heavens and count the stars—if indeed you can count them." Then he said to him, "So shall your offspring be." Abram BELIEVED the Lord, and he credited it to him as righteousness.

Genesis 15:5 & 6 (NIV)

So they took away the stone (at Lazarus' grave). And Jesus lifted up His eyes and said, Father, I thank You that You have heard Me. Yes, I know You always hear and listen to Me; but I have said this on account of and for the benefit of the people standing around, so that they may BELIEVE You did send Me—that You have made Me Your Messenger.

John 11:41 & 42 (Amplified)

For anyone who comes to God must BELIEVE that he exists and that he rewards those who search for him.

Hebrews 11:6 (NEB)

> *Once* again the Gospel Message
> From the Saviour you have heard;
> Will you heed the invitation?
> Will you turn unto the Lord?
> Let your will to God be given,
> Trust in Christ's atoning blood;
> Look to Jesus now in heaven,
> Rest on His unchanging Word.
> Come BELIEVING! Come BELIEVING!
> Come to Jesus, look and live!
>
> *(by Daniel Whittle)*

Adore and Praise God that He can be BELIEVED.

THE GOD WHO SAID "BELIEVE"

*B*ut as many as received Him, to them He gave the right to become the children of God, even to those who BELIEVE in His name.

John 1:12 (NKJ)

*T*his is what the Scripture says: The word is near you; it is in your mouth and in your heart. That is the teaching of faith that we are telling. If you use your mouth to say, "Jesus is Lord," and if you BELIEVE in your heart that God raised Jesus from the dead, you will be saved.

Romans 10:8 & 9 (NCV)

*F*or God loved the world so much that he gave his only Son, so that everyone who BELIEVES in him may not die but have eternal life.

John 3:16 (Good News)

*A*nd he said to them, "Go to all the world and preach the gospel to every creature: he who BELIEVES and is baptized shall be saved, but he who will not BELIEVE shall be condemned."

Mark 15:15 & 16 (Moffatt)

*T*hen I listened and He said, it was for you I bled,
And with me He sweetly pled, to BELIEVE it:
This is now salvation's day, sin has all been put away,
This is what I heard Him say, Oh, believe it!

I could then withstand no more, for I saw my sins He bore,
So I entered by the door, and BELIEVED it:
Now I'm happy all the day, I can sing as well as pray,
For my sins are washed away, I BELIEVE it.

(by John Ferguson)

Adore and Give glory to a BELIEVABLE God.

THE GOD WHO SAID "BELIEVE"

*L*et not your hearts be disquieted: you BELIEVE—BELIEVE in God and also in me. In my Father's house there are many abodes; were it not so, would I have told you I was going to prepare a place for you? And when I go and prepare a place for you, I will come back and take you to be with me, so that you may be where I am.

John 14:1-3 (Moffatt)

*T*here are many other signs that Jesus worked and the disciples saw, but they are not recorded in this book. These are recorded so that you may BELIEVE that Jesus is the Christ, the Son of God, and that BELIEVING this you may have life through his name.

John 20:30 & 31 (NJB)

"*E*veryone who calls on the name of the Lord shall be saved." Now then, how shall they invoke Him in whom they have no faith? And how shall they BELIEVE in One of whom they have not heard? Again, how shall they listen without a preacher? But how shall they preach unless they are sent? Just as it is written, "How lovely are the feet of those who publish the glad, good news.

Romans 10:13-15 (Berkeley)

*J*ust as I am, without one plea, but that Thy blood was shed for me,
And that Thou biddest me come to Thee, O Lamb of God, I come! I come!
Just as I am and waiting not to rid my soul of one dark blot,
To Thee whose blood can cleanse each spot, O Lamb of God, I come! I come!

Just as I am Thou wilt receive, wilt welcome, pardon, cleanse, relieve,
Because Thy promise I BELIEVE, O Lamb of God, I come! I come!
Just as I am, Thy love unknown hath broken every barrier down:
Now to be Thine, yea Thine alone, O Lamb of God, I come! I come!

(by Charlotte Elliott)

Adore God because he is BELIEVABLE.

THE GOD WHO SAID "BELIEVE"

*J*esus says to him, (Thomas) Because you have seen me and at present have me within the range of your vision, you have BELIEVED, with the result that you are in a state of BELIEF. Spiritually prosperous are those who, not having seen, yet BELIEVED.

John 20:29 (Wuest)

*A*nd Abraham BELIEVED God, and it was reckoned unto him for righteousness.

Romans 4:3 (Phillips)

*A*nd of this gospel I was appointed a herald and an apostle and a teacher. That is why I am suffering as I am. Yet I am not ashamed, because I know whom I have BELIEVED, and am convinced that he is able to guard what I have entrusted to him for that day.

2 Timothy 1:11 & 12 (NIV)

*W*e BELIEVE with our hearts, and we are made right with God. And we use our mouths to say that we BELIEVE, and so we are saved.

Romans 10:10 (NCV)

I know not why God's wondrous grace to me He hath made known,
Nor why, unworthy, Christ in love redeemed me for His own.
I know not how his saving faith to me He did impart,
Nor how BELIEVING in His Word wrought peace with-in my heart.

I know not how the Spirit moves, Convincing men of sin,
Revealing Jesus through the Word, Creating faith in Him.
I know not when my Lord may come, At night or noonday fair,
Nor if I'll walk the vale with Him, Or "meet Him in the air."

But "I know whom I have BELIEVED,
And am persuaded that He is able
To keep that which I've committed
Unto Him against that day."

(by Daniel W. Whittle)

Begin praying with adoration to the God of BELIEF.

THE GOD WHO GIVES BREAD

BREAD—Baked and leavened food made of a mixture whose basic constituent is flour or meal. (Webster)

*T*hen Melchizedek king of Salem brought out BREAD and wine; he was the priest of God Most High. "And he blessed him and said: Blessed be Abram of God Most High, Possessor of heaven and earth: And blessed be God Most High, Who has delivered your enemies into your hand."

Genesis 14:18-20 (NKJ)

*T*hen Yahweh said to Moses, "Now I will rain down BREAD for you from the heavens. Each day the people are to go out and gather the day's portion."

Exodus 16:4 (NJB)

*P*ray then like this—Our Heavenly Father, may your name be honored: May your kingdom come, and your will be done on earth as it is in Heaven. Give us this day the BREAD we need.

Matthew 6:9-11 (Phillips)

> *B*reak Thou the BREAD of life, O Lord to me,
> That hid within my heart Thy word may be:
> Mold each inward thought, from self set free,
> And let my steps be all controlled by Thee.
>
> Bless Thou the truth, O Lord to me, to me,
> As Thou didst bless the BREAD by Galilee:
> Then shall all bondage cease, All fetters fall;
> And I shall find my peace, My All in All.
>
> *(by Mary A. Lathbury)*

Adore the God who gives BREAD.

THE GOD WHO GIVES BREAD

BREAD—The word BREAD in the Bible is used in a very wide sense, occurring as our food,... In strictness it denotes baked food, especially loaves. (Unger's Bible Dictionary.)

(*Abram* speaking to angels from God) "Please let a little water be brought and wash your feet, and rest yourselves under a tree; and I will bring a piece of BREAD, that you may refresh yourselves;

Genesis 18:4 & 5a (NAS)

For the Lord hath chosen Zion; he hath desired it for his habitation. This is my rest for ever: here will I dwell; for I have desired it. I will abundantly bless her provision: I will satisfy her poor with BREAD.

Psalm 132:13-15 (KJ)

While they were eating, Jesus took the BREAD, gave a prayer of thanks, broke it, and gave to his disciples. "Take and eat it," he said; "this is my body."

Matthew 26:26 (GN)

> *According* to Thy gracious word, in deep humility
> This would I do, O Christ my Lord, I would remember Thee.
> Thy body given for my sake, my BREAD from heaven shall be:
> Thy testamental cup I take, and thus remember Thee.
>
> Remember Thee, and all Thy pains, and all Thy love to me;
> Yea, while a breath—a pulse remains, would I remember Thee
> And when, O Lord, Thou comest again, and I Thy glory see,
> Forever as the Lamb once slain, I will remember Thee.
>
> *(by James Montgomery)*

Adore and Praise God for providing our daily BREAD.

THE GOD WHO GIVES BREAD

BREAD—Bread was a term for the whole meal; as ground grain is for all that is eaten at any time. The best was made of wheat, ground and sifted, leavened and baked. Poorer kinds were made of barley, rye, beans, and lentils. The bread was kneaded with the hands or the feet, in a trough. (Smith's Bible Dictionary)

*R*ather, is not this the fast that I have chosen: to loose the bonds of wickedness, to undo the bands of the yoke, to let the oppressed go free, and that you break every enslaving yoke. Is it not to divide your BREAD with the hungry, and bring the homeless poor into your house? When you see the naked that you cover him, and that you hide not yourself from the needs of your own flesh and blood?

Isaiah 58:6 & 7 (Amplified)

*J*esus said, "I tell you the truth, it was not Moses who gave you BREAD from heaven; it is my Father who is giving you the true BREAD from heaven. God's BREAD is the One who comes down from heaven and gives life to the world.

John 6:32 (NCV)

*I*s not the cup of thanksgiving for which we give thanks a participation in the blood of Christ? And is not the BREAD that we break a participation in the body of Christ?

1 Corinthians 10:16 (NIV)

> *H*ere conscience ends its strife, and faith delights to prove
> The sweetness of the BREAD of Life, the fullness of Thy love.
> That blood that flowed for sin in symbol here we see,
> And feel the blessed pledge with-in that we are loved of Thee.
>
> O, if this glimpse of love is so divinely sweet,
> What will it be, O Lord, above, Thy gladdening smile to meet!
> To see Thee face to face, Thy perfect likeness wear,
> And all Thy ways of wondrous grace through endless years declare.
>
> *(by Frederick Oakley)*

Begin your prayer time in adoration of the BREAD of Life.

THE GOD WHO GIVES BREAD

BREAD—The word BREAD is used figuratively in such expressions as "BREAD of sorrows" "BREAD of tears"—sorrow and tears are like one's daily BREAD, they form so great a part of life. The BREAD of "wickedness" and "of deceit" denote in like manner that wickedness and deceit are a part of the daily life. (Today's Dictionary of the Bible)

*V*ain is it to rise early for your work, and keep at work so late, gaining your BREAD with anxious toil! God's gifts come to his loved ones while they sleep.

Psalm 127:2 (Moffatt)

*Y*ou have fed us with SORROW AND TEARS, and have made us the scorn of the neighboring nations. They laugh among themselves.

Psalm 80:5 (Paraphrased)

*F*or they eat the BREAD of wickedness, And drink the wine of violence.

Proverbs 4:17 (NKJ)

*B*READ obtained by falsehood is sweet to man, But afterward his mouth will be filled with gravel.

Proverbs 20:17 (NAS)

The following words have been chosen because no matter what sorrow or tears or wickedness or deceit people experience it can be overcome through God's "Amazing grace."

*A*mazing grace! How sweet the sound, that saved a wretch like me!
I once was lost, but now am found, was blind, but now I see.
'Twas grace that taught my heart to fear, and grace my fears relieved.
How precious did that grace appear the hour I first believed!

Through many dangers, toils and snares, I have already come;
Tis grace hath brought me safe thus far, and grace will lead me home.
When we've been there ten thousand years, bright shining as the sun,
We've no less days to sing God's praise than when we first begun.

(by John Newton)

Adore and Praise God for His Amazing Grace over all sorrow, tears and bitterness.

THE GOD WHO GIVES BREAD

*M*en ate the BREAD of angels; he sent them all the food they could eat.

Psalm 78:25 (NIV)

*G*o, eat your BREAD with joy, And drink your wine with a merry heart; For God has already accepted your works.

Ecclesiastes 9:7 (NKJ)

*A*nd when one of those who were reclining at the table with Him heard this, he said to Him, "Blessed is everyone who shall eat BREAD in the kingdom of God."

Luke 14:15 (NAS)

*T*he teaching I gave you is the same teaching I received from the Lord: On the night when the Lord Jesus was handed over to be killed, he took BREAD and gave thanks for it. Then he broke the BREAD and said, "This is my body; it is for you. Do this to remember me." In the same way, after they ate, Jesus took the cup. He said, "This cup is the new agreement that is sealed with the blood of my death. When you drink this, do it to remember me." Every time you eat this BREAD and drink this cup you are telling others about the Lord's death until he comes.

1 Corinthians 11:23-26 (NCV)

*B*reak Thou the BREAD of life, O Lord, to me.
That hid with-in my heart Thy word may be:
Mold Thou each inward thought, from self set free,
And let my steps be all controlled by Thee.

Open Thy word of truth that I may see
Thy message written clear and plain for me;
Then in sweet fellowship walking with Thee
Thine image on my life engraved will be.

(by Mary A. Lathbur)

Begin your prayer time adoring and praising the God who is the BREAD of life.

THE GOD WHO GIVES BREAD

It was near the time of the Passover, the great Jewish Festival. Raising his eyes and seeing a large crowd coming toward him, Jesus said to Philip, "Where are we to buy BREAD to feed these people?" This he said to test him; Jesus himself knew what he meant to do. Philip replied, "Twenty pounds would not buy enough BREAD for every one of them to have a little." One of the disciples, Andrew, the brother of Simon Peter, said to him, "There is a boy here who has five BARLEY LOAVES and two fishes; but what is that among so many?" Jesus said, "Make the people sit down." There was plenty of grass there, so the men sat down, about five thousand of them. Then Jesus took the LOAVES, gave thanks, and distributed them to the people as they sat there. He did the same with the fishes, and they had as much as they wanted.

John 6:5-11 (NEB)

Truly I assure you, the believer has eternal life. Your ancestors ate the MANNA in the desert and they died; this is the BREAD that comes down from heaven, so that anyone who eats of it may not die. I am the LIVING BREAD that came down from heaven. If anyone eats of this BREAD, he will live forever. And the BREAD, which for the life of the world I give, is My Flesh.

John 6:47-51 (Berkeley)

Here, O our Lord, we see Thee face to face
Here would we touch and handle things unseen;
Here grasp with firmer hand the eternal; grace
And all our weariness upon Thee lean.

Here would we feed upon the BREAD of God.
Here drink with Thee the royal wine of heaven;
Here would we lay aside each earthly load,
Here taste afresh the calm of sin forgiven.

(by Horatius Bonar)

Begin prayer with adoration and awe of the BREAD provided from God.

THE GOD WHO CLEANSES

CLEAN—free from contamination, corruption, flaws and pollution.

*W*ash me thoroughly (and repeatedly) from my iniquity and guilt, and CLEANSE me and make me wholly pure from my sin.

Psalm 52:2 (Amplified)

I shall pour clean water over you and you shall be CLEANSED; I shall CLEANSE you of all your defilement and all your idols.

Ezekiel 36:25 (NJB)

If we confess our sins, he is faithful and just, he forgives our sins and CLEANSES us from all iniquity.

1 John 1:9 (Moffatt)

Search me, O God, and know my heart today;
Try me, O Saviour, know my thoughts I pray.
See if there be some wicked way in me;
CLEANSE me from every sin and set me free.

Lord, take my life and make it wholly Thine;
Fill my poor heart with Thy great love divine.
Take all my will, my passion, self and pride;
I now surrender, Lord in me abide.

(by J. Edwin Orr)

Begin your prayer time adoring and worshipping the God who CLEANSES us from sin.

THE GOD WHO CLEANSES

CLEANSE—To purify, make clean, free from filth, impurity, guilt and infection. (Webster)

*H*ow can a young man CLEANSE his way? By taking heed according to Your word.

Psalm 119:9 (NKJ)

*T*hen a leper came to him, knelt down before him, and said, "Sir, if you want to, you can make me CLEAN." Jesus reached out and touched him. "I do want to," he answered. "Be CLEAN!" At once he was CLEAN from his leprosy.

Matthew 8:2 & 3 (Good News)

*H*usbands, love your wives as Christ loved the Church and gave himself for it to make it belong to God. Christ used the word to make the church CLEAN by washing it with water,

Ephesians 5:25 & 26 (NCV)

I praise Thee, Lord, for CLEANSING me from sin;
Fulfil Thy Word and make me pure with-in.
Fill me with fire where once I burned with shame
Grant my desire to magnify Thy name.

O, Holy Ghost, revival comes from Thee;
Send a revival—start the work in me.
Thy word declares Thou wilt supply our need;
For blessings now, O Lord, I humbly plead.

(by J. Edwin Orr)

Begin you prayer time with adoration of God's CLEANSING.

THE GOD WHO CLEANSES

*H*ave mercy on me, O God, according to your unfailing love; according to your compassion blot out my transgressions. Wash away all my iniquity and CLEANSE me from sin.

Psalm 51:1 & 2 (NIV)

"*I* am the real vine, and my father is the gardener. Every barren branch of mine he cut away; and every fruiting branch he CLEANS, to make it more fruitful still. You have already been CLEANSED by the word that I spoke to you."

John 15:1-3 (NEB)

"*S*o, by virtue of the blood of Jesus, you and I, my brothers, may now have confidence to enter the holy place by a fresh and living way, which he has opened up for us by himself passing through the curtain, that is, his own human nature. Further, since we have a great High Priest set over the household of God, let us draw near with true hearts and fullest confidence, knowing that our inmost souls have been WASHED by the sprinkling of. His blood just as our bodies are purified by the CLEANSING of clean water."

Hebrews 11:19-22 (Phillips)

> *N*earer, still nearer, close to my heart,
> Draw me my Saviour, so precious Thou art;
> Fold me, O fold me close to Thy breast,
> Shelter me safe in that "Haven of Rest."
>
> Nearer, still nearer, nothing I bring,
> Naught as an offering to Jesus my King;
> Only my sinful contrite heart,
> Grant me the CLEANSING Thy blood doth impart.
>
> *(by Lelia N. Morris)*

Begin you prayer time adoring and praising the God who CLEANSES us.

THE GOD OF THE CITY

■ CITY—An inhabited place of greater size, population, or importance than a town or village.

*T*here is a river, the streams whereof shall make glad the CITY of God, the holy place of the tabernacles of the most High.

Psalm 46:4 (KJ)

*I*n that day shall this song be sung in the land of Judah; We have a strong CITY; the Lord sets up salvation as walls and bulwarks.

Isaiah 26:1 (Amplified)

*Y*ou have come to mount Sion, the CITY of the living God, the heavenly Jerusalem, to myriads of angels in festal gathering, to the assembly of the first-born registered in heaven, to the God of all as judge, to the spirits of men made perfect, to Jesus who mediates the new covenant, and to the sprinkled blood whose message is nobler than Abel's.

Hebrews 12:22-24 (Moffatt)

*G*lorious things of thee are spoken, Zion CITY of our God;
He whose word can not be broken formed thee for His own abode:
On the Rock of Ages founded, what can shake thy sure repose?
With salvation's walls surrounded, Thou mayest smile at all thy foes.

Saviour, if of Zion's CITY I, through grace a member am,
Let the world deride or pity—I will glory in Thy name.
Fading is the world-ling's pleasure, all his boasted pomp and show;
Solid joys and lasting treasure none but Zion's children know.

(John Newton)

Begin your prayer time adoring and praising the God who abides in the CITY.

THE GOD OF THE CITY

CITIES OF REFUGE—When the Israelites had come into the land of Canaan they were to choose towns conveniently situated as "CITIES OF REFUGE," to which the manslayer who had killed a person by accident might flee. (Unger's)

*N*ow some of the families of the sons of Kohath were given CITIES as their territory from the tribe of Ephraim. And they gave them one of the CITIES OF REFUGE, Shechem with its common lands, in the mountains of Ephraim.

1 Chronicles 6:66 & 67a (NKJ)

*I*f Yahweh does not build the house, in vain the masons toil; If Yahweh does not guard the CITY, in vain the sentries watch.

Psalm 127:1 (NJB)

*A*nd I saw heaven new in quality and an earth new in quality, for the first heaven and the first earth passed away. And the sea does not exist any longer. And the CITY, the Holy CITY, Jerusalem, the new one in quality, I saw coming down out of heaven from God, having been prepared as a bride who has been adorned for her groom.

Revelation 20:1 & 2 (Wuest)

*I*n the land of fadeless day lies a "CITY foursquare,"
It shall never pass away, and there is no "night there."
God shall "wipe away all tears;" there's no death no pain, nor fears;
And they count not time by years, for there is "no night there."

All the gates of pearl are made, In the "city foursquare,"
All the streets with gold are laid, and there is "no night there."
God shall "wipe away all tears;" there's no death, no pain, nor fears;
And they count not time by years, for there is "no night there.

(by John R. Clements)

Begin you prayer time adoring God for providing us with a heavenly CITY OF REFUGE.

THE GOD OF THE CITY

CITY—In the most ancient times the only distinction between village and CITY was that an assemblage of houses and buildings surrounded by a wall was reckoned a CITY, and without such surroundings a village. (Unger)

*W*hen the trumpets sounded, the people shouted, and at the sound of the trumpet, when the people gave a loud shout, the wall collapsed; so every man charged straight in, and they took the CITY. They devoted the CITY to the Lord.

Joshua 6:20 & 21a (NIV)

*Y*ou are a light that gives light to the world. A CITY that is built on a hill cannot be hidden.

Matthew 5:14 (NCV)

*A*ll these persons died in the faith. They were not yet in possession of the things promised, but they had seen them far ahead and hailed them, and confessed themselves no more than strangers or passing strangers on earth. Those who use such language show plainly that they are looking for a country of their own. If their hearts had been in the country they had left, they could have found opportunity to return. Instead, we find them longing for a better country—I mean, the heavenly one. That is why God is not ashamed to be called their God; for he has a CITY ready for them.

Hebrews 11:13-16 (NEB)

*A*nd the gates shall never close to the "CITY foursquare,"
There life's crystal river flows and there is no night there.
God shall "wipe away all tears;" there's no death, no pain, nor fears;
And the count no time by years, for there is "no night there."

There they need no sunshine bright, in that "CITY foursquare,"
For the Lamb is all the light, and there is "no night there."
God shall "wipe away all tears;" there's no death, no pain, nor fears:
And they count not time by years, for there is "no night there."

(by John R. Clements)

Begin your prayer time adoring God for being the light in the "CITY foursquare."

THE GOD OF THE CITY

Hebrew CITIES, The cities of Palestine were, judging from the large number mentioned in Joshua, relatively small, like most CITIES of ancient times. They were like oriental CITIES of today, built with narrow crooked streets, with many squares near the gates, where markets and courts were held. The government of Jewish CITIES was vested in a council of elders. (Unger's)

*N*ow Boaz went up to the gate and sat down there, and behold the close relative of whom Boaz spoke was passing by, so he said, "Turn aside friend, sit down here." And he turned aside and sat down. And he took ten men of the elders of the CITY and said, "Sit down here." So they sat down.

Ruth 4:1 & 2 (NAS)

*O*ne night the Lord spoke to Paul in a vision and told him, "Don't be afraid! Speak out! Don't quit! For I am with you and no one can harm you. Many people here in this CITY belong to me." So Paul stayed there the next year and a half, teaching the truths of God.

Acts 18:9-11 (Paraphrased)

*H*appy are those who wash their robes, for they have the right to the tree of life and the freedom of the gates of the CITY.

Revelation 22:14 (Phillips)

*W*hen my life work is ended, and I cross the swelling tide,
When the bright and glorious morning I shall see;
I shall know my Redeemer when I reach the other side
And His smile will be the first to welcome me.

I shall know Him, I shall know him,
And redeemed by His side I shall stand,
I shall know Him, I shall know Him
By the prints of the nails in His hand.

Through the gates to the CITY in a robe of spotless white,
He will lead me where no tears will ever fall;
In the glad song of ages I shall mingle with delight;
But I long to meet my Saviour first of all.

(by Fanny J. Crosby)

Begin your prayer time adoring the God who provides a heavenly CITY.

THE GOD WHO CLOTHES

CLOTHE—To put garments on; to invest with raiment; to cover with dress (Webster)

The Lord is King, He is CLOTHED in majesty. The Lord is CLOTHED in majesty and armed with strength. The world is set, and it cannot be moved.

Psalm 93:1 (NCV)

The Lord God made coats of skin and CLOTHED them.

Genesis 3:21 (KJ)

"Think of the lilies; they neither spin nor weave; yet I tell you, even Solomon in all his splendor was not ATTIRED like one of these. But if that is how God CLOTHES the grass, which is grown in the field today, and tomorrow is thrown on the stove, how much more will He CLOTHE you!"

Luke 12:27 & 28 (NEB)

> O worship the King, all glorious above,
> O gratefully sing His power and His love;
> Our shield and Defender, the Ancient of Days,
> Pavilioned in splendor, and girded with praise.
>
> O tell of His might, O sing of His grave,
> Whose ROBE is the light, whose canopy space,
> His chariots of wrath the deep thunderclouds form,
> And dark is His path on the wings of the storm.
>
> *(by Robert Grant)*

Begin you prayer time adoring God for the way He CLOTHES Himself.

THE GOD WHO CLOTHES

🈲 CLOTHES synonyms—Apparel, array, attire, dress, garments, raiment, vesture, habit, garb. (Webster)

*B*less Yahweh, my soul. Yahweh my God, how great you are! CLOTHED in majesty and glory, wrapped in a robe of light!

Psalm 104:1 (NJB)

I put on righteousness and it CLOTHED me; My justice was like a ROBE and a turban.

Job 29:14 (NKJ)

*S*ix days after this Jesus took with Him Peter and James and John, and led them up on a high mountain, apart by themselves. And He was transfigured before them and became resplendent with divine brightness. And His GARMENTS became glistening, intensely white, as no fuller (cloth dresser) on earth could bleach them.

Mark 9:2 & 3 (Amplified)

> *W*ith harps and with viols, there stands a great throng
> In the presence of Jesus, and sings this new song:
> Unto Him who hath loved us and washed us from sin
> Unto Him be the glory for ever. Amen.
>
> All these once were sinners, defiled in his sight,
> Now ARRAYED in pure GARMENTS in praise they unite.
> Aloud in His praises our voices shall ring,
> So that others believing, this new song shall sing.
>
> *(by Arthur T. Pierson)*

Begin you prayer time adoring and giving praise to the God who ADORNS us in white.

February 29

THE GOD WHO CLOTHES

I will also CLOTHE her priests with salvation: and her saints shall shout for joy.

Psalm 132:16 (KJ)

"*I* was hungry and you fed me, thirsty and you gave me drink; I was a stranger and you received me in your homes, naked and you CLOTHED me; I was sick and you took care of me, in prison and you visited me.

Matthew 25:35 & 36 (Good News)

You younger members must also submit to the elders. Indeed all of you should defer to one another and wear the OVERALL of humility in serving each other.

Peter 5:5 (Phillips)

For we know that if the earthly tent which is our house is torn down, we have a building from God, a house not made with hands, eternal in the heavens. For indeed in this house we groan, longing to be CLOTHED with our dwelling from heaven.

2 Corinthians 5:1 & 2 (NAS)

> *Thine* be the glory, risen, conquering Son,
> Endless is victory Thou o'er death hast won;
> Angels in bright RAIMENT rolled the stone away,
> Kept the folded GRAVE-CLOTHES, where Thy body lay.
>
> Lo! Jesus meets us, risen from the tomb;
> Lovingly He greets us, scatters fear and gloom;
> Let the church with gladness, hymns of triumph sing,
> For the Lord now liveth, death hast lost its sting.
>
> *(by Edmond L. Budry)*

Begin your prayer time adoring God for how He has clothed us.

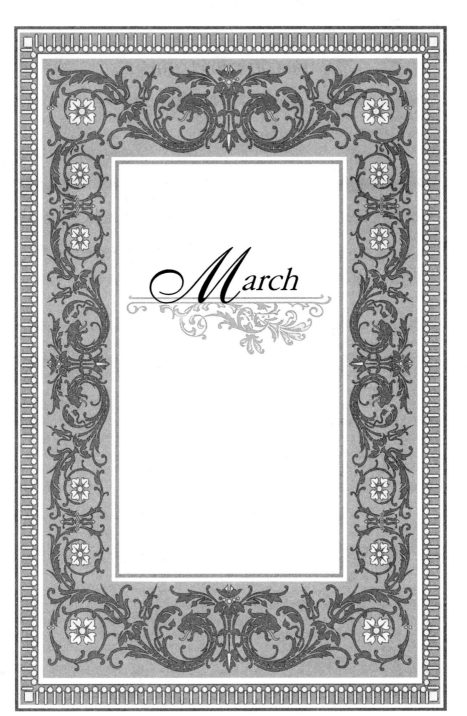

March

THE GOD WHO CLOTHES

*H*ow good and pleasant it is when brothers live together in unity! It is like precious oil poured on the head, running down on the beard, running down on Aaron's beard, down on the collar of his ROBES.

Psalm 133:1 & 2 (NIV)

"*T*hree days ago," said Cornelius, "at this very hour I was praying in my house at three o'clock in the afternoon, when a man stood before me in SHINING DRESS, saying, "Cornelius, your prayer has been heard, your alms are remembered by God.""

Acts 10:30 & 31 (Moffatt)

*A*nd the angel said unto them, Stop being afraid. For behold, I am bringing you good tidings of great joy, which joy is of such a nature that it shall pertain to all people, because there was born to you a Saviour who is Christ, the Lord, in the city of David. And this shall be an unusual and distinguishing token of identification for you; you shall find a new born infant which has been wrapped in CLOTH BANDS, and lying in a feeding trough.

Luke 2:10 & 11 (Wuest)

*T*hen I saw heaven thrown open and a white horse appeared. Its Rider is called Faithful and True; justly He sentences and wages war. His eyes are a fire-flame and on His head are many diadems with a name inscribed which no one knows except Himself. The ROBE He is wearing is sprinkled with blood and His appointed title is: The Word of God. On white horses and DRAPED in fine linen, white and pure, the heavenly armies follow Him.

Revelation 19:11-14 (Berkeley)

*T*he countless multitude on High, that tune their songs to Jesus name,
All merit of their own deny, and Jesus' worth alone proclaim.
Firm on the ground of sovereign grace, they stand before Jehovah's throne;
The only song in that blest place Is, "Thou art worthy! Thou alone!"

With spotless ROBES of purest white, and branches of triumphal palm,
They shout, with transports of delight, heavens ceaseless universal psalm;
"Salvation's glory all be paid To Him who sits upon the throne,
And to the Lamb whose blood was shed; Thou! Thou art worthy! Thou alone!"

(by Archibald Rutherford)

Begin your prayer time adoring the God who washed your ROBES white.

THE GOD WHO COMFORTS AND CONSOLES

▓ COMFORT—support, consolation under calamity, distress or danger. That which gives strength, or support in distress, difficulty, danger or infirmity. (Webster)

*Y*es, though I walk through the (deep, sunless) valley of the shadow of death, I will fear or dread no evil; for You are with me; Your rod (to protect) and Your staff (to guide), they COMFORT me.

Psalm 23:4 (Amplified)

*C*OMFORT ye, COMFORT ye my people, saith your God. Speak ye COMFORTABLY to Jerusalem, and cry unto her, that her warfare is accomplished, that her iniquity is pardoned: for she hath received of the Lord's hand double for all her sins.

Isaiah 40:1 & 2 (KJ)

*P*raise be to the God and Father of our Lord Jesus Christ, God is the Father who is full of mercy and all COMFORT. He COMFORTS us every time we have trouble, so when others have trouble, we can COMFORT them with the same COMFORT God gives us.

2 Corinthians 1:3 & 4 (NCV)

*U*nder His wings I am safely abiding;
Though the night deepens and tempests are wild,
Still I can trust Him; I know He will keep me;
He has redeemed me, and I am His child

Under His wings, what a refuge in sorrow!
How the heart yearningly turns to His rest!
Often when earth has no balm for my healing,
There I find COMFORT, and there I am blest

Under His wings, under His wings,
Who from His love can sever?
Under His wings my soul shall abide,
Safely abide forever.

(by William O. Cushing)

Begin your prayer time adoring the God who CONSOLES and COMFORTS.

THE GOD WHO COMFORTS AND CONSOLES

▦ COMFORT synonyms—consolation, solace, encouragement and support. (Webster)

*R*emember the word you pledged your servant, on which you have built my hope. This has been my COMFORT in my suffering: that your promise gives me life.

Psalm 119:49 & 50 (NJB)

*S*ay it again: "The Lord of Hosts declares that the cities of Israel will again overflow with prosperity, and the Lord will again COMFORT Jerusalem and bless her and live in her."

Zechariah 1:17 (Paraphrased)

*I*f then our common life in Christ yields anything to stir the heart, any loving CONSOLATION, any sharing of the spirit, any warmth of affection or compassion, fill up my cup of happiness by thinking and feeling alike, with the same love for one another, the same turn of mind, and a common care for unity.

Philippians 2:1 & 2 (NEV)

*E*very day the Lord Himself is near me with a special mercy for each hour;
All my cares He fain would bear and cheer me,
He whose name is Counsellor and Power
The protection of His child and treasure is a charge that on Himself He laid;
As thy days, thy strength shall be in measure,
This the pledge to me He made.

Help me then in every tribulation so to trust Thy promises, O Lord,
That I lose not faith's sweet CONSOLATION
Offered me within Thy holy word.
Help me Lord, when toil and trouble meeting; e'er to take, as from a Father's hand,
One by one, the days, the moments fleeting,
Till I reach the promised land.

(by Lina Sandell Berg)

Begin your prayer time adoring God for the COMFORT and CONSOLATION He gives.

THE GOD WHO COMFORTS AND CONSOLES

COMFORT—Hebrew, naham, to COMFORT, give forth sighs; Greek, parakaleo, to call alongside to help. Our English word is from the Latin confortare (con cortis) to strengthen much, and means to ease, encourage, inspirit, enliven. (Unger's Bible Dictionary)

*S*end me a sign of your favor. When those who hate me see it they will loose face because you help and COMFORT me.

Psalm 86:17 (LB)

*I*ndeed, the Lord will COMFORT Zion: He will COMFORT all her waste places. And her wilderness He will make like Eden, and her desert like the garden of the Lord; joy and gladness will be found in her, thanksgiving and sound of a melody.

Isaiah 51:3 (NAS)

*B*ut God, the ENCOURAGER of the downhearted, did CONSOLE us by the arrival of Titus, and not merely by his arrival, but by the ENCOURAGEMENT he received from you, for he related how you are longing for us, your sorrow, your zeal for me, all of which turned out for my greater joy.

2 Corinthians 7:6 & 7 (Berkeley)

*F*or the blessed Holy Spirit, sent by Thee from heaven above;
We would join to praise Thee, Father, for this matchless gift of love.
Then He showed us that the Saviour, On the cross had born our sin;
And when we, by faith received Him, sealed us, and now dwells within.

O, forbid that we should grieve Him by neglect or willful sin;
Grant that we may know the fullness of this heavenly Guest within!
For the Holy Spirit's presence, COMFORTER and Guide divine;
From our hearts we join to praise Thee for this gracious Gift of Thine!

(by Alfred P. Gibbs)

Begin you prayer time with adoration to the COMFORTING God.

THE GOD WHO COMFORTS AND CONSOLES

COMFORTER—the designation of the Holy Spirit. The same Greek word *parakletos*, thus rendered is translated "Advocate" as applicable to Christ. It means properly "one who is summoned to the side of another" to help him in a court of justice by defending him. (Today's Dictionary of the Bible)

I have said all these things while I am still with you. But the one who is coming to stand by you, the HOLY SPIRIT whom the Father will send in my name, will be your teacher and will bring to your minds all that I have said to you."

John 14:25 & 26 (Phillips)

*H*owever, I am telling you nothing but the truth when I say, it is profitable—good, expedient, advantageous—for you that I go away. Because if I do not go away, the COMFORTER (COUNSELLOR, HELPER, ADVOCATE, INTERCESSOR, STRENGTHENER, STANDBY) will not come to you—into close fellowship with you. But if I go away, I will send Him to you—to be in close fellowship with you.

John 16:7 (Amplified)

*M*y little children, these things I write to you, that you may not sin. And if anyone sins, we have an ADVOCATE with the Father, Jesus Christ the righteous.

1 John 2:1 (NKJ)

O spread the tidings round where ever man is found,
Wherever human hearts and human woes abound;
Let every Christian tongue proclaim the joyful sound:
The COMFORTER has come!

Lo, the great King of Kings, with healing in His wings,
To every captive soul a full deliverance brings;
And through the vacant cells the song of triumph rings:
The COMFORTER has come!

(by Frank Bottome)

Begin your prayer time with adoration to the God who provided a personal CONSOLER.

THE GOD WHO COMFORTS AND CONSOLES

Shout for joy, O heavens, rejoice, O earth! For the Eternal has CONSOLED his people and pitied his folklorn folk.

Isaiah 49:13 (Moffatt)

For this is what the Lord says: "I will extend peace to her like a river, and the wealth of nations like a flooding stream; you will nurse and be carried on her arm and dandled on her knees. As a mother COMFORTS her child, so will I COMFORT you; and you will be COMFORTED over Jerusalem."

Isaiah 66:12 & 13 (NIV)

And behold, there was a man in Jerusalem whose name was Simeon, and this man was righteous and one who reverenced God and was pious, looking expectantly toward that which will afford COMFORT and refreshment for Israel.

Luke 2:25 (Wuest)

Now may our Lord Jesus Christ Himself, and God our Father, Who loved us and gave us everlasting CONSOLATION and encouragement and well-founded hope through (His) grace (unmerited favor), COMFORT and encourage your hearts and strengthen them—make them steadfast and keep them unswerving—in every good work and word.

2 Thessalonians 2:16 & 17 (Amplified)

Oh, the best friend to have is Jesus,
When the cares of life upon you roll;
He will heal the wounded heart,
He will strength and grace impart.

What a friend I have found in Jesus!
Peace and COMFORT to my soul He brings;
Leaning on His mighty arm,
I will fear no ill nor harm.

(by Peter P. Bilhorn)

Begin your prayer time in adoration to the God of COMFORT.

THE GOD WHO COMFORTS AND CONSOLES

In the multitudes of my thoughts within me thy COMFORTS delight my soul.

Psalm 94:19 (KJ)

Then you will say on that day, "I will give thanks to Thee, O Lord; For although Thou wast angry with me, Thine anger is turned away, And Thou dost COMFORT me."

Isaiah 12:1 (NAS)

As Christ's cup of suffering overflows, and we suffer with him, so also through Christ our CONSOLATION overflows. If distress be our lot, it is the price we pay for your CONSOLATION, for your salvation; if our lot be CONSOLATION, it is to help us to bring you COMFORT, and strength to face with fortitude the same sufferings we now endure.

2 Corinthians 1:5 & 6 (NEB)

Thus God, determining to show more abundantly to the heirs of promise the immutability of His counsel, confirmed it by an oath, that by two immutable things in which it is impossible for God to lie, we might have strong CONSOLATION, who have fled for refuge to lay hold of the hope set before us.

Hebrews 6:17 & 18 (NKJ)

Let me at Thy throne of mercy
Find a sweet relief;
Kneeling there in deep contrition,
Help my unbelief.

Thou the spring of all my COMFORT,
More than life to me,
Whom have I on earth beside Thee?
Whom in heaven but Thee?

(by Fanny J. Crosby)

Begin you prayer time adoring the God who COMFORTS and CONSOLES.

THE GOD WHO COUNSELS

COUNSEL—To give advice; to advise; to exhort, warn, admonish or instruct. (Webster)

*Y*ou guide me with your COUNSEL, and afterward you will take me into glory.

Psalm 73:24 (NIV)

*F*or there is a child born for us, a son given to us and dominion is laid on his shoulders; and this is the name they give him; Wonderful COUNSELOR, Mighty God, Eternal Father, Prince of Peace.

Isaiah 9:5 & 6 (NJB)

*A*las, Lord God! Behold, You made the heavens and the earth by Your great power and by Your stretched out arm! There is nothing too hard or too wonderful for You, Who shows loving-kindness to thousands, and recompenses the iniquity of the fathers into the bosom of their children after them. The great, the Mighty God, the Lord of hosts is His name, Great in COUNSEL and mighty in deeds; Whose eyes are open upon all the ways of the sons of men, to reward or repay to each according to his ways and according to the fruits of his doings.

Jeremiah 32:17-19 (Amplified)

*L*ord, speak to me, that I may speak
In living echoes of Thy tone;
As thou hast sought, so let me seek
Thy erring children lost and lone.

O TEACH me, Lord, that I may TEACH
The precious things Thou doest impart;
And wing my words, that they may reach
The hidden depths of many a heart.

(by Frances R. Havergal)

Begin your prayer time adoring the God who gives COUNSEL.

THE GOD WHO COUNSELS

COUNSELOR, In general, an advisor upon any matter. (Unger's Bible Dictionary)

I praise the Lord because he ADVISES me. Even at night I feel his LEADING.

Psalm 16:17 (NCV)

*(C*hrist) in whom also we have obtained an inheritance, being predestined according to the purpose of Him who works all things according to the COUNSEL of His will.

Ephesians 1:11 (NKJ)

*T*herefore judge nothing before the time, until the Lord come, who both will bring to light the hidden things of darkness, and will make manifest the COUNSELS of the hearts: and then shall every man have praise of God.

1 Corinthians 4:5 (KJ)

*F*or the blessed Holy Spirit
Sent by Thee from above;
We would join to praise Thee, Father,
For this matchless Gift of Love.

Now He seeks to TEACH and GUIDE us,
From Thy precious holy word;
And empowers us for the service
Of our Saviour, Christ, the Lord.

(by Alfred P. Gibbs)

Begin your prayer time adoring the God who COUNSELS, INSTRUCTS, TEACHES and GUIDES.

THE GOD WHO COUNSELS

I will INSTRUCT you and teach you what is the road to take; I will give you COUNSEL, O humble soul.

Psalm 32:8 (Moffatt)

All this also comes from the Lord Almighty, wonderful in COUNSEL and magnificent in wisdom.

Isaiah 28:29 (NIV)

Every scripture is God-breathed, and is profitable for TEACHING, for conviction, for improvement, for TRAINING with respect to righteousness, in order that the man of God may be complete, fitted out for every good work.

2 Timothy 3:16 & 17 (Wuest)

My ADVICE to you is to buy from me that gold which is purified in the furnace so that you may be rich, and the white garments to wear so that you may hide the shame of your nakedness, and salve to put on your eyes to make you see.

Revelation 3:18 (Phillips)

Father, grant Thy Holy Spirit
In our hearts may rule today,
Grieved not, quenched not, but unhindered
Hold us beneath His mighty sway.

He it is who works within us,
TEACHING rebel hearts to pray;
He whose holy intercessions
Rise for us both night and day.

(by E. Margaret Clarkson)

Begin your prayer time adoring the God who ADVISES, TEACHES, COUNSELS GUIDES and TRAINS.

GOD OUR COVER

COVER—To overspread, to hide, to shelter. (Webster)

If you live in the shelter of Elyon and make your home in the shadow of Shaddai, you can say to Yahweh, "My refuge, my fortress, my God in whom I trust!" He rescues you from the snares of fowlers hoping to destroy you; he COVERS you with his feathers, and you find shelter underneath his wings.

Psalm 91:1-4 (NJB)

"So it shall be, while My glory passes by, that I will put you in the cleft of the rock, and will COVER you with My hand while I pass by.

Exodus 33:22 (NKJ)

Spiritually prosperous are those whose lawlessnesses were put away and whose sins were COVERED.

Romans 4:7 (Wuest)

The Lord's our Rock, in Him we hide,
A SHELTER in the time of storm;
Secure what ever ill betide,
A SHELTER in the time of storm.

A shade by day, defense by night,
A SHELTER in the time of storm;
No fears alarm, no foes affright,
A SHELTER in the time of storm.

(by Vernon J. Charlesworth)

Begin your prayer time in adoration to the God who provides your SHELTER.

GOD OUR COVER

COVER synonyms—overspread, cloak, shield, protect, shelter, hide, mark. (Webster)

Bless—affectionately, gratefully praise—the Lord, O my soul! O Lord my God, You are very great! You are clothed with honor and majesty: Who COVER Yourself with light as with a garment, Who has stretched out the heavens like a curtain or a tent,

Psalm 104:1 & 2 (Amplified)

For I am the Lord your God, who churns up the sea so that its waves roar— the Lord Almighty is his name. I have put my words in thy mouth, and have COVERED you with the shadow of my hand—I who set the heavens in place, who layed the foundations of the earth, and who say unto Zion, "You are my people."

Isaiah 51:15 & 16 (NIV)

If I had not come and spoken unto them, they had not had sin: but now they have no cloke (cloak) for their sin.

John 15:22 (KJ)

A wonderful Saviour is Jesus my Lord,
A wonderful Saviour to me;
He hideth my soul in the cleft of the rock,
Where river of pleasure I see.

He hideth my soul in the cleft of the rock
That shadows a dry, thirsty land;
He hideth my life in the depths of His love,
And COVERS me there with His hand.

(by Fanny J. Cosby)

Begin your prayer time adoring the God who is a COVER for your sins.

GOD OUR COVER

*H*ow blessed is he whose transgression is forgiven, Whose sin is COVERED.

Psalm 32:1 (NAS)

*H*e spread out a cloud above them to SHIELD them from the burning sun, and gave them a pillar of flame at night to give them light.

Psalm 105:39 (Living Bible)

*N*obody lights a lamp and then COVERS it with a basin or puts it under a bed. On the contrary, he puts it on a lamp-stand so that those who come in may see the light. For there is nothing that will not become public, nothing under COVER that will not be made known and brought into the open.

Luke 8:16 & 17 (NEB)

*A*t all times carry faith as a SHIELD; with it you will be able to put out all the burning arrows shot by the evil one.

Ephesians 6:16 (Good News)

O worship the King, all glorious above,
O gratefully sing His power and His love;
Our SHIELD and Defender, the Ancient of days,
Pavilioned in splendor, and girded with praise.

The earth, with its store of wonders untold,
Almighty, Thy power hath founded of old;
Hath stablished it fast by a changeless decree,
And round it hath cast, like a MANTLE the sea.

(by Robert Grant)

Begin your prayer time adoring the God who is your SHIELD.

GOD OUR COVER

*F*or You have formed my inward parts; You have COVERED me in my mother's womb. I will praise You, for I am fearfully and wonderfully made; Marvelous are Your works, And that my soul knows very well.

Psalm 139:13 & 14 (NKJ)

*F*or you have been a SHELTER and a refuge for me, a strong tower against the adversary.

Psalm 61:3 (Amplified)

*A*nd if someone wants to sue you and take your TUNIC, let him have your CLOAK as well.

Matthew 5:40 (NIV)

*T*hou art my HIDING PLACE and my SHIELD; I wait for Thy word.

Psalm 119:114 (NAS)

*W*ith numberless blessings each moment He crowns,
And filled with His fullness divine,
I sing in my rapture, oh glory to God
For such a Redeemer as mine!

When CLOTHED in His brightness, transported I rise
To meet Him in clouds of the sky,
His perfect salvation, His wonderful love,
I'll shout with the millions on high.

(by Fanny J. Crosby)

Begin your prayer time adoring the God who is you COVERING, SHIELD, HIDING-PLACE and CLOAK.

THE GOD WHO WEARS A CROWN
AND WHO GIVES CROWNS

CROWN—An ornament worn on the head by kings and those having sovereign power, as a badge of their office. Regal power; sovereignty; kingly government or imperial domain. (Webster)

*N*ow in my vision I saw a white cloud and sitting on it, one like a son of man with a gold CROWN on his head and a sharp sickle in his hand.

Revelation 14:14 (NJB)

*S*piritually prosperous is the man who remains steadfast under trial, because after he has met the test and has been approved, he shall receive the CROWN, namely, that CROWN which has to do with life (eternal life), which (CROWN) He promised to those who love Him.

James 1:12 (Wuest)

O Lord, the king rejoices in your strength. How great is his joy in the victories you give! You have granted him the desire of his heart and have not withheld the request of his lips. You welcomed him with rich blessings and placed a CROWN of pure gold on his head.

Psalm 21:1-3 (NIV)

> *C*ROWN Him with many CROWNS, the Lamb upon the throne:
> Hark! how the heavenly anthem drowns all music but its own!
> Awake, my soul, and sing of Him who died for thee,
> And hail Him as thy matchless King Through all eternity.
>
> CROWN Him the Lord of love: behold his hands and side
> Rich wounds, yet visible above, in beauty glorified;
> No angel in the sky can fully bear that sight,
> But downward bends his wondering eye at mysteries so bright.

(by Matthew Bridges)

Begin your prayer time adoring the CROWNED king.

THE GOD WHO WEARS A CROWN
AND WHO GIVES CROWNS

CROWN—literally, something set apart, consecration. Is supposed to mean a diadem. It was applied to the plate of gold in front of the high priest's miter; also to the diadem which Saul wore into battle, and which was brought to David... used at the coronation. (Unger's Bible Dictionary)

For the Lord hath chosen Zion; he hath desired it for his habitation. This is my rest forever: here will I dwell; for I have desired it. I will abundantly bless her provision: I will satisfy her poor with bread. I will also clothe her priests with salvation: and her saints shall shout aloud for joy. There will I make the horn of David to bud: I have ordained a lamp for mine anointed. His enemies will I clothe with shame: but upon himself shall his CROWN flourish.

Psalm 132:13-18 (KJ)

Every athlete in training submits to strict discipline; he does so in order to be CROWNED with a wreath that will not last; but we do it for one that will last forever.

1 Corinthians 9:25 (Good News)

So my brothers whom I love and long for, my joy and my CROWN, do stand firmly in the Lord, and remember how much I love you.

Philippians 4:1 (Phillips)

CROWN Him the Lord of life: who triumphed over the grave,
Who rose victorious in the strife for those He came to save;
His glories now we sing, Who died and rose on high,
Who died eternal life to bring and lives that death may die.

CROWN Him the Lord of years, the Potentate of time,
Creator of the rolling spheres, ineffably sublime!
All hail, Redeemer hail! For Thou hast died for me;
Thy praise shall never, never fail through-out eternity.

(by Matthew Bridges)

Begin your prayer time praising the God who gives us CROWNS.

THE GOD WHO WEARS A CROWN
AND WHO GIVES CROWNS

CROWN of thorns, our Lord was crowned with one, in mockery by the Romans... the object was to insult... probably made with the abundant thorny nabk bush... whose flexible round branches could easily be platted into the form of a crown. (Today's Dictionary of the Bible)

*U*sing thorny branches, they made a CROWN, put it on his head, and put a stick in his right hand. Then the soldiers bowed before Jesus and made fun of him, saying, "Hail, King of the Jews!"

Matthew 27:29 (NCV)

*A*nd instantly I was, in spirit, there in heaven and saw—oh, the glory of it!—a throne and someone sitting on it! Great bursts of light flashed forth from him as from a glittering diamond, or from a shining ruby, and a rainbow glowing like an emerald encircled his throne. Twenty-four smaller thrones surrounded his, with twenty-four Elders sitting on them: all were clothed in white, with golden CROWNS upon their heads.

Revelation 4:2-4 (TLB)

*T*hen I saw heaven wide open, and there before me was a white horse; and its rider's name was Faithful and True, for he is just in judgment and just in war. His eyes flamed like fire, and on his head were many DIADEMS.

Revelation 19:11 & 12 (TEB)

*C*ROWNED with thorns upon the tree, silent in Thine agony;
On Thy grief and sore amaze, Saviour, I would fix my gaze!
Sin atoning Sacrifice, Thou art precious in mine eyes;
Thou alone my rest shall be, now and through eternity.

(by H. Gratton Guiness)

Begin you prayer time giving praises to the Saviour who was willing to wear a CROWN of thorns for you.

THE GOD WHO WEARS A CROWN
AND WHO GIVES CROWNS

DIADEM (bound around) CROWN The original meaning rolled together, or around, like the modern eastern headdress. (Smith's Bible Dictionary)

The simple acquire folly, but the prudent are CROWNED with knowledge. The evil bow before the good, and the wicked (stand suppliant) at the gates of the (uncompromisingly) righteous. The poor is hated even by his own neighbor, but the rich has many friends. He who despises his neighbors sins (against God, his fellow man and himself) but happy—blessed and fortunate— is he who is kind and merciful to the poor. Do they not err who devise evil and wander from the way of life? But loving-kindness and mercy, loyalty and faithfulness shall be to those who devise good. In all labor there is profit, but idle talk leads only to poverty. The CROWN of the wise is their wealth of wisdom, but the foolishness of (self-confident) fools is (nothing but) folly.

Proverbs 14:18-24 (Amplified)

What is man that Thou art mindful of him, or a son of man that Thou lookest after him? For a little while Thou hast ranked him lower than the angels; with glory and honor hast Thou CROWNED him; all things hast Thou subjected underneath his feet.

Hebrews 2:6-8 (Berkeley)

By faith we see Him lifted up, On the cross! On the cross!
He drinks for us the bitter cup, On the cross! On the cross!
The rocks do rend, the mountains quake, while Jesus doth atonement make,
While Jesus suffers for our sake, On the cross! On the Cross!

But now He is risen, ascended, CROWNED, On the throne! On the throne!
Heaven's highest place for Him is found, On the throne! On the throne!
Our hearts we low in worship bow, And join, as one, to hail Him now:
"Worthy, O Lamb of God, art Thou!" On the throne! On the throne!

(by Joseph Hopkins)

Begin you prayer time adoring the worthy CROWNED Lamb of God.

arch 19

THE GOD OF THE NIGHT AND DAY:
THE LIGHT AND THE DARKNESS

■ DAY That part of the time of the earth's revolution on its axis, in which a given area is presented to the sun. NIGHT That part of the natural DAY when the sun is below the horizon. (Webster)

God said, "let there be LIGHT", and there was light. God saw that the LIGHT was good, and God divided LIGHT from DARKNESS. God called the LIGHT "DAY", and the DARKNESS he called "NIGHT". Evening came and morning came: the first day.

Genesis 1:3 & 4 (NJB)

You are my lamp, O Lord; the Lord turns my DARKNESS into LIGHT.

2 Samuel 22:29 (NIV)

You yourselves used to be in the DARKNESS, but since you have become the Lord's people who are in the LIGHT. So you must live like people who belong to the LIGHT.

Ephesians 5:8 (Good News)

Walk in the LIGHT! so shalt thou know that fellowship of love.
His Spirit only can bestow Who reigns in LIGHT above.
Walk in the LIGHT! and thou shalt find thy heart made truly His,
Who dwells in cloudless LIGHT enshrined, in whom no DARKNESS is.

Walk in the LIGHT! and thou shalt own thy DARKNESS passed away.
Because that LIGHT on thee shone in which is perfect DAY.
Walk in the LIGHT! thy path shall be a path, though thorny, bright;
For God, by grace, shall dwell in thee, and God Himself is LIGHT.

(by Bernard Barton)

Begin your prayer time with adoring the God who provides both physical and spiritual LIGHT.

THE GOD OF THE NIGHT AND DAY:
THE LIGHT AND THE DARKNESS

LIGHT That form of motion or energy capable of affecting the organs of sight and thus rendering visible the objects from which it proceeds. DARKNESS Absence of light; obscurity; gloom. (Webster)

"While the earth remains, seedtime and harvest, and cold and heat, and summer and winter, and DAY and NIGHT shall not cease.

Genesis 8:22 (NAS)

The people that walked in DARKNESS have seen a great LIGHT: they that dwell in the shadow of death, upon them hath the LIGHT shined.

Isaiah 9:2 (KJ)

With joy constantly giving thanks to the Father who qualified you for the portion of the share of the inheritance of the saints in the sphere of the LIGHT; who transferred us out of the tyrannical rule of DARKNESS and transferred us into the kingdom of the Son of His love.

Colossians 1:12 & 13 (Wuest)

Give me this DAY the pardon of my sin,
Cleanse Thou my soul, and make me pure with-in;
I know no fear if Thou art by my side,
Stay ever close beside me, be my guide!

Give me this DAY the comfort of Thy grace,
Let me but see the radiance of Thy face;
Keep me, O Father, in Thy perfect love,
Grant me a resting place with Thee above!

(by Rob Roy Perry)

Begin your prayer time giving thanks to God for the LIGHT He provides.

THE GOD OF THE NIGHT AND DAY,
THE LIGHT AND DARKNESS

LIGHT came also naturally to typify true religion and the felicity it imparts and the glorious inheritance of the redeemed. (Today's Dictionary of the Bible)

The heavens proclaim God's splendor, the sky speaks of his handiwork; DAY after DAY takes up the tale, NIGHT after NIGHT make him known.

Psalm 19:1 & 2 (Moffatt)

Who are these who sit in DARKNESS, in the shadow of death, crushed by misery and slavery? They rebelled against the Lord, scorning him who is the God above all gods.

Psalm 107:10 & 11 (Paraphrased)

But you, my friends, are not in the DARK, that the DAY should overtake you like a thief. You are all children of LIGHT, children of DAY.

1 Thessalonians 5:4 & 5 (NEB)

> The whole world was lost in the DARKNESS of sin;
> The LIGHT of the world is Jesus;
> Like sunshine at noonday His GLORY shone in,
> The LIGHT of the world is Jesus.
>
> Come to the Light, 'tis shining for thee;
> Sweetly the LIGHT has dawned upon me;
> Once I was blind, but now I can see;
> The LIGHT of the world is Jesus.
>
> *(by Philip Bliss)*

Begin your prayer time adoring God as the LIGHT of the world.

THE GOD OF THE DAY AND NIGHT,
OF THE LIGHT AND THE DARKNESS

🔳 DAY of Christ is the period connected with reward and blessing of saints at the coming of Christ for His own. (Unger's)

A single DAY spent in your Temple is better than a thousand anywhere else! I would rather be a doorman of the Temple of my God than live in the palaces of wickedness.

Psalm 84:10 (Living Bible)

*B*ut you are a chosen race, a royal priesthood, a dedicated nation, (God's) own purchased, special people, that you may set forth the wonderful deeds and display the virtues and perfections of Him Who called you out of DARKNESS into His marvelous LIGHT.

1 Peter 2:9 (Amplified)

*I*n this way our witnessing of Christ has been confirmed in you, so that you are falling behind in no Christian grace, while awaiting the appearing of our Lord Jesus Christ. And He will establish you to the finish, so that no blame may be yours at the DAY of our Lord Jesus Christ.

1 Corinthians 1:6-8 (Berkeley)

*N*o DARKNESS have we who in Jesus abide,
The LIGHT of the world is Jesus.
We walk in the LIGHT while we follow our Guide,
The LIGHT of the world is Jesus.

No need of the sunlight in heaven we're told
The LIGHT of the world is Jesus.
The Lamb is the LIGHT in the City of God,
The LIGHT of the world is Jesus.

(by Philip P. Bliss)

Begin your prayer time adoring the LIGHT of the world.

THE GOD OF THE NIGHT AND DAY;
THE LIGHT AND DARKNESS

DAY of the Lord—refers to the final consummation of the kingdom of God and his triumph over his foes at the time he delivers his people. (Today's)

This is the DAY that the Lord has made. Let us rejoice and be glad in it.

Psalm 118:24 (NCV)

Be silent in the presence of the Lord God; For the DAY of the Lord is at hand, For the Lord has prepared a sacrifice; He has invited His guests.

Zephaniah 1:7 (NAS)

But there is one thing, my friends, that you must never forget: that with the Lord, "a DAY" can mean a thousand years, and a thousand years is like a DAY.

2 Peter 3:8 (NJB)

DAY by DAY and with each passing moment,
Strength I find to meet my trials here;
Trusting in my Father's wise bestowment
I've no cause for worry or for fear.

He whose heart is kind beyond all measure
Gives unto each DAY what He deems best,
Lovingly its part of pain and pleasure,
Mingling toil with peace and rest.

(by Lina Sandell Berg)

Begin your prayer time with adoration for the God who gives us what He thinks best for each DAY.

THE GOD OF THE NIGHT AND THE DAY,
THE LIGHT AND THE DARKNESS

LIGHT synonyms—radiance, beam, gleam, flash, brightness, brilliancy, splendor, blaze, illumination, lamp. (Webster)

_If_ I say, "Surely the DARKNESS will hide me and the LIGHT become night around me," even the DARKNESS will not be dark to you; the NIGHT will shine like DAY, for DARKNESS is as LIGHT to you.

Psalm 139:11 & 12 (NIV)

But you are a chosen race, the King's priests, the holy nation, God's own people, chosen to proclaim the wonderful acts of God, who called you from DARKNESS into his own marvelous LIGHT.

1 Peter 2:9 (GN)

This then is the message which we have heard of him, and declare unto you, that God is LIGHT, and in him is no DARKNESS at all. If we say that we have fellowship with him, and walk in DARKNESS, we lie, and do not the truth: But if we walk in the LIGHT, we have fellowship one with another, and the blood of Jesus Christ his Son, cleanseth us from all sin.

1 John 1:5-7 (KJ)

Every DAY the Lord Himself is near me
With a special mercy for each hour;
All my cares He fain would bear and cheer me,
He whose name is Counselor and Power.

The protection of His child and treasure
Is a charge that on Himself He laid;
"As thy DAYS thy strength shall be in measure,"
This the pledge to me He made

(by Lina Sandell Berg)

Begin your prayer time adoring the God who gives you DAILY strength.

THE GOD OF NIGHT AND DAY;
LIGHT AND DARKNESS

DARKNESS synonyms—dimness, obscurity, gloom (Webster)

The Lord gives voice before His army, For His camp is very great; For strong is the One who executes His word. For the DAY of the Lord is great and very terrible; Who can endure it?

Joel 2:11 (NKJ)

Again, a commandment, one new in quality, I am writing to you, which is true in Him, and in you, because the DARKNESS is being caused to be passed away, and the LIGHT, the genuine LIGHT already is SHINING.

1 John 2:8 (Wuest)

Give us this DAY our daily bread.

Matthew 6:11 (NAS)

In case one builds on this foundation gold, silver, precious stones, wood, hay stubble, each one's work will come to evidence, for the DAY will bring it to LIGHT; by the FIRE it shall be revealed. Of what ever quality each one's work may be, the FIRE will test it.

1 Corinthians 3:12 & 13 (Berkeley)

> Help me then in every tribulation
> So to trust Thy promises, O Lord,
> That I lose not faith's sweet consolation
> Offered me within Thy holy word.
>
> Help me Lord, when toil and trouble meeting;
> E'er to take, as from a father's hand
> One by one, the DAYS, the moments fleeting,
> Till I reach the promised land.
>
> *(by Lima Sandell Berg)*

Begin you prayer time with adoration to the God who walks with us through each DAY.

THE GOD OF NIGHT AND DAY; LIGHT AND DARKNESS

*W*hile DAYLIGHT lasts, we must be busy with the work of Him who sent me; NIGHT comes when no one can do any work.

John 9:4 (Moffatt)

*A*nd we have the prophetic word (made) firmer still. You will do well to pay close attention to it as to a LAMP shining in a dismal (squalid, dark) place, until the DAY breaks through (the gloom) and the morning Star rises (comes into being) in your hearts.

2 Peter 1:19 (amplified)

*A*nd I will cause strange demonstrations in the heavens and on the earth— blood and fire and clouds of smoke; the sun shall turn black and the moon blood-red before that awesome DAY of the Lord arrives.

Acts 2:19 & 20 (TLB)

*I*n all the world around me I see His loving care,
And though my heart grows weary, I never will despair;
I know that He is leading through all the stormy blast,
The DAY of His appearing will come at last,

He lives, He lives, Christ Jesus lives TODAY!
He walks with me and talks with me along life's narrow way.
He lives, He lives, salvation to impart!
You ask me how I know He lives? He lives within my heart

(by Alfred H. Ackley)

Begin your prayer time praising the God of the NIGHT and DAY.

GOD OUR DELIVERER

⌗ DELIVER—to free, to release, to set at liberty; to rescue or save. (Webster)

*B*ut the Lord looks after those who fear him, those who put their hope in his love. He SAVES them from death and spares their lives in times of hunger.

Psalm 33:18 & 19 (NCV)

*S*ing to the Lord; praise the Lord! For He has DELIVERED the life of the poor and needy from the hand of evildoers.

Jeremiah 20:13 (Amplified)

"*T*his is how you should pray: "Our Father in heaven, hallowed be your name, your kingdom come, your will be done on earth as it is in heaven. Give us this day our daily bread. Forgive us our debts, as we also have forgiven out debtors. And lead us not into temptation, but DELIVER us from the evil one.""

Matthew 6:9-13 (NIV)

'*T*is the grandest theme through the ages rung;
'Tis the grandest theme for a mortal tongue;
'Tis the grandest theme that the world e'er sung,
Our God is able to DELIVER thee.

He is able to DELIVER thee;
Though by sin oppressed,
Go to Him for rest;
Our God is able to DELIVER thee.

(by William A. Ogden)

Begin your prayer time adoring the God who is able to DELIVER.

GOD OUR DELIVERER

DELIVER—synonyms: Free, save, rescue, emancipate, release, discharge, liberate. (Webster)

And Yahweh said, "I have seen the miserable state of my people in Egypt, I have heard their appeal to be free of their slave-drivers. Yes, I am well aware of their sufferings. I mean to DELIVER them out of the hands of the Egyptians and bring them up out of that land to a land rich and broad, a land where milk and honey flow, the home of the Canaanites, the Hittites, the Amorites, the Perizzites, the Hivites and the Jebusites."

Exodus 3:7 & 8 (NJB)

He shall call upon me, and I will answer him; I will be with him in trouble; I will DELIVER him and honor him.

Psalm 91:15 (KJ)

And the Lord will RESCUE me from all evil, and take me safely into his heavenly kingdom. To him be the glory for ever and ever. Amen.

2 Timothy 4:18 (Good News)

'Tis the grandest theme in the earth or main;
'Tis the grandest theme for a mortal strain;
'Tis the grandest theme, tell the world again,
"Our God is able to DELIVER thee."

'Tis the grandest theme, let the tidings roll
To the guilty heart, to the sinful soul;
Look to God in faith He will make thee whole,
"Our God is able to DELIVER thee."

(by William A. Ogden)

Begin your prayer time adoring the God who is able to DELIVER you.

GOD OUR DELIVERER

*C*ommit yourself to the Lord; let Him DELIVER him; let Him RESCUE him, because He delights in him.

Psalm 22:8 (NAS)

*W*hen wisdom enters your heart, And knowledge is pleasant to your soul, Discretion will preserve you; Understanding will keep you, to DELIVER you from the ways of evil,

Proverbs 2:10-12a (NKJ)

*A*nd forgive us our debts as we have forgiven our debtors. And lead us not into temptation but DELIVER us from the evil one. (For thine is the kingdom and the power and the glory forever. Amen)

Matthew 6:12 & 13 (Berkeley)

*T*he Lord knows how to be DELIVERING the godly out of testing and temptation but to be reserving the unrighteous for the day of judgment to be punished.

2 Peter 2:9 (Wuest)

*R*ESCUE the perishing, care for the dying,
Snatch them in pity from sin and the grave;
Weep o'er the erring one, lift up the fallen,
Tell them of Jesus the mighty to SAVE.

RESCUE the perishing, duty demands it;
Strength for thy labor the Lord will provide;
Back to the narrow way patiently win them;
Tell the poor wanderer a Saviour has died.

(by Fanny J. Crosby)

Begin your prayer time adoring the God who DELIVERS you, who RESCUES you.

GOD OUR DELIVERER

I am under vows to thee, O God: I will pay thee my offering of praise, for thou hast SAVED my life from death, and my feet from stumbling

Psalm 56:12 & 13 (Moffatt)

*S*o the Lord raised up leaders among the Israelis to RESCUE them from the tyranny of the Syrians; and then Israel lived in safety again as they had in former days,

2 Kings 13:5 (TLB)

*F*rom Thessalonica the word of the Lord rang out; and not in Macedonia and Achaia alone, but everywhere your faith in God has reached men's ears. No words of ours are needed, for they by themselves spread the news of our visit to you and its effect: how you turned from idols, to be servants of the living God, and to wait expectantly for the appearance from heaven of his Son Jesus, whom he raised from the dead, Jesus our DELIVERER from the terrors of judgment to come.

1 Thessalonians 1:8-10 (NEB)

*B*ut now, by dying to what once bound us, we have been RELEASED from the law so that we serve in the new way of the Spirit, and not in the old way of the written code.

Romans 7:6 (NIV)

> *T*hough many are slighting Him,
> Still He is waiting,
> Waiting the penitent child to receive;
> Plead with them earnestly,
> Plead with them gently,
> He will forgive if they only believe.
>
> RESCUE the perishing,
> Care for the dying;
> Jesus is merciful,
> Jesus will SAVE.

(by Fanny J. Crosby)

Begin your prayer time adoring the God who RELEASED us from the binding law.

GOD OUR DELIVERER

*G*reat DELIVERANCE giveth he to his king; and showeth mercy to his anointed, to David, and to his seed for evermore.

Psalm 18:50 (KJ)

*T*here is no wisdom or understanding or counsel (that can prevail) against the Lord. The horse is prepared for the day of battle, but DELIVERANCE and victory are of the Lord.

Proverbs 21:30 & 31 (Amplified)

*T*ruly, in our own hearts we believed we would die. But this happened so we would not trust in ourselves but in God, who raises people from the dead. God SAVED us from these great dangers of death, and he will continue to SAVE us.

2 Corinthians 1:9 & 10 (NCV)

*B*eloved, when I give all diligence to write unto you of the common salvation, it was needful for me to write unto you, and exhort you that ye should earnestly contend for the faith which was once DELIVERED unto the saints.

Jude 3 (KJ)

> *S*AVED by the blood of the crucified One!
> Now ransomed from sin and a new work begun,
> Sing praises to the Father and praise to the Son,
> SAVED by the blood of the crucified One!
>
> SAVED by the blood of the crucified One
> All hail to the Father, all hail to the Son,
> All hail to the Spirit, the great three in one!
> SAVED by the blood of the crucified One.
>
> *(by S. J. Henderson)*

Begin your prayer time adoring the God who SAVED, DELIVERED you from the penalty of sin.

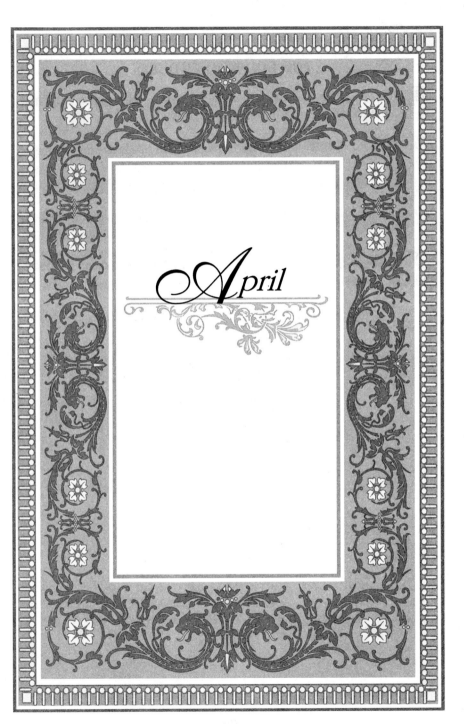

THE GOD WHO ENDURES

ENDURE—to last, to continue in the same state without ever perishing; to remain; to abide, to bear with patience. (Webster)

*B*ut the Lord ABIDES forever; He has established his throne for judgment.

Psalm 9:7 (NAS)

*H*is name shall ENDURE forever; His name shall continue as long as the sun. And men shall be blessed in Him; All nations shall call him blessed.

Psalm 72:17 (NKJ)

*Y*es, Yahweh is good, his love is EVERLASTING, his faithfulness ENDURES from age to age.

Psalm 100:5 (NJB)

O God, our help in ages past,
Our hope for years to come,
Our shelter from the stormy blast,
And our eternal home.

Before the hills in order stood,
Or earth received her frame,
From EVERLASTING Thou art God
To ENDLESS years the same.

(by Isaac Watts)

Begin your prayer time adoring the God who ENDURES FOREVER.

THE GOD WHO ENDURES

ENDURE synonyms—bear, last, suffer, remain, continue, sustain, undergo.
(Webster)

O thou Eternal, throned forever, from age to age thy fame ENDURES.

Psalm 102:12 (Moffatt)

*M*ay the glory of the Lord ENDURE forever; may the Lord rejoice in his works.

Psalm 104:31 (NIV)

*B*ut the Word of the Lord (divine instruction, the Gospel) ENDURES forever.
And this word is the good news which was preached to you.

1 Peter 1:25 (Amplified)

> *W*hen hoary time shall pass away,
> And earthly thrones and kingdoms fall;
> When men who here refuse to pray,
> On rocks and hills and mountains call;
>
> God's love, so sure, shall still ENDURE,
> All measureless and strong;
> Redeeming love to Adams race
> The saints' and angels song.
>
> *(by F.M. Lehman)*

Begin your prayer time adoring the Good whose love ENDURES.

THE GOD WHO ENDURES

*T*hank the Lord because he is good. His love CONTINUES FOREVER.

1 Chronicles 16:35

*I*t came to pass, as the trumpeters and singers were as one, to make one sound to be heard in praising and thanking the Lord; and when they lifted up their voice with the trumpet and cymbals and instruments of music, and praised the Lord saying, For he is good; for his mercy ENDURETH forever: that then the house was filled with a cloud, even the house of the Lord; So that the priests could not minister by reason of the cloud: for the glory of the Lord had filled the house of God.

2 Chronicles 5:13 & 14 (KJ)

*F*or his anger LASTS only a moment, but his favor LASTS a lifetime; weeping may REMAIN for a night, but rejoicing comes in the morning.

Psalm 30:5 (NIV)

*O*h, give thanks to the Lord, for He is good; his loving kindness CONTINUES FOREVER.

Psalm 136:1 (Paraphrased)

I know of a Name, A beautiful name,
That unto a Babe was given;
The stars glittered bright through-out that glad night,
And angels praised God in heaven.

The One of that Name, my Saviour became,
My Saviour of Calgary;
My sins nailed Him there, My burdens He bare,
He SUFFERED all this for me.

(by Jean Perry)

Begin you prayer time adoring God because of His ENDURING love, mercy, favor joy and kindness. Then thank Him because His anger LASTS only a short time.

THE GOD WHO ENDURES

*W*ealth and riches are in his house, And his righteousness ENDURES forever.

Psalm 112:3 (NAS)

*Y*our sovereignty is an eternal sovereignty, your empire LASTS from age to age. Always true to his promises, Yahweh shows love in all he does.

Psalm 145:13 (NJB)

*A*nd what of ourselves? With all these witnesses to faith around us like a cloud, we must throw off every encumbrance, every sin to which we cling, and run with resolution the race for which we are entered, our eyes fixed on Jesus on whom faith depends from start to finish: Jesus who, for the sake of joy that laid ahead of him, ENDURED the cross, making light of its disgrace, and has taken his seat at the right hand of the throne of God.

Hebrews 12:1 & 2 (NEB)

*T*herefore I (am ready to) persevere and stand my ground with patience and ENDURE everything for the sake of the elect (God's chosen), so that they too may obtain (the) salvation which is in Christ Jesus with (the reward of) eternal glory.

2 Timothy 2:10 (Amplified)

*T*o Calvary, Lord, in spirit now
Our grateful souls repair,
To dwell upon Thy dying love,
And taste its sweetness there.

There through Thine hour of deepest woe,
Thy SUFFERING spirit passed;
Grace there its wondrous victory gained,
And love ENDURED at last.

(by Edward Denny)

Begin your prayer time adoring the God who ENDURED SUFFERING.

THE GOD WHO IS ESTABLISHED
AND WHO ESTABLISHES

ESTABLISH—To make steadfast, firm, or stable; to settle on a firm or permanent basis, either to originate and settle, or to settle what is already originated; to set or fix unalterably. (Webster)

The Lord reigneth, he is clothed with majesty; the Lord is clothed with strength, wherewith he has girded himself: the world also is STABLISHED, that it cannot be moved. Thy throne is ESTABLISHED of old: thou art from everlasting.

Psalm 92:1 & 2 (KJ)

For the promises of God in Him are Yes, and in Him Amen, to the glory of God through us. Now He who ESTABLISHES us with you in Christ and has anointed us in God, who has also sealed us and given us the Spirit in our hearts as a deposit.

2 Corinthians 1:20-22 (NKJ)

Thou sayest, "I make a compact with my chosen, I swear to my servant David, to make his dynasty endure, to MAKE HIS THRONE LAST FOR ALL TIME"; and heaven is praising, O Eternal, heavens own host, the marvel of thy faithfulness."

Psalm 89:3-5 (Moffatt)

> O worship the King, all glorious above,
> O gratefully sing His power and His love;
> Our Shield and Defender, the Ancient of Days,
> Pavilioned in splendor and girded with praise.
>
> The earth, with its store of wonder untold,
> Almighty, Thy power hath founded of old;
> Hath STABLISHED it fast by a changeless decree,
> And round it hath cast, like a mantle the sea.
>
> *(by Robert Grant)*

Begin your prayer time adoring the God who ESTABLISHED the world and all that is in it.

THE GOD WHO IS ESTABLISHED
AND WHO ESTABLISHES

ESTABLISH—synonyms: Plant, fix, settle, found, organize, confirm, institute, prove, substantiate, constitute. (Webster)

(You have said) I have made a covenant with My chosen one, I have sworn to David My servant. Your seed I will ESTABLISH forever, and build up your throne for all generations. Selah (pause and calmly think of that)!

Psalm 89:3 & 4 (Amplified)

"Nevertheless, I will remember My covenant with you in the days of your youth, and I will ESTABLISH an everlasting covenant with you."

Ezekiel 16:60 (NAS)

The point of what we are saying is this: We do have such a high priest, who sat down at the right hand of the throne of the Majesty in heaven, and who serves in the sanctuary, the true tabernacle set up by the Lord, not by man. Every high priest is appointed to offer both gifts and sacrifices, and so it was necessary for this one also to have something to offer. If he were on earth he would not be a high priest, for there are already men who offer the gifts prescribed by the law. They serve at a sanctuary that is a copy and shadow of what is in heaven. This is why Moses was warned when he was about to build the tabernacle: "See to it that you make everything according to the pattern shown you on the mountain." But the ministry Jesus has is superior to theirs as the covenant of which he is mediator is superior to the old one, and it is FOUNDED on better promises.

Hebrews 8:1-6 (NIV)

Thou son of God, eternal Word,
Who heaven and earth's FOUNDATIONS laid,
Upholding by Thy word and power
The universe Thy hands have made.

Exalted to the Father's throne,
With glory and with honor crowned,
All at Thy glorious name shall bow,
As Lord of all by each be owned.

(by Inglis Fleming)

Begin your prayer time adoring the God who FOUNDED a better covenant.

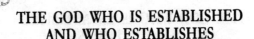

THE GOD WHO IS ESTABLISHED
AND WHO ESTABLISHES

*A*nd the dream was repeated to Pharaoh twice because the thing is ESTABLISHED by God, and God will·shortly bring it to pass.

Genesis 41:32 (NKJ)

I waited and waited for Yahweh, now at last he has stooped to me and heard my cry for help. He has pulled me out of the horrible pit, out of the slough of the marsh, has SETTLED my feet on a rock and steadied my steps.

Psalm 40:1 & 2 (NJB)

*H*ave the roots (of your being) firmly and deeply planted (in Him)—fixed and FOUNDED in Him—being continually built up in Him, becoming increasingly more confirmed and ESTABLISHED in the faith, just as you were taught, and abounding and overflowing in it with thanksgiving.

Colossians 2:7 (Amplified)

*A*nd so·were the churches ESTABLISHED in the faith, and increased in number daily.

Acts 16:5 (KJ)

*H*ow firm a FOUNDATION, ye saints of the Lord,
Is laid for your faith in His excellent word!
What more can He say than to you He has said,
To you, who for refuge to Jesus have fled.

The soul that on Jesus hath leaned for repose,
I will not, I will not desert to his foes;
That soul, though all hell should endeavor to shake,
I'll never, no never, no never forsake.

(from Rippon's selection of hymns)

Begin your prayer time adoring God for ESTABLISHING your faith.

THE GOD WHO IS ESTABLISHED
AND WHO ESTABLISHES

*T*he Lord will ESTABLISH you as his holy people, as he promised you on oath, if you keep the commands of the Lord your God and walk in his ways.

Deuteronomy 28:9 (NIV)

I will sing always of the Eternal's love, telling all ages of thy faithfulness; for thy love thou hast promised to be everlasting, and thy faithfulness is firmly FIXED in heaven.

Psalm 89:1 & 2 (Moffatt)

*F*orever, O Lord, Your word is settled in heaven, Your faithfulness endures to all generations; You ESTABLISHED the earth and it abides.

Psalm 119:89 & 90 (NKJ)

*D*o not be carried about by different and varied and alien teachings; for it is good for the heart to be ESTABLISHED and ennobled and strengthened by means of grace (God's favor and spiritual blessing) and not (be devoted to) foods (rules of diet and ritualistic meals) which bring no (spiritual) benefit or profit to those who observe them.

Hebrews 13:9 (Amplified)

> *I*'m pressing on the upward way,
> New heights I'm gaining every day;
> Still praying as I'm onward bound,
> Lord PLANT my feet on higher ground.
>
> Lord, lift me up and let me stand
> by faith on heaven's table land;
> A higher plane than I have found
> "Lord, PLANT my feet on higher ground."
>
> *(by Johnson Oatman, Jr.)*

Begin your prayer time adoring the God who can PLANT His love in you.

THE GOD WHO FORGIVES

FORGIVE—To pardon; to remit, as an offense or debt; to overlook (an offense) and treat (the offender) as not guilty. (Webster)

*T*hen if my people will humble themselves and pray, and search for me, and turn from their wicked ways, I will hear them from heaven and FORGIVE their sins and heal their land.

2 Chronicles 7:14 (Paraphrased)

*A*t times the land will become so dry that no food will grow, or a great sickness will spread among the people. Sometimes all the crops will be destroyed by locusts or grasshoppers. Your people will be attacked in their cities by their enemy or will become sick. When any of these things happen, the people will become truly sorry. If your people spread their hands in prayer toward this Temple, then hear their prayers from your home in heaven. FORGIVE and treat each person as he should be treated because you know what is in everyone's heart.

1 Kings 8:37-39 (NCV)

*I*f we confess our sins, He is so faithful and just as to FORGIVE us our sins and to cleanse us from all unrighteousness.

1 John 1:9 (Berkeley)

*G*reat God of wonders! all Thy ways
Are matchless, God-like and divine;
But the bright glories of Thy grace
Above thine other wonders shine.

In wonder lost, with trembling joy
We take the PARDON of our God:
PARDON for crimes of deepest dye,
A PARDON bought with Jesus blood.

(by Samuel Davies)

Contemplate the wonder of FORGIVENESS, and adore the God who PARDONS sinners.

THE GOD WHO FORGIVES

FORGIVE—synonyms—Pardon, absolve, remit, cancel, release. (Webster)

For You, Lord are good, and ready to FORGIVE, And abundant in mercy to all those who call upon You.

Psalm 86:5 (NKJ)

If any of you is in trouble let him pray. If anyone is flourishing let him sing praises to God. If anyone is ill he should send for the church elders. They should pray over him, anointing him with oil in the Lord's name. Believing prayer will save the sick man: the Lord will restore him and any sins he has committed will be FORGIVEN.

James 5:13-16 (Phillips)

For in Christ our RELEASE is secured and our sins are FORGIVEN through the shedding of his blood.

Ephesians 1:7 (NEB)

They nailed my Lord upon a tree
And left Him, dying there:
Through love He suffered there for me;
'Twas love beyond compare.

"FORGIVE them, O FORGIVE!" He cried,
Then bowed His sacred head;
O Lamb of God! my sacrifice!
For me Thy blood was shed.

(by C. Austin Miles)

Begin your prayer time adoring the God who shed His blood for your FORGIVENESS.

THE GOD WHO FORGIVES

FORGIVENESS of sin, one of the constituent parts of justification. In PARDONING sin, God ABSOLVES the sinner from the condemnation of the law, and that on account of the work of Christ, he removes the guilt of sin, or the sinner's actual liability to eternal wrath on account of it. (Today's Dictionary of the Bible)

*B*lessed is he whose transgression is FORGIVEN, whose sin is covered.

Psalm 32:1 (NKJ)

*F*or he rescued us from the power of darkness and brought us safe into the kingdom of his dear son, by whom we are set free and our sins are FORGIVEN.

Colossians 2:13 & 14 (GN)

*B*ut arise and stand upon your feet; for I have appeared to you for this purpose, that I might appoint you to serve as (My) minister and to bear witness both to what you have seen of Me and to that in which I will appear to you. Choosing you out (selecting you for myself) and delivering you from among this (Jewish) people and the Gentiles to whom I am sending you, to open their eyes, that they may turn from darkness to light, and from the power of Satan to God, so that they may receive FORGIVENESS and RELEASE from their sins and a place and portion among those who are consecrated and purified by faith in Me.

Acts 26:16-18 (Amplified)

> *B*lessed be the name of Jesus!
> I'm so glad He took me in;
> He's FORGIVEN my transgressions,
> He has cleansed my heart from sin.
>
> I will praise Him! I will praise Him!
> Praise the Lamb for sinners slain;
> Give Him glory, all ye people,
> For His blood can wash away each stain.
>
> *(by M.J. Harris)*

Begin you prayer time adoring God for FORGIVING you.

THE GOD WHO FORGIVES

FORGIVENESS—Divine forgiveness.. is one of the most complicated and costly undertakings, demanding complete satisfaction to meet the demands of God's outraged holiness. (Unger's Bible Dictionary)

If you, O Lord, kept a record of sins, O Lord, who could stand? But with you there is FORGIVENESS; therefore you are feared.

Psalm 130:3 & 4 (NIV)

Get rid of all bitterness, passion, and anger. No more shouting or insults! No more hateful feelings of any sort! Instead, be kind and tender-hearted to one another, and forgive one another, as God has FORGIVEN you in Christ.

Ephesians 4:31 & 32 (GN)

If you forgive men their trespasses, then your heavenly Father will FORGIVE you; but if you do not forgive men, your Father will not FORGIVE your trespasses either.

Matthew 6:15 & 16 (Moffatt)

> He all my griefs has taken, and all my sorrows borne;
> In temptation He's my strong and mighty tower;
> He has all my sins FORGIVEN, and Him I do adore
> From my heart, and now He keeps me by His power.
>
> Though all the world forsake me, and Satan tempt me sore,
> Through Jesus I shall safely reach the goal:
> He's the Lily of the Valley the Bright and Morning Star,
> He's the fairest of ten thousand to my soul.
>
> *(by Charles W. Fry)*

Begin your prayer time adoring the FORGIVING God.

THE GOD WHO FORGIVES

$\mathcal{B}$less Yahweh, my soul, bless his holy name, all that is in me! Bless Yahweh, my soul, and remember all his kindnesses; in FORGIVING all your offenses, in curing all your diseases, in redeeming your life from the pit, in crowning you with loving tenderness, in filling your years with prosperity, in renewing your youth like an eagle's.

Psalm 103:1-6 (NJB)

$\mathcal{T}$o the Lord our God belong compassion and FORGIVENESS, for we have rebelled against Him;

Daniel 9:9 (NAS)

$\mathcal{A}$nd He said to her, Your sins are FORGIVEN! Then those who were at table with Him began to say among themselves, Who is this, Who even FORGIVES sins? But Jesus said to the woman, Your faith has saved you; go (enter) into peace—in freedom from all the distresses that are experienced as a result of sin.

Luke 7:48-50 (Berkeley)

$\mathcal{I}$t should then be clear to you, Brother-men, that through this one FORGIVENESS of sin is announced to you. In Him every believer is ABSOLVED from everything from which you could not be absolved by the law of Moses.

Acts 13:38 & 39 (Amplified)

$\mathcal{T}$hough your sins be as scarlet,
They shall be white as snow;
Though they be red like crimson,
They shall be as wool!

He'll FORGIVE you transgressions,
And remember them no more;
"Look unto Me, ye people,"
Saith the Lord your God.

(Fanny J. Crosby)

Begin your prayer time in adoration to the God who FORGIVES and remembers no more.

THE GOD WHO FORGIVES

I acknowledged my sin to You, And my iniquity I have not hidden. I said, "I will confess my transgressions to the Lord," And you FORGAVE the iniquity of my sin.

Psalm 32:5 (NKJ)

*L*ord, if you keep in mind our sins then who can ever get an answer to his prayers? But you FORGIVE! What an awesome thing this is! That is why I wait expectantly, trusting God to help, for he has promised.

Psalm 130:3 & 4 (Paraphrased)

*G*od has chosen you and made you his holy people. He loves you. So always do these things: Show mercy to others, be kind, humble, gentle, and patient. Get along with each other, and forgive each other. If someone does wrong to you, forgive that person because the Lord FORGAVE you.

Colossians 3:12-13 (NCV)

*A*gain Jesus said, "Peace be with you! As the Father has sent me, I am sending you." And with that he breathed on them and said, "Receive the Holy Spirit. If you forgive anyone his sins, they are FORGIVEN; if you do not forgive them, they are not forgiven.

John 20:21-23 (NIV)

*T*here is never a day so dreary,
There is never a night so long,
But the soul that is trusting Jesus
Will somewhere find a song.

There is never a guilty sinner,
There is never a wondering one,
But that God in mercy PARDON
Through Jesus Christ, His Son.

(by Anna B. Russell)

Begin your praying time adoring God for complete FORGIVENESS.

THE GOD WHO IS GREAT

GREAT—Expressing a large, extensive, or unusual degree of anything; vast; sublime; dignified; noble. (Webster)

*F*or the Lord is GREAT and greatly to be praised; He is also to be feared above all gods.

1 Chronicles 16:25

*H*ow GREAT are your doings, O Lord! Your thoughts are very deep.

Psalm 92:5 (Amplified)

*T*his is what I shall tell my heart, and so recover hope: the favors of Yahweh are not all past, his kindnesses are not exhausted; every morning they are renewed; GREAT is his faithfulness.

Lamentations 3:21-23 (NJB)

> *G*REAT God of wonders! all Thy ways
> Are matchless, God-like, and divine;
> But the bright glories of Thy grace
> Above thine other wonders shine.
>
> In wonder lost, with trembling joy,
> We take the pardon of our God:
> Pardon for crimes of deepest dye,
> A pardon bought with Jesus blood.
>
> *(by Samuel Davies)*

Adore God for His GREATNESS.

THE GOD WHO IS GREAT

GREAT synonyms; Big, wide, excellent, immense, bulky, majestic, grand, eminent, noble, powerful. (Webster)

*W*hen the Lord brought back the captives who returned to Zion, we were like those who dream (it seemed so unreal). Then was our mouth filled with laughter, and our tongue was singing. Then they said among the nations, The Lord has done GREAT things for them.

Psalm 126:1 & 2 (Amplified)

*H*owbeit Jesus suffered him not, but saith unto him, Go home to thy friends, and tell them how GREAT things the Lord hath done for thee, and hath had compassion on thee.

Mark 5:19 (KJ)

I ask that your minds may be opened to see his light, so that you will know what is the hope to which he Has called you, how rich are the wonderful blessings he promises his people, and how very GREAT is his power at work in us who believe.

Ephesians 1:18 & 19a (Good News)

> *G*REAT God, we sing that mighty hand
> by which supported still we stand;
> The opening year Thy mercy shows;
> That mercy crowns it till it close.
>
> In scenes exalted or depressed
> Thou art our joy, and Thou our rest;
> Thy goodness all our hopes shall raise,
> Adored through all our changing days.
>
> *(by Philip Doddridge)*

Begin you prayer time with adoring God for His GREATNESS.

THE GOD WHO IS GREAT

The GREAT day of the Lord is near—near and coming quickly. Listen! The cry on the day of the Lord will be bitter, the shouting of the warrior there.

Zephaniah 1:14 (NIV)

Bless the Eternal, O my soul! Eternal One, my God, Thou art most GREAT, arrayed in glorious majesty.

Psalm 104:1 (Moffatt)

And as He was getting into the boat, the man who had been demon-possessed was entreating Him that he might accompany Him. And He did not let him, but He said to him, "Go home to your people and report to them what GREAT things the Lord has done for you, and how He had mercy on you.

Mark 5:18 & 19 (NAS)

If we receive the witness of men, the witness of God is GREATER; for this is the witness of God which He has testified of His Son.

1 John 5:9 (NKJ)

> To God be the glory, GREAT things He hath done,
> So loved He the world that He gave us His Son,
> Who yielded His life an atonement for sin,
> And opened the Life-gate that all may go in.
>
> O perfect redemption, the purchase of blood,
> To every believer the promise of God;
> The vilest offender who truly believes,
> That moment from Jesus a pardon receives.
>
> *(by Fanny J. Crosby)*

Begin your prayer time adoring the GREAT God.

THE GOD WHO IS GREAT

He said, "Praise the Lord. He has saved you from the Egyptians and their king, and He has saved the people from the power of the Egyptians. Now I know the Lord is GREATER than all gods, because He did this to those who looked down on Israel."

Exodus 18:10 & 11 (NCV)

How precious also are Thy thoughts to me, O God! How VAST is the sum of them!

Psalm 139:17 (NAS)

Nathaniel answered him, Rabbi, as for you, you are the son of God. As for you, King you are of Israel. Answered Jesus and said to him, Because I said to you that I saw you down under the fig tree you are believing? GREATER things than these you shall see. And He says to him, Most, assuredly, I am saying to you, you shall see heaven opened and the angels of God ascending and descending upon the Son of Man.

John 1:49-51 (Wuest)

And here is how to measure it—the GREATEST love is shown when a person lays down his life for his friends.

John 15:13 (Paraphrased)

GREAT things He hath taught us, GREAT things He hath done,
And great our rejoicing through Jesus the Son;
But purer, and higher, and GREATER will be
Our wonder, our transport, when Jesus we see.

Praise the Lord, praise the Lord, Let the earth hear His voice!
Praise the Lord, praise the Lord, Let the people rejoice!
O come to the Father through Jesus the Son,
And give Him the glory, GREAT things He hath done.

(by Fanny J. Crosby)

Begin you prayer time in adoring the GREAT God.

THE GOD WHO IS GREAT

Thy right hand, O Lord, is become glorious in power: thy right hand, O Lord, hath dashed in pieces the enemy. And in GREATNESS of thine excellency thou hast overthrown them that rose up against thee: thou setest forth thy wrath, which consumed them as stubble.

Exodus 15:6 & 7 (KJ)

Every day (with its new reasons) will I bless You—affectionately and gratefully praise You; yes, I will praise your name for ever and ever.. GREAT is the Lord and highly to be praised, and His GREATNESS is (so vast and deep as to be) unsearchable.

Psalm 145:2 & 3 (Amplified)

But you, my children, are of God's family, and you have mastery over these false prophets, because he who inspires you is GREATER then he who inspires the godless world.

1 John 4:4 (NEB)

They were singing the song of Moses, the servant of God, and the song of the Lamb: "Lord, God Almighty, How GREAT and wonderful are your deeds! King of all nations, How right and true are your ways!

Revelation 15:3 (GN)

The God of Abraham praise, Who reigns enthroned above;
Ancient of everlasting days, and God of love.
Jehovah, GREAT I AM, by earth and heaven confessed;
I bow and bless the sacred Name, forever blest.

The whole triumphant host give thanks to God on high;
"Hail, Father, Son and Holy Ghost!" They ever cry.
Hail, Abraham's God and mine! I join the heavenly lays;
All might and majesty are Thine, and endless praise.

(by Daniel ben Judah)

Begin your prayer time adoring the GREAT I AM.

THE GOD WHO IS GREAT

*W*ho is this who comes from Edom, with dyed garments from Bozrah, This One who is glorious in His apparel, Traveling in the GREATNESS of His strength? "I who speak in righteousness, mighty to save."

Isaiah 63:1 (NKJ)

*O*ne generation will commend your works to another; they will tell of your mighty acts. They will speak of the glorious splendor of your majesty, and I will meditate on your wonderful works. They will tell of the power of your awesome works, and I will proclaim your GREAT deeds.

Psalm 145:4-6 (NIV)

*B*ut God is so rich in mercy, that on account of His GREAT love with which He loved us, He made us who were dead in trespasses, alive in unison with Christ.—by grace you have been saved.

Ephesians 2:4 & 5 (Berkeley)

*T*hen I heard a GREAT voice from the throne crying, "See! The home of God is with men, and He will live among them. They shall be his people, and God himself shall be with them,

Revelation 21:3 (Phillips)

*G*uide us, O Thou GREAT Jehovah, Pilgrims through this barren land;
We are weak, but Thou art mighty; hold us by Thy powerful hand:
Bread of Heaven, feed us now and evermore

Saviour, come! we long to see Thee, long to dwell with Thee above;
And to know, in full communion, all the sweetness of Thy love;
Come, Lord Jesus! take Thy waiting people home

(by William Williams)

Begin your prayer time adoring the GREAT God.

GOD'S HAND

▓ HAND—performance, handiwork; workmanship; that is, the effect for the cause. To lead, guide or help with the hand. (Webster)

You protect me with your saving shield. You support me with your right HAND. You have stooped to make me great.

Psalm 18:35 (NCV)

And David said to Gad, "I am in great distress. Please let us fall into the HAND of the Lord, for his mercies are great; but do not let me fall into the hand of man."

2 Samuel 24:14 (NKJ)

So they sent the ark of God to Ekron. As the ark of God was entering Ekron, the people of Ekron cried out, "They have brought the ark of the god of Israel around to us to kill us and our people." So they called together all the rulers of the Philistines and said, "Send the ark of the God of Israel away; let it go back to its own place, or it will kill us and our people. "For death had filled the city with panic; God's HAND was very heavy upon it.

1 Samuel 5:10 & 11 (NIV)

> Saviour! I follow on, guided by Thee,
> Seeing not yet the HAND that leadeth me;
> Hushed be my heart and still, fear I no future ill;
> Only to do Thy will, my will shall be.
>
> Riven the rock for me, thirst to relieve,
> Manna from heaven falls fresh every eve;
> Never a pang severe causeth my eye to tear,
> But Thou dost whisper near, "Only believe!"
>
> *(by Charles S. Robinson)*

Begin your prayer time adoring God for His guiding HAND.

GOD'S HAND

*B*ut I put my trust in you, Yahweh, I say, "You are my God". My days are in your HAND, rescue me from the hands of my enemies and persecutors; let your face smile on your servant, save me in your love.

Psalm 31:14-16 (NJB)

*T*he king's heart is in the HAND of the Lord, as the rivers of water: he turneth it whithersoever he will.

Proverbs 21:1 (KJ)

*S*tephen being under the control of the Holy Spirit, having fixed his gaze into heaven, saw God's glory and Jesus standing at the right HAND of God, and said, Behold, I see the heavens which have opened, and the Son of Man standing on the right HAND of God.

Acts 7:55 & 56 (Wuest)

*T*hou, Lord, in the beginning hast laid the foundation of the earth. And the heavens are the work of thy HANDS.

Hebrews 1:10 (Phillips)

*O*ften to Marah's brink have I been brought;
Shrinking the cup to drink, help I have sought;
And with the prayer's ascent, Jesus the branch hath rent
Quickly relief hath sent, sweetening the draught.

Saviour! I long to walk closer with Thee;
Led by Thy guiding HAND, ever to be;
Constantly near Thy side, constantly purified,
Living for Him who died freely for me!

(by Charles S. Robinson)

Begin your prayer time adoring the guiding HAND of God.

GOD'S HAND

The havens are telling of the glory of God; And their expanse is declaring the work of His HAND.

Psalm 19:1 (NAS)

Then, by the good HAND of our God upon us, they brought us a man of understanding, of the sons of Mahli the son of Levi, the son of Israel, namely Sherebiah, with his sons and brothers, eighteen men.

Ezra 8:18 (NKJ)

Who will be the accuser of God's chosen ones? It is God who pronounces acquittal: then who can condemn? It is Christ—Christ who died, and more than that, was raised from the dead—who is at God's right HAND, and indeed pleads our cause.

Romans 8:33 & 34 (NEB)

Write a letter to the leader of the church at Ephesus and tell him this: "I write to inform you of a message from him who walks among the churches and holds their leaders in his right HAND.

Revelation 2:1 (Paraphrased)

Rise, my soul, thy God directs thee;
Stranger hands no more impede;
Pass thou on; His HANDS protect thee,
Strength that has the captive freed.

Light Divine surrounds thy going:
God Himself shall mark the way:
Secret blessings, richly flowing,
Lead to everlasting day.

(by J.N. Darby)

Adore God for His leading HANDS.

GOD'S HAND

*L*et Your HAND be upon the man of Your right HAND, Upon the son of man whom You made strong for Yourself.

Psalm 80:17 (NKJ)

*L*isten to me, Jacob, Israel whom I have called: I am evermore the same, I am the first and I the last; my HAND laid the foundations of the earth, my right HAND spread the skies above; whenever I call them, they answer to the summons.

Isaiah 48:12 & 13 (Moffatt)

*A*nd He said to them, Why are you disturbed and troubled, and why do such doubts and questions arise in your hearts? See My HANDS and My feet, that it is I Myself; feel of and handle Me and see, for a spirit does not have flesh and bones as you see that I have.

Luke 24:38 & 39 (Amplified)

*T*his One, after offering for our sins one sacrifice of perpetual efficacy, took His seat at the right HAND of God.

Hebrews 10:12 (Berkeley)

*H*e leadeth me, O blessed thought!
O words with heavenly comfort fraught!
What-e'er I do, where-e'er I be,
Still 'tis God's HAND that leadeth me!

Sometimes "mid scenes of deepest gloom,
Sometimes where E-den's bowers bloom,
by waters still, o'er troubled sea,
Still 'tis His HAND that leadeth me!

(Joseph H. Gilmore)

Adore God for allowing his HANDS to receive nail prints.

GOD'S HAND

*C*ome, let us sing for joy to the Lord; let us shout aloud to the Rock of our Salvation.

Let us come before him with thanksgiving and extol him with music and song. For the Lord is the great God, the great King above all gods. In his HAND are the depths of the earth, and the mountain peaks belong to him. The sea is his, for he made it, and his HANDS formed the dry land.

Psalm 95:1-5 (NIV)

*B*ehold the Lord's HAND is not shortened, that it cannot save; neither is his ear heavy that it cannot hear.

Isaiah 59:1 (KJ)

*F*or we know who said, "I will take revenge, I will repay"; and who said, "The Lord will judge his people." It is a terrible thing to fall into the HANDS of the living God.

Hebrews 10:30 & 31 (Good News)

*"C*ome" said Jesus. Then Peter got out of the boat and started walking towards Jesus across the water, but as soon as he felt the force of the wind, he took fright and began to sink. "Lord! save me!" he cried. Jesus put out his HAND at once and held him. "Man of little faith," he said "why did you doubt?"

Matthew 14:29-31 (NJB)

> *L*ord, I would clasp Thy HAND in mine,
> Nor ever murmur nor repine,
> Content whatever lot I see,
> Since 'tis Thy HAND that leadeth me!
>
> And when my task on earth is done,
> When, by Thy grace, the victory's won,
> E'en death's cold wave I will not flee,
> Since God through Jordan leadeth me!
>
> *(Joseph H. Gilmore)*

Begin praying with adoration to the God who stretches His HAND out to us.

GOD'S HAND

But now, O Lord, Thou art our Father, we are the clay, and Thou our potter; and all of us are the work of Thy HAND.

Isaiah 64:8 (NAS)

The one whom God corrects is happy, so do not hate being corrected by the Almighty. God hurts, but he also bandages up; he injures, but his HANDS also heal.

Job 5:17 & 18 (NCV)

I (John the Baptist) indeed baptize you with water unto repentance, but He who is coming after me is mightier than I, whose sandals I am not worthy to carry. He will baptize you with the Holy Spirit and fire. His winnowing fan is in His HAND, and He will thoroughly purge His threshing floor, and gather His wheat into the barn; but He will burn up the chaff with unquenchable fire.

Matthew 3:11 & 12 (NKJ)

When I saw him, I fell in a dead faint at his feet, but he touched me with his right HAND and said, "Do not be afraid; it is I, the First and the Last; I am the Living One," I was dead and now I am to live for ever and ever, and I hold the keys of death and of the underworld.

Revelation 1:17 & 18 (NJB)

Put thou thy trust in God,
In duty's path go on;
Walk in His strength with faith and hope,
So shall thy work be done.

Commit thy ways to Him,
Thy works into his HANDS,
And rest on His unchanging word,
Who heaven and earth commands.

(by Paul Gerhardt)

Begin your prayer time adoring the God who holds our life in His HANDS.

THE GOD WHO HEARS

HEAR—To perceive by the ear; to receive an impression of through the auditory organs; as, to hear sound; to hear a voice; to hear words. To listen; to harken; to attend. (Webster)

*A*nswer me when I call, O God of my righteousness! Thou hast relieved me in my distress; Be gracious to me and HEAR my prayer.

Psalm 4:1 (NAS)

*Y*es, the Lord HEARS the good man when he calls to him for help, and saves him out of all his troubles.

Psalm 34:17 (Paraphrased)

*C*ome and listen, all you who fear God, while I tell you what the Lord has done for me: when I uttered my cry to him and high praise was on my tongue, had I been guilty in my heart the Lord would never have heard me. But God not only HEARD me he LISTENED to my prayer.

Psalm 66:16-19 (NJB)

> *I*n the secret of His presence, how my soul delights to hide!
> Oh, how precious are the lessons which I learn at Jesus side!
> Earthly cares can never vex me, neither trials lay me low;
> For when Satan comes to tempt me, to the secret place I go.
>
> Only this I know: I tell Him all my doubts, my griefs and fears:
> Oh, how patiently He LISTENS! and my drooping soul He cheers:
> Do you think He never reproves me? What a false friend He would be,
> If He never, never told me of the sins which He must see.
>
> *(by Ellen Lakshmi Gorch)*

Begin you prayer time adoring the God who HEARS.

THE GOD WHO HEARS

The Lord said, "I have seen the troubles my people suffered in Egypt, and I have HEARD their cries when the Egyptian slave masters hurt them. I am concerned about their pain, and I have come down to save them from the Egyptians.

Exodus 3:7 & 8a (NCV)

Does he who implanted the ear not HEAR? Does he who formed the eye not see?

Psalm 94:9 (NIV)

We know positively that God does not HEAR sinners, but if anyone be a worshipper of God and His will is habitually doing, this one He HEARS.

John 9:31 (Wuest)

But the angel said to him, "Have no fear Zacharias, because your prayer has been HEARD; your wife Elizabeth will bear you a son, whom you will call John.

Luke 1:13 (Berkeley)

HEAR my cry, O Lord!
Lord, vouch safe Thy loving kindness,
HEAR me in my supplication,
Consider my distress.

Oh, regard me with compassion,
And forgive me all my sin.
Let Thy promise be my refuge
Oh, be gracious and redeem me.

(by Alfred Wooler)

Begin your prayer time adoring the God who HEARS our supplications.

THE GOD WHO HEARS

*P*raise waiteth for thee, O God, in Sion: and unto thee shall the vow be performed: O thou that HEAREST prayer, unto thee shall all flesh come.

Psalm 65:1 & 2 (KJ)

vs. 19,21,23,25,27,30,33,35 & 39 (each begin with "then HEAR from heaven").
vs 40
"*N*ow, my God, I pray, let Your eyes be open and let Your EARS BE ATTENTIVE to the prayer made in this place.

2 Chronicles 6:19-40 (NKJ)

"*B*y myself I can do nothing. As I HEAR, I judge, and my judgment is true because I do not live to please myself but to do the will of the Father who sent me.

John 5:3 (Phillips)

*S*o they took away the stone. And Jesus lifted up His eyes and said, Father, I thank You that You have HEARD me. Yes, I know You always HEAR and LISTEN to Me; but I have said this on account of and for the benefit of the people standing around, so that they may believe You did send Me—that You have made Me Your messenger.

John 11:41 & 42 (Amplified)

'*T*is the blessed hour of prayer, when our hearts lowly bend,
And we gather to Jesus, our Saviour and Friend;
If we come to Him in faith, His protection share,
What a balm for the weary! O how sweet to be there!

'Tis the blessed hour of prayer, when the Saviour draws near,
With a tender compassion His children to HEAR;
When He tells us we may cast at His feet every care,
What a balm for the weary! O how sweet to be there!

(by Fanny J. Crosby)

Adore God for HEARING our every prayer.

THE GOD WHO HEARS

*W*hen the righteous cry for help, the Lord HEARS, and delivers them out of their trouble and distress.

Psalm 34:17 (Amplified)

"*O* Eternal, pray remember how I have lived ever mindful of thee, honestly and heartily, and how I have done what was right in thy sight!" Hezekiah wept aloud. Then this word came from the Eternal to Isaiah: "Go and give Hezekiah this message from the Eternal, the God of his father David, "I have HEARD your prayers, I have seen your tears, and I now add fifteen years to your life.""

Isaiah 15:5-7 (Moffatt)

I (Jesus) do not call you servants any longer, because a servant does not know what his master is doing. Instead, I call you friends, because I have told you everything I HEARD from my Father.

John 15:15 (Good News)

I will confess, praise and give thanks to You, for You have HEARD and answered me, and have become my salvation and deliverer.

Psalm 118:21 (Amplified)

Saviour, like a Shepherd lead us,
Much we need Thy tender care;
In Thy pleasant pastures feed us,
For our use Thy folds prepare:
Blessed Jesus, Blessed Jesus,
Thou hast bought us, Thine we are.

We are Thine; do Thou befriend us,
Be the guardian of our way;
Keep Thy flock, from sin defend us,
Seek us when we go astray;
Blessed Jesus, Blessed Jesus,
HEAR, O HEAR us when we pray.

(by Dorothy A. Thrupp)

Begin your prayer time adoring the God who HEARS our every petition.

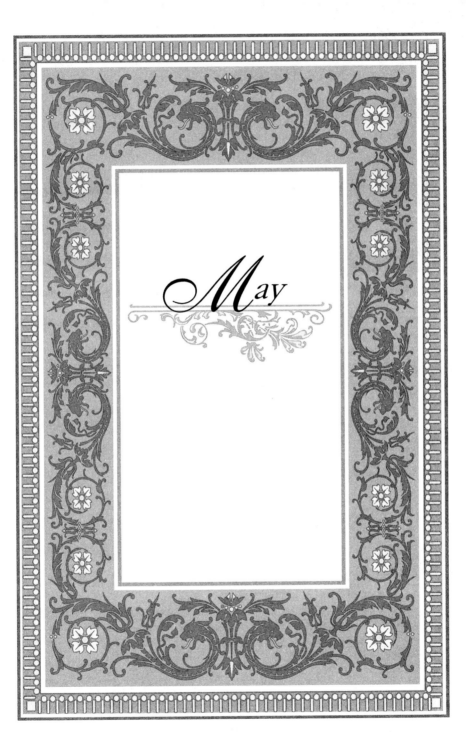

May

THE GOD OF HEAVEN

HEAVEN—The region or expanse which surrounds the earth, and which appears above and around us, like an immense arch or vault, in which are seen the sun, moon stars; the firmament; the sky. (Webster)

God made the VAULT, and it divided the waters above the VAULT, from the waters under the VAULT. God called the VAULT "HEAVEN". Evening came and morning came: the second day.

Genesis 1:7 & 8 (NJB)

The Lord looks down from HEAVEN on all mankind to see if there are any who are wise, who want to please God.

Psalm 14:2 (Paraphrased)

Let your light shine among the people so that they may observe your lofty actions and give glory to your HEAVENLY Father.

Matthew 5:16 (Berkeley)

> Praise, my soul, the King of HEAVEN,
> To His feet thy tribute bring;
> Ransomed, healed, restored, forgiven,
> Who, like me, His praise should sing? Alleluia!
> Alleluia! Praise the Everlasting King!
>
> Praise Him for His grace and favor
> To our fathers in distress;
> Praise Him, still the same forever,
> Slow to chide and swift to bless. Alleluia!
> Alleluia! Glorious in His faithfulness.
>
> *(by Henry F. Lyte)*

Begin your prayer time adoring the God who created the HEAVENS.

THE GOD OF HEAVEN

⊞ HEAVEN—Among Christians, the part of space in which the omnipresent Jehovah is supposed to show sensible manifestations of his glory; the habitation of God and the residence of angels and blessed spirits. (Webster)

*W*hy, although HEAVEN, the highest HEAVEN belongs to the Eternal your God, and the earth with all it holds, yet the Eternal set his heart in love upon your fathers, and chose their descendants after them, chose you out of all the nations?

Deuteronomy 10:14 & 15 (Moffatt)

*F*or ever, O Lord, thy word is settled in HEAVEN.

Psalm 119:89 (KJ)

*B*ut you have come to Mount Zion, even to the city of the living God, HEAVENLY Jerusalem, and to an innumerable multitude of angels, to a festal gathering, and to the assembly of the first-born who are enrolled in HEAVEN, and to God the Judge of all, and to the spirits of just men who have been brought to completeness and to Jesus, the mediator of a new testament, and to blood of sprinkling which speaks better things than the blood of Abel (i.e., the animal blood which he shed sacrificially).

Hebrews 12:22-24 (Wuest)

> *T*he God of Abraham praise, Who reigns enthroned above;
> Ancient of everlasting days, and God of love.
> Jehovah, great I Am, by earth and HEAVEN confessed;
> I bow and bless the sacred Name, forever blest.
>
> The whole triumphant host give thanks to God on high.
> "Hail, Father, Son, and Holy Ghost!" They ever cry.
> Hail, Abraham's God and mine! I join the HEAVENLY lays;.
> All might and majesty are Thine, And endless praise.
>
> *(by Daniel ben Judah)*

Begin your prayer time adoring God and the HEAVENLY home He has prepared.

THE GOD OF HEAVEN

🔲 HEAVEN—Scriptures evidently specify three HEAVENS, since "the third HEAVEN" is revealed to exist. It is logical that a third HEAVEN cannot exist without a first and a second. Scripture does not describe specifically the first and second. The first however, apparently refers to the atmospheric heavens of the fowl. The second heaven may be the stellar spaces. It is the abode of all supernatural beings. The third HEAVEN is the abode of the Triune God. (Unger's Bible Dictionary)

The HEAVENS declare the glory of God; And the firmament shows His handiwork.

Psalm 19:1 (NKJ)

"For behold, I create new HEAVENS and a new earth; And the former things shall not be remembered or come to mind.

Isaiah 65:17 (NAS)

I know a man in Christ who fourteen years ago, whether in the body or out of the body I do not know, God knows, was caught up to the third HEAVEN.

2 Corinthians 12:2 (Amplified)

The spacious FIRMAMENT on high,
With all the blue, ethereal SKY,
And spangled HEAVENS, a shining frame,
The great Original proclaim:

The unwearied sun, from day to day,
Does his Creator's power display;
And publishes to every land
The work of an Almighty hand.

(by Joseph Addison)

Begin your prayer time adoring the God who dwells in HEAVEN.

THE GOD OF HEAVEN

■ HEAVEN—In HEAVEN the blessedness of the righteous consists in the possession of "life everlasting," "an eternal weight of glory", an exemption from all suffering forever, a deliverance from all evils and from the society of the wicked, bliss without end, the "fullness of joy" forever. The believer's heaven is not only a state of everlasting blessedness, but also a place—"a place prepared" for them. (Today's Dictionary of the Bible)

This what the Lord says: "HEAVEN is my throne and earth is my footstool. Where is the house you will build for me? Where will my resting place be? Has not my hand made all these things, and so they came into being?" Says the Lord.

Isaiah 66:1 & 2 (NIV)

We know that our body—the tent we live in here on earth will be destroyed. But when that happens God will have a house for us. It will not be a house made by human hands; instead, it will be a home in HEAVEN that will last forever.

2 Corinthians 5:1 (NCV)

Praise be to the God and Father of our Lord Jesus Christ, who in his mercy gave us new birth into a living hope by the resurrection of Jesus Christ from the dead! The inheritance to which we are born is one that nothing can destroy or spoil or wither. It is kept for you in HEAVEN.

1 Peter 1:3 & 4 (NEB)

The people of the Lord Are on their way to HEAVEN;
They there obtain their great reward, the prize will there be given.
'Tis conflict here below, 'tis triumph there, and peace;
On earth we wrestle with the foe, in HEAVEN our conflicts cease.

'Tis gloom and darkness here, 'tis light and joy above;
There all is pure and all is clear, there all is peace and love.
Then let us joyful sing, the conflict is not long;
We know in HEAVEN we'll praise our King, in one eternal song.

(by Thomas Kelly)

Begin your prayer time adoring God for preparing a place in HEAVEN for the people who have accepted His Son as their Saviour.

THE GOD OF HEAVEN

⊞ HEAVEN—1. Rakia, firmament 2. Shamayim, the HEAVENS 3. Marom, high region 4. Arabah, the HEAVEN (Smith's Bible Dictionary; showing the various words for HEAVEN found in the Bible)

*D*eclare his glory among the nations, his marvelous deeds among the peoples. For great is the Lord and most worthy of praise; he is to feared above all gods. For all the gods of the nations are idols, but the Lord made the HEAVENS. Splendor and majesty are before him; strength and joy in HIS DWELLING PLACE.

1 Chronicles 16:24-26 (NIV)

*B*ut the day of the Lord will come; it will come, unexpected as a thief. On that day the HEAVENS will disappear with a great rushing sound, the elements will disunitegrate in flames, and the earth with all that is in it will be laid bare.

2 Peter 3:10 (NEB)

*T*herefore, rejoice, O HEAVENS, and all you who live in the HEAVENS! But alas for the earth and the sea, for the devil has come down to you in great fury, knowing that his time is short.

Revelation 12:12 (Phillips)

*W*hen all my labors and trials are o'er,
When by the gift of His infinite grace,
And I am safe on that beautiful shore,
I am accorded in HEAVEN a place,
Just to be near the dear Lord I adore,
Just to be there and to look on His face,
Will through the ages be glory for me.
Will through the ages be glory for me.

Friends will be there I have loved long ago;
Joy like a river around me will flow;
Yet, just a smile from my Saviour I know,
Will through the ages be glory for me.

(by Charles H. Gabriel)

Begin your prayer time with adoration for the God of HEAVEN.

GOD OUR HELP

🀫 HELP—To lend strength or means toward; to aid; to assist. (Webster)

*O*ur soul awaits Yahweh, he is our HELP and shield; our hearts rejoice in him, we trust in his holy name.

Psalm 33:20 & 21 (NJB)

*G*od is our refuge and strength, a very present HELP in trouble.

Psalm 46:1 (KJ)

*I*mmediately having cried out, the father of the little boy was saying, I am believing. Be HELPING my weakness of faith.

Mark 9:24 (Wuest)

*T*he HELPER will come—the Spirit of truth, who comes from the father. I will send him from the Father, and he will speak about me.

John 15:26 (Good News)

> *O* God, our HELP, in ages past,
> Our hope for years to come,
> Our shelter from the stormy blast,
> And our eternal home!
>
> Under the shadow of Thy throne
> Thy saints have dwelt secure;
> Sufficient is Thine arm alone,
> And our defense is sure.
>
> *(by Isaac Watts)*

Begin your prayer time adoring the God who is our HELPER.

GOD OUR HELP

HELP—synonyms—Assist, aid, succor, relieve.

*U*nless the Lord had given HELP, I would soon have dwelt in the place of the dead.

Psalm 94:17 (NIV)

*T*hen Samuel took a stone and erected it between Mispah and Jeshanah, naming it HELPSTONE. "This is witness," he said, "that the Eternal has HELPED us."

1 Samuel 7:12 (Moffatt)

*H*e has put down the mighty from their thrones, and exalted those of low degree. He has filled and satisfied the hungry with good things, and the rich He has sent away empty handed—without a gift. He has laid hold on His servant Israel (to HELP him, to espouse his cause), in remembrance of His mercy.

Luke 1:52-54 (Amplified)

A thousand ages, in Thy sight,
Are like an evening gone;
Short as the watch that ends the night,
Before the rising sun.

O God, our HELP in ages past,
Our hope for years to come,
Be Thou our guide while life shall last,
And our eternal home.

(by Isaac Watts)

Begin your prayer time adoring the God who HELPS.

GOD OUR HELP

O Israel, trust in the Lord; He is their HELP and their shield.

Psalm 115:9 (NKJ)

*O*ur HELP comes from the Lord, who made heaven and earth.

Psalm 124:8 (NCV)

*T*ruly, truly, I say to you, he who believes in Me, the works that I do shall he do also; and greater works than these shall he do; because I go to the Father. And whatever you ask in My name, that will I do, that the Father may be glorified in the Son. If you ask Me anything in My name, I will do it. If you love Me, you will keep my commandments. And I will ask the Father, and He will give you another HELPER, that He may be with you forever; that is the Spirit of truth, whom the world cannot receive, because it does not behold Him or know Him, but you know Him because He abides with you, and will be in you.

John 14:12-17 (NAS)

*I*mmortal, invisible, God only wise,
In light inaccessible hid from our eyes,
Most blessed, most glorious, the Ancient of Days,
Almighty, victorious, Thy great name we praise.

Great Father of glory, pure Father of light,
Thine angels adore Thee, all veiling their sight;
All praise we would render: O HELP us to see
'Tis only the splendor of light hideth Thee.

(by Walter Chalmers Smith)

Begin your prayer time adoring The Almighty because He provided us with a HELPER.

GOD OUR HELP

*F*or the Lord is our defense; and the Holy One of Israel is our king. Then thou spakest in vision to thy holy one, and saidst, I have laid HELP upon one that is mighty; I have exalted one chosen out of the people.

Psalm 89:18 & 19 (KJ)

*B*ut now God himself comes to HELP me, the Lord, supporter of my life.

Psalm 54:4 (NJB)

*W*e, therefore, can confidently say: The Lord is my HELPER; I will not fear: What shall man do unto me?

Hebrews 13:6 (Phillips)

*A*lso, the Spirit HELPS us with our weakness. We do not know how to pray as we should. But the Spirit himself speaks to God for us, even begs God for us with deep feelings that words cannot explain.

Romans 8:26 (NCV)

> *H*oly Ghost with light divine,
> Dwelling in this heart of mine;
> Take all doubts and fears away,
> As I tread the narrow way.
>
> Holy Ghost with power divine,
> Strengthen this weak heart of mine
> When my prayers I can't express
> Thou dost AID in my distress.
>
> *(by Andrew Reed)*

Begin your prayer time adoring God for giving us the Holy Spirit as an AID to prayer.

THE GREAT I AM

I AM—a name of God. Literally God is he who is, the absolute I, the self-existent One. (Unger's)

Moses said to God, "Suppose I go to the Israelites and say to them, "The God of your fathers has sent me to you," and they ask me, "What is his name?" Then what shall I tell them? God said to Moses, "I AM who I AM." This is what you are to say to Israelites: I AM has sent me to you."

Exodus 3:13 & 14 (NIV)

The Lord, the King of Israel, says—yes, it is Israel's Redeemer, the Lord of Hosts, who says it—I AM the First and Last; there is no other God.

Isaiah 44:6 (Paraphrased)

Jesus said to them, "I AM the bread of life. Whoever comes to me shall never be hungry, and whoever believes in me shall never be thirsty.

John 6:35 (NEB)

> *Glory* to God on high!
> Peace upon earth and joy,
> Good will to man.
> We who God's blessings prove,
> HIS NAME all names above,
> Sing, now, the Saviour's love,
> Too vast to scan.
>
> *(by Thomas Kelly)*

Begin your prayer time adoring the great I AM.

THE GREAT I AM

*N*ow when Abram was ninety-nine years old, the Lord appeared to Abram and said to him, I AM God Almighty; walk before Me and be blameless.

Genesis 17:1 (NAS)

*H*e (Isaac) then made his way up to Beersheba, and that very night the Eternal appeared to him saying, I AM the God of your Father Abraham: fear not, I AM with you and I will bless you and multiply your descendants, for the sake of my servant Abraham.

Genesis 26:24 (Moffatt)

*F*or where two or three of you come together in my name, I AM there with them.

Matthew 18:19 (Good News)

*T*hen Jesus spoke to them again, I AM the light of the world; My follower will not walk around in darkness, but has the Light of life.

John 8:12 (Berkeley)

I AM the Door,
I AM the Door,
by me if any man enter in
He shall be saved.

I AM the Door, the words are but four,
Millions are in, but there's room for more,
The door's open wide,
Come right inside, and thou shalt be saved.

(Author unknown)

Begin your prayer time adoring the great I AM.

THE GREAT I AM

I will not execute the fierceness of My anger, I will not again destroy Ephriam. For I AM God, and not man, The Holy One in your midst; And I will not come with terror.

Hosea 11:9 (NKJ)

*H*ear, O My people, and I will speak; O Israel, I will testify to you and against you; I AM God, your God.

Psalm 50:7 (Amplified)

*H*e was saying to them, As for you, from beneath you are. As for myself, from above I AM. As for you, of this world you are. As for myself, I AM not of this world. Therefore I said to you, You shall die in your sins, for if you do not believe that I AM, you shall die in your sins.

John 8:23 & 24 (Wuest)

"*L*ook," said the Jews to him, "you are not fifty yet—and has Abraham seen you?" "I tell you in solemn truth," returned Jesus, "before there was an Abraham, I AM".

John 8:57 & 58 (Phillips)

> *H*e died! He died! the lowly man of sorrows,
> On whom were laid our many griefs and woes;
> Our sins He bore beneath God's awful billows,
> And He hath triumphed over all our foes.
> "I AM He that liveth, and was dead;
> And behold, I AM am alive forevermore.
>
> *(by C. Russel Hurditch)*

Begin you prayer time adoring the GREAT I AM.

THE GREAT I AM

I will make them want to know me, that I AM the Lord. They will be my people, and I will be their God, because they will return to me with their whole hearts.

Jeremiah 24:7 (NCV)

I AM Yahweh, unrivaled; there is no other God beside me.

Isaiah 45:5 (NJB)

I AM the Door. Anyone, who enters in through Me will be saved—will live; he will come in and he will go out (freely), and will find pasture.
I AM the Good Shepherd. The good shepherd risks and lays down his (own) life for the sheep.

John 10:9 & 11 (Amplified)

I AM he that liveth, and was dead; and behold, I AM alive for evermore, Amen; and have the keys of hell and of death.

Revelation 1:18 (KJ)

> *He* lives! He lives!
> What glorious consolation!
> Exalted at His Father's own right hand;
> He pleads for us,
> And by His intercession,
> Enables all His saints by grace to stand.
> I AM He that liveth, and was dead;
> And behold, I AM alive for ever more.
>
> *(by C. Russell Hurditch)*

Begin your prayer time adoring the living GREAT I AM.

THE GREAT I AM

*J*esus told her, I AM the one who raises the dead and gives them life again. Anyone who believes in me, even though he dies like anyone else, shall live again.

John 11:25 (Paraphrased)

*J*esus answered, "I AM the way and the truth and the life. No one comes to the Father except by me."

John 14:6 (NIV)

*O*n his way to Damascus, as he came near the city, a light from the sky suddenly flashed all around him. He fell to the ground and heard a voice saying to him, "Saul, Saul! Why do you persecute me?" "Who are you, Lord?" he asked. "I AM Jesus, whom you persecute," the voice said.

Acts 9:33-5 (Good News)

I AM the Alpha and the Omega, the first and the last, the beginning and the end. I, Jesus, have sent my angel to you with this testimony for the churches. I AM the root and scion of David, the bright morning star.

Revelation 22:13 & 16 (NEB)

*T*he God of Abraham praise,
Who reigns enthroned above;
Ancient of everlasting days,
And God of love.

Jehovah, great I AM,
by earth and heaven confessed;
I bow and bless the sacred name,
Forever blest.

(by Daniel ben Judah)

Begin your prayer time adoring the GREAT I AM.

THE GOD OF JUSTICE

JUSTICE—lawful, rightful, just. (Webster)

*T*he Rock! His work is perfect, For all His ways are JUST; A God of faithfulness and without injustice. Righteous and upright is He.

Deuteronomy 32:4 (NAS)

*I*nspire the king, O God, with thine own JUSTICE, endow his majesty with thine own equity, that he may rule thy folk aright and deal out JUSTICE to the poor.

Psalm 72:1 & 2 (Moffatt)

*B*y myself I can do nothing; I judge only as I hear, and my judgment is JUST, for I seek not to please myself but him who sent me.

John 5:30 (NIV)

> *T*here's a wideness in God's mercy,
> Like the wideness of the sea;
> There's a kindness in His JUSTICE,
> Which is more than liberty.
>
> There is welcome for the sinner,
> And more graces for the good;
> There is mercy with the Saviour;
> There is healing in His blood.
>
> *(by Frederick W. Faber)*

Begin you prayer time adoring a JUST God.

THE GOD OF JUSTICE

JUSTICE synonyms—Equity, law impartiality, fairness, right, reasonableness, propriety, uprightness, integrity (Webster)

*G*ood and UPRIGHT is the Lord: therefore will he teach sinners in the way.

Psalm 25:8 (KJ)

*T*herefore the Lord will wait, that He may be gracious to you; And therefore He will be exalted, that He may have mercy on you. For the Lord is a God of JUSTICE; Blessed are all those who wait for Him.

Isaiah 30:18 (NKJ)

*N*ow I, Nebuchadnezzar, praise and extol and honor the King of Heaven, all of Whose works are faithful and RIGHT, and His ways are JUST; and those who walk in pride He is able to abase and humble.

Daniel 4:37 (Amplified)

*T*here's a wideness in God's mercy,
Like the wideness of the sea;
There's a kindness in His JUSTICE,
Which is more than liberty.

For the love of God is broader
Than the measure of man's mind;
And the heart of the Eternal
Is most wonderfully kind.

(Frederick W. Faber)

Adore the Son of God for meeting the demand for JUSTICE in regarding your sin.

THE GOD OF JUSTICE

JUSTICE of God. In theology, as in the Scriptures, the terms JUSTICE and RIGHTEOUSNESS are used synonymously. The JUSTICE of God is both an essential and a relative attribute of the divine existence. It is a necessary outflow from the holiness of God. (Unger's)

*F*or the Lord is RIGHTEOUS; He loves RIGHTEOUSNESS; the upright will behold His face.

Psalm 11:7 (NAS)

*S*ince all have sinned and are falling short of honor and glory which God bestows and receives. (All) are JUSTIFIED and made UPRIGHT and in RIGHT standing with God, freely and gratuitously by His grace (His unmerited favor and mercy), through the redemption which is (provided) in Christ Jesus.

Romans 3:23 & 24 (Amplified)

*T*hey were singing the song of Moses, the servant of God, and the song of the Lamb, as they chanted: "Great and marvelous are thy deeds, O Lord God, sovereign over all;
JUST and true are thy ways, thou king of the ages. Who shall not revere thee, Lord, and do homage to thy name? For thou alone art holy. All nations shall come and worship in thy presence, for thy JUST dealings stand revealed.

Revelation 15:3 (NEB)

*T*here's a wideness in God's mercy,
Like the wideness of the sea;
There's a kindness in His JUSTICE,
Which is more than liberty.

If our love were but more simple,
We should take Him at His word,
And our lives would be all sunshine
In the sweetness of our Lord.

(by Frederick W. Faber)

Begin your prayer time adoring the God who tempers JUSTICE with mercy.

THE GOD OF KINDNESS

KINDNESS—Good will; benevolence; that temper or disposition which delights in contributing to the happiness of others.

*B*lessed be the Lord, For He has shown me His marvelous KINDNESS in a strong city.

Psalm 31:21 (NKJ)

*F*or the mountains may depart and the hills disappear, but my KINDNESS shall not leave you. My promise of peace for you will never be broken, says the Lord who has mercy upon you.

Isaiah 54:10 (Paraphrased)

*B*ut when the KINDNESS and love of God our Savior appeared, he saved us. It was not by any good works that we ourselves had done, but because of his own mercy that he saved us through the washing by which the Holy Spirit gives us new birth and new life.

Titus 3:4 & 5 (Good News)

> *A*wake, my soul, to joyful lays,
> And sing thy great Redeemer's praise;
> He justly claims a song from thee,
> His loving KINDNESS, oh, how free!
>
> He saw me ruined by the fall,
> Yet loved me not withstanding all;
> He saved me from my lost estate,
> His loving KINDNESS, oh, how great!
>
> *(by Samuel Medly)*

Begin your prayer time adoring the God of KINDNESS.

May 19

THE GOD OF KINDNESS

Synonyms for KIND—Tender, affectionate, well-disposed, courteous, tender-hearted. (Webster)

*B*ut they and our fathers were insolent and obstinate, they would not listen to thy commands and refused to obey; thy wonderful deeds with them they forgot; they were obstinate, and they appointed one to lead them back to their bondage in Egypt. Yet thou art a God ready to pardon, KIND and pitiful, slow to be angry and rich in mercy; thou didst not abandon them.

Nehemiah 9:16 & 17 (Moffatt)

O praise the Lord, all you nations! Praise Him all you people! For His mercy and loving-KINDNESS are great toward us, and the truth and faithfulness of the Lord endure forever. Praise the Lord!—Hallelujah!

Psalm 117 (Amplified)

*B*ut when the KINDNESS of God our Saviour and his love towards man appeared, he saved us in his own mercy—not by virtue of any moral achievements of ours, but by the cleansing power of a new birth and the moral renewal of the Holy Spirit.

Titus 3:4 & 5 (Phillips)

*W*hen trouble, like a gloomy cloud,
Has gathered thick and thundered loud,
He near my soul has always stood,
His loving KINDNESS, oh, how good!

Soon shall we mount and soar away
To the bright realms of endless day,
And sing, with rapture and surprise,
His loving KINDNESS, in the skies.

Begin your prayer time adoring God's loving KINDNESS.

THE GOD OF KINDNESS

⊞ LOVING-KINDNESS—Hebrew word is hesed, desire, ardor. In a good sense hesed is zeal toward anyone, kindness, love. Of God toward men, goodness, mercy grace. (Unger's)

*G*od says, "I left you for a time, but with great KINDNESS I will bring you back again. I became very angry and hid from you for a time, but I will show you mercy with KINDNESS forever, says the Lord who saves you.

Isaiah 54:7 & 8 (NCV)

*A*nd he prayed to the Lord and said, "Please Lord, was not this what I said while I was still in my own country? Therefore to forestall this I fled to Tarshish, for I knew that Thou art a gracious and compassionate God, slow to anger and abundant in LOVINGKINDNESS, and one who relents concerning calamity.

Jonah 4:2 (NAS)

*F*or this very reason, make every effort to add to your faith goodness; and to goodness, knowledge; and to knowledge, self-control; and to self, control, perseverance; and to perseverance, godliness; and to godliness, brotherly-KINDNESS; and to brotherly-KINDNESS, love.

2 Peter 1:5-7 (NIV)

*I*n TENDERNESS He sought me,
Weary and sick with sin,
And on His shoulders brought me
Back to His fold again.
While angels in His presence sang
Until the courts of heaven rang.

Oh, the love that sought me!
Oh, the blood that bought me!
Oh, the grace that brought me to the fold,
Wondrous grace that brought me to the fold!

(by W. Spencer Walton)

Begin your prayer time adoring the God of KINDNESS.

GOD'S KINGDOM

KINGDOM—The territory or country subject to a king; the territory under the dominion of a king or monarch. (Webster's)

*T*hine, O lord, is the greatness, and the power, and the glory, victory and majesty: for all that is in heaven and in earth is thine; thine is the KINGDOM, O Lord, and thou art exalted as head above all.

1 Chronicles 29:11 (KJ)

*A*ll the ends of the earth will remember and turn to the Lord, and all families will bow down before him, for DOMINION belongs to the Lord and he rules over the nations.

Psalm 22:27 & 28 (NIV)

*I*n due course John the Baptist arrived, preaching in the Judean desert; "You must change your hearts—for the KINGDOM of heaven has arrived!"

Matthew 3:1 & 2 (Phillips)

> *L*o! He comes, from heaven descending,
> Once for favored sinners slain!
> Thousand thousand saints attending
> Swell the triumph of His train!
>
> Yea, Amen, let all adore Thee,
> High on Thine exalted throne;
> Saviour, take the power and glory,
> Claim the KINGDOMS for Thine own
>
> *(Author unknown)*

Begin your prayer time adoring the King of the KINGDOM.

GOD'S KINGDOM

▦ KINGDOM of God; KINGDOM of heaven. The "KINGDOM of God" is evidently a more comprehensive term than the KINGDOM of heaven" and embraces all created intelligences both in heaven and on earth who are willingly subject to God and thus in fellowship with him. (Unger's)

In heaven has the Eternal fixed his throne, and his DOMINION covers all the world.

Psalm 103:19 (Moffatt)

But Jesus said, Permit the children, and stop forbidding them to come to me, for of such is the KINGDOM of heaven.

Matthew 19:14 (Wuest)

(*After* all), the KINGDOM of God is not a matter of (getting the) food and drink (one likes), but instead, it is righteousness—that state which makes a person acceptable to God—and heart-peace and joy in the Holy Spirit.

Romans 14:17 (Amplified)

When He cometh, when He cometh to make up His jewels,
All His jewels, precious jewels, His loved and His own.
Like the stars of the morning, His bright crown adorning,
They shall shine in their beauty, Bright gems for His crown.

He will gather, He will gather the gems for His KINGDOM;
All the pure ones, all the bright ones, His loved and His own.
Little children, little children, who love their Redeemer,
Are the jewels, precious jewels, His loved and His own.

(by William O. Cushing)

Begin your prayer time adoring the King of the KINGDOM.

GOD'S KINGDOM

🔲 KINGDOM of God denotes 1. Christ's mediatorial authority, or his rule on earth; 2. the blessings and advantages of all kinds that flow from his rule; 3. the subjects of the KINGDOM taken collectively, or the church. (Today's)

*Y*ahweh, all your creatures thank you, and your faithful bless you. Kingly and glorious they proclaim you, they affirm your might. Let mankind learn your acts of power, and the majestic glory of your sovereignty, your EMPIRE lasts from age to age.

Psalm 145:10-13 (NJB)

*T*his is the way you should pray: Our Father in heaven: May your name be kept holy, May your KINGDOM come, May your will be done on earth as it is in heaven.

Matthew 6:9 & 10 (Good News)

"*T*hy throne, O God, is forever and ever, and the scepter of Thy KINGDOM is a scepter of absolute fairness.

Hebrews 1:8 (Berkeley)

*F*ar away in the depths of my spirit tonight
Rolls a melody sweeter than psalm;
In celestial-like strains it unceasingly falls
O'er my soul like an infinite calm.

And me thinks when I rise to that City of peace,
Where the Author of peace I shall see,
That one strain of the song which the ransomed will sing,
In that heavenly KINGDOM shall be:

Peace! Peace! wonderful peace,
Coming down from the Father above;
Sweep over my spirit forever, I pray,
In fathomless billows of love.

(by W. D. Cornell)

Begin your prayer time adoring the King of the KINGDOM.

GOD'S KINGDOM

"*This* decision is by the decree of the watchers, And the sentence by the word of the holy ones, In order that the living may know That the Most High rules in the KINGDOM of men, Gives it to whomever He will, And sets over it the lowest of men."

Daniel 4:17 (NKJ)

The deliverers will ascend Mount Zion To judge the mountain of Esau, And the KINGDOM will be the Lord's.

Obadiah 21 (NAS)

All the more then, my friend, exert yourself to clinch God's choice and calling of you. If you behave so, you will never come to grief. Thus you will be afforded full and free admission into the eternal KINGDOM of our Lord and Saviour Jesus Christ.

2 Peter 1:10 & 11 (Wuest)

Then the seventh angel blew his trumpet. And there were loud voices in heaven saying: The power to RULE THE WORLD now belongs to our Lord and his Christ, and he will rule for ever and ever.

Revelation 11:15 (NCV)

Speak to my soul, Lord Jesus, speak now in tenderest tone;
Whisper in loving kindness; "Thou art not left alone."
Open my heart to hear Thee, quickly to hear Thy voice,
Fill Thou my soul with praises, let me in Thee rejoice.

Speak to Thy children ever, lead in the holy way;
Fill them with joy and gladness, teach them to watch and pray.
May they in consecration yield their whole lives to Thee,
Hasten Thy coming KINGDOM, till our dear Lord we see.

(by L.L. Piclett)

Begin your prayer time adoring the God whose KINGDOM will never pass away.

THE LAW OF GOD

🔲 LAW—A general rule of action or conduct established or enforced by a sovereign authority. (Webster)

*T*he LAW of the Lord is perfect, restoring the whole person; the testimony of the Lord is sure, making wise the simple and willing.

Psalm 19:7 (Amplified)

*M*any people will come and say, "Come, let us go up to the mountains of the Lord, to the house of the God of Jacob. He will teach us his ways, so that we will walk in his paths." The LAW will go out from Zion, the word of the Lord from Jerusalem.

Isaiah 2:3 (NIV)

*B*ut he who with eagerness and concentration has pored over the perfect LAW, the LAW of liberty, and has continued in it, not having been a hearer who forgets but a doer who works, this person shall be prospered spiritually in his doing.

James 1:25 (Wuest)

*H*oly Bible, book divine, precious treasure, thou art mine;
Mine to tell me whence I came; mine to punish or reward.
Mine to chide me when I rove; mine to show a Savior's love;
Mine thou art to guide and guard; mine to punish or reward.

Mine to comfort in distress, suffering in this wilderness;
Mine to show, by living faith, man can triumph over death.
Mine to tell of joys to come, and the rebel sinners doom;
O thou Holy Book divine, precious treasure, thou art mine.

(by John Burton)

Begin you prayer time adoring the God who gave the LAW as a *guide.

THE LAW OF GOD

LAW—The Moral LAW is the revealed will of God as to human conduct, binding on all men until the end of time. (Today's)

For the COMMANDMENT is a lamp, and the teaching is light; And reproofs for discipline are a way of life.

Proverbs 6:23 (NAS)

For Yahweh is our judge, Yahweh our LAW GIVER, Yahweh our King and our Saviour.

Isaiah 33:22 (DV)

"*Teacher*," he asked, "which is the greatest COMMANDMENT in the LAW? Jesus answered," "You must love the Lord your God with all your heart, and with all your soul, and with all your mind." This is the greatest and most important COMMANDMENT. The second most important COMMANDMENT is like it: "You must love your neighbor as yourself." The whole LAW of Moses and the teachings of the prophets depends on these two COMMANDMENTS."

Matthew 22:36-40 (Good News)

Lamp of our feet whereby we trace our path, when want to stray;
Stream from the fount of heavenly grace, brook by the traveler's way.
Bread of our souls , whereon we feed, true manna from on high;
Our *guide and chart, wherein we read of realms beyond the sky.

Pillar of fire, through watches dark, or radiant cloud by day;
When waves would overwhelm our tossing bark our anchor and our stay.
Word of the ever living God, will of His glorious son;
Without our Lord how could earth be trod, Or heaven itself be won

(by Bernard D. Barton)

Begin your prayer time adoring the God who gave the LAW to be our daily guide.

THE LAW OF GOD

▓ LAW—Hebrew, torah, teaching, instruction, a term employed almost 200 times in the Bible and signifying the revealed will of God with respect to human conduct. (Unger's)

*M*y covenant was with him, one of life and peace, and I gave them to him that he might fear Me; so he feared Me and was reverent before my name. The LAW of truth was in his mouth, and injustice was not found in his lips. He walked with me in peace and equity, and turned many away from iniquity.

Malachi 2:5 & 6 (NKJ)

*W*ell then, whatever you would have men do to you, do just the same to them; that is the meaning of the Law and the prophets.

Matthew 7:12 (Moffatt)

*B*ut the man who looks into the perfect mirror of God's LAW, the LAW of liberty, and makes a habit of so doing, is not the man who sees and forgets. He puts the LAW into practice and he wins true happiness.

James 1:25 (Phillips)

> *F*ulfillment of the LAW, O happy situation,
> Jesus has bled, and there is remission;
> Cursed by the LAW and bruised by the fall
> Grace has redeemed us once for all.
>
> Now we are free—there's no condemnation,
> Jesus provides a perfect salvation;
> "Come unto Me," O hear his sweet call,
> Come, and He saves us once for all.
>
> *(by Philip P. Bliss)*

Adore the God who fulfilled for us the requirements of the LAW through His Son.

THE LAW OF GOD

🔲 LAW—Greek nomos. The term law is used for the Old Testament as a whole. (Today's Dictionary of the Bible)

*H*earken unto me, ye that know righteousness, the people in whose heart is my LAW; fear ye not the reproach of men, neither be ye afraid of their revilings.

Isaiah 51:7 (KJ)

*W*hat ever the LAW says it says to those who are inside the LAW, that every mouth may be shut and all the world made answerable to God; for no person will be acquitted in his sight on the score of obedience to LAW. What the LAW imparts is a consciousness of sin. But now we have a righteousness of God disclosed apart from the LAW altogether; it is attested by the LAW and the prophets, but it is righteousness of God which comes from believing in Jesus Christ. And it is meant for all who have faith. No distinctions are drawn.

Romans 1:19-22 (Moffatt)

*D*o not malign one another, brothers. One who maligns or criticizes his brother, maligns the LAW and criticizes the LAW but if you criticize the LAW you are not its practicer but its judge. There is one LAWGIVER and Judge— He who has power to save and to destroy. But who are you to be judging your neighbor?

James 4:11 & 12 (Berkeley)

> *H*ark sinner, hark! we have tidings so true,
> Tidings of pardon and blessing for you!
> God in his word says that Christ on the tree
> Died for guilty sinners and "Salvation is free."
>
> Guilty by LAW you are, yet know very well
> Jesus has suffered to save you from hell;
> Though condemned, now justified you may be,
> Jesus paid the ransom, and "Salvation is free."
>
> *(Author unknown)*

Adore God for the Living LAW.

THE GOD OF LIFE

LIFE—That which makes ALIVE, or causes growth and development. The duration of existence, usefulness, or efficiency. (Webster)

The time came when the Lord God formed a man's body from the dust of the ground and breathed into it the breath of LIFE. And man became a LIVING person.

Genesis 2:7 (Living Bible)

Thou hast granted me LIFE and loving kindness; And Thy care has preserved my spirit.

Job 10:12 (NAS)

In the beginning (before all time) was the Word (Christ), and the Word was with God, and the Word was God Himself. He was present originally with God. All things were made and came into existence through Him; and without Him was not even one thing made that has come into being. In Him was LIFE and the LIFE was the Light of men.

John 1:1-4 (Amplified)

Sing them over again to me, wonderful words of LIFE
Let me more of their beauty see, wonderful words of LIFE.
Words of LIFE and beauty, Teach me faith and duty:
Beautiful words, wonderful words, wonderful words of LIFE.

Christ, the blessed One, gives to all wonderful words of LIFE;
Sinner, list to the loving call, wonderful words of LIFE.
All so freely given, wooing us to heaven;
Beautiful words, wonderful words, wonderful words of LIFE.

(by Philip P. Bliss)

Begin your prayer time adoring the God of LIFE.

THE GOD OF LIFE

LIFE—1. That which is physical or natural. 2. Eternal. This is the gift of God as a result of faith in Jesus Christ. 3. Absolute LIFE. God in Christ, as self-existent or absolute LIFE is the Source of all LIFE. (Unger's)

Yahweh God caused to spring up from the soil every kind of tree, enticing to look at and good to eat, with the tree of LIFE and the tree of the knowledge of good and evil in the middle of the garden.

Genesis 2:9 (NJB)

For even as the Father raises the dead back to LIFE, in the same way the Son gives LIFE to those he wants to.

John 5:21 (Good News)

This treasure, however, we possess within utensils of mere clay—an evidence that the unparalleled power is of God and not from us. We are hedged in from every side, but we live no cramped lives; we suffer embarrassments but we do not despair; we are persecuted but not deserted; struck down but not destroyed; all the while bearing about in the body the death-marks of (the Lord) Jesus, so that by our bodies the LIFE of Jesus may be shown.

2 Corinthians 4:7-10 (Berkeley)

Break Thou the bread of LIFE, dear Lord to me,
As Thou didst break the loaves beside the sea.
With-in the sacred page I seek Thee Lord;
My spirit pants for Thee, O LIVING Word.

Break Thou the bread of LIFE, O Lord to me,
That hid within my heart Thy word may be:
Mold Thou each inward thought, from self set free,
And let my steps be all controlled by Thee.

(by Mary A. Lathbury)

Begin your prayer time adoring the God who gives LIFE.

May 31

THE GOD OF LIFE

LIFE—generally of physical life; used also figuratively for immortality. (Today's Dictionary of the Bible)

*B*ut now ask the beasts, and they will tell you; and the birds of the air, and they will tell you; or speak to the earth, and it will teach you; and the fish of the sea will explain to you, who among all these does not know that the hand of the Lord has done this, in whose hand is the LIFE of every living thing, and the breath of all mankind?

Job 12:7-10 (NKJ)

*S*o people receive God's promise by having faith. This happens so the promise can be a free gift. Then all of Abraham's children can have that promise. It is not only for those who live under the law of Moses but for anyone who lives with faith like that of Abraham, who is the father of us all. As it is written in the Scriptures: "I am making you a father of many nations. This is true before God, the God Abraham believed, the God who gives LIFE to the dead and who creates something out of nothing.

Romans 4:16 & 17 (NCV)

*A*nd this is the testimony, that LIFE eternal God gave us. And this LIFE is in His Son. The one who has the Son has the LIFE. The one who does not have the Son of God the LIFE he does not have.

1 John 5:11 & 12 (Wuest)

*O*h, what a Saviour, that He died for me!
From condemnation He hath made me free;
"He that believeth on the Son," saith He
"Hath everlasting LIFE."

All my iniquities on Him were laid.
All my indebtedness by Him were paid;
All who believe on Him, the Lord hath said,
"Hath everlasting LIFE."

(by James McGranaham)

Begin you prayer time adoring the God who gives everlasting LIFE.

*J*une

THE GOD WHO GIVES LIFE

LIFE—Hay or Chay, (Hebrew), living thing; Nephesh (Hebrew) soul, mind, heart. (Smith's)

This is my comfort and consolation in my affliction, that Your word has revived me and given me LIFE.

Psalm 119:50 (Amplified)

For as the Father has LIFE-GIVING power in himself, so has the Son, by the Father's gift.

John 5:26 (NEB)

I could see no Temple in the city, for the Lord, the Almighty God, and the Lamb are themselves the Temple. The city has no need for the light of the sun or moon, for the splendor of God fills it with light and its radiance is the Lamb. The nations will walk in its light, and the kings of the earth will bring their glory into it. The city's gates shall stand open day after day—and there will be no night there. Into the city they will bring the splendors and the honors of the nations. But nothing unclean, no one who deals in filthiness and lies, shall ever at any time enter it—only those whose names are written in the Lamb's book of LIFE.

Revelation 21:22-27 (Phillips)

I've a message from the Lord, Hallelujah!
The message unto you I'll give;
'Tis recorded in His word, Hallelujah!
It is only that you look and LIVE.

LIFE is offered unto you, Hallelujah!
Eternal LIFE thy soul shall have,
If you'll only look to Him, Hallelujah!
Look to Jesus who alone can Save.

(by William A. Ogden)

Begin your prayer time adoring the God who can give you eternal LIFE.

THE GOD WHO GIVES LIFE

Surely goodness and love will follow me all the days of my LIFE, and I will dwell in the house of the Lord forever.

Psalm 23:6 (NIV)

What gives LIFE is the Spirit; flesh is of no avail at all. The words I have uttered to you are spirit and LIFE.

John 6:63 (Moffatt)

For David speaketh concerning him, I foresaw the Lord always before my face, for he is on my right hand, that I should not be moved: therefore did my heart rejoice, and my tongue was glad; moreover also my flesh shall rest in hope: because thou wilt not leave my soul in hell, neither wilt thou suffer thine Holy One to see corruption. Thou has made known to me the ways of LIFE; thou shalt make me full of joy with thy countenance.

Acts 2:25-28 (KJ)

Blessed are those who wash their robes, that they may have the right to the tree of LIFE, and may enter by the gates into the city.

Revelation 22:14 (NAS)

LIFE, LIFE of love poured out fragrant and holy!
LIFE, amid rude thorns of earth, stainless and sweet!
LIFE, whence God's face of love, glorious but lowly,
Shines forth to bow us, Lord, low at Thy feet.

Death, death of stricken love, wrath's sea exploring!
Death, LIFE'S mysterious death—deep meeting deep!
Death, whence Thy bursting heart fills ours—outpouring
All, all in worship, Lord, low at Thy feet.

(by Frank Allaben)

Begin your prayer time adoring the God whose Son gave up His LIFE so that you may have eternal LIFE.

THE GOD WHO GIVES LIFE

*A*nd you are to say to this people, "Yahweh says this: Look, I now set in front of you the way of LIFE and the way of death.

Jeremiah 21:8 (JB)

*J*esus assured her, I am the Resurrection and the LIFE, the believer in Me will live even when he dies, and everyone who lives and believes in Me shall never, never die.

John 11:25 & 26 (Berkeley)

*T*his is a true saying, to be completely accepted and believed: Christ Jesus came into the world to save sinners. I am the worst of them, but it was for this very reason that God was merciful to me, in order that Christ Jesus might show his full patience with me, the worst of sinners, as an example for all those who would later believe in him and receive eternal LIFE.

1 Timothy 1:15 & 16 (Good News)

*G*uard and keep yourselves in the love of God; expect and patiently wait for the mercy of our Lord Jesus Christ, the Messiah (which will bring you) unto LIFE eternal.

Jude 21 (Amplified)

> *J*esus LIVES and so shall I.
> Jesus LIVES, and death is now
> Death! thy sting is gone forever!
> But my entrance into glory.
> He who deigned for me to die,
> Courage, then, my soul, for thou
> LIVES, the band of death to sever.
> Hast a crown of LIFE before thee;
> He shall raise me with the just:
> Thou shalt find thy hopes were just;
> Jesus is my hope and trust.
> Jesus is the Christian's Trust.
>
> *(by Christian F. Gellert)*

Begin your prayer time adoring God for the gift of LIFE.

THE LORD

🔲 LORD—A master; a person possessing supreme power and authority; a ruler, a governor. (Webster)

Then Moses and the children of Israel sang this song to the LORD, and spoke saying: "I will sing unto the LORD, for he has triumphed gloriously! The horse and rider He has thrown into the sea! The LORD is my strength and song, and he has become my salvation; He is my God, and I will praise Him; My father's God and I will exalt Him.

Exodus 15:1 & 2 (NKJ)

O come, let us sing to the LORD; let us make a joyful noise to the rock of our salvation.

Psalm 95:1 (Amplified)

And there were shepherds in that very region bivouacking in the fields under the open sky, and guarding their flock during the appointed night watches. And an angel of the LORD took his stand at their side, and the glory of the LORD shone round about them, and they feared a great fear. And the angel said to them, Stop being afraid. For behold, I am bringing you good tidings of great joy, which joy is of such a nature that it shall pertain to all people, because there was born to you today a Saviour who is Christ, the LORD, in the city of David.

Luke 2:8-11 (Wuest)

> *Holy,* Holy, Holy! LORD God Almighty!
> Early in the morning our song shall rise to Thee;
> Holy, Holy, Holy! Merciful and Mighty!
> God in Three Persons, blessed Trinity!
>
> Holy, Holy, Holy! LORD God Almighty!
> All Thy works shall praise Thy name, in earth, and sky, and sea
> Holy, Holy, Holy! Merciful and Mighty!
> God in Three Persons, blessed Trinity!
>
> *(by Reginald Heber)*

Begin your prayer time adoring the Almighty LORD.

THE LORD

🔲 LORD—Jehovah (Hebrew, Yahweh) This is used as a proper name of God. (Adonai, Hebrew) emphatic THE LORD and by many regarded as the plural of LORD. It is used chiefly in the Pentateuch. (Unger's)

*M*ay people all over the earth know that the LORD is God, and that there is no other God at all.

1 Kings 8:30 (Paraphrased)

*C*ome, let us sing for joy to the LORD; let us shout aloud to the Rock of our salvation. For the LORD is a great God, the great King above all gods.

Psalm 95:1 & 3 (NIV)

A great crowd followed them as they were leaving Jericho, and two blind men who were sitting by the roadside, hearing it was Jesus who was passing by, cried out, "Have pity on us LORD, you Son of David!" The crowd tried to hush them up, but this only made them cry out more loudly still, "Have pity on us, LORD, you Son of David!" Jesus stood quite still and called out to them, "What do you want me to do?" "LORD, let us see again!" And Jesus, deeply moved with pity, touched their eyes. At once their sight was restored, and they followed him.

Matthew 20-24 (Phillips)

> *G*ive to the LORD of Lords renown
> Give to our God immortal praise!
> The King of kings with glory crown
> Mercy and truth are all His ways;
> His mercies ever shall endure
> Wonders of grace to God belong,
> When lords and kings are known no more.
> Repeat His mercies in your song.
>
> *(by Isaac Watts)*

Begin your prayer time adoring the LORD.

THE LORD

LORD—Hebrew adon—means one possessed of absolute control. The old plural form of this Hebrew word is adonai. From a reverence for the name "Jehovah," the Jews, in reading their Scriptures, whenever adon occurred, always pronounced it adonai. (Today's Dictionary of the Bible)

Thou alone art the LORD. Thou hast made the heavens, the heaven of heavens with all their host, the earth and all that is on it, the seas and all that is in them, and the heavenly host bows down before Thee.

Nehemiah 9:6 (NAS)

Hark! a din among the mountains, as of a mighty host. Hark! 'tis the uproar of empires, of nations gathering; for the LORD of hosts is mustering a battle array.

Isaiah 13:4 (Moffatt)

The Sabbath came for man's sake; not man for the Sabbath, so that the Son of Man is LORD also of the Sabbath.

Mark 2:27 & 28 (Berkeley)

> My God, how wonderful Thou art,
> Thy majesty how bright,
> How beautiful Thy mercy seat,
> In depths of burning light!
>
> Yet I may love Thee, too, O LORD,
> Almighty as Thou art,
> For Thou hast stooped to ask of me
> The love of my poor heart.
>
> *(by Frederick William Faber)*

Begin your prayer time adoring the LORD.

THE LORD

■ LORD—Elohim—The plural is used in Hebrew to enlarge and intensify the idea expressed by the singular. It is not the gods, but is the strongest of all strong beings, the fullness of divine perfections, the sum of all the powers of all imaginable gods. (Smith's)

*A*nd Elijah came to all the people, and said, "How long will you falter between two opinions? If the LORD is God, follow Him; but if Baal, then follow him." But the people answered him not a word.

1 Kings 18:21 (NKJ)

*T*he LORD is near to near to all who call upon Him sincerely and in truth.

Psalm 145:18 (Paraphrased)

"*W*hy do you keep calling me "LORD, LORD"—and never do what I tell you?

Luke 6:26 (NEB)

*C*rown Him the LORD of years, the POTENTATE of time,
Creator of the rolling spheres, ineffably sublime!
All hail, Redeemer hail! For Thou has died for me;
Thy praise shall never, never fail throughout eternity

Crown Him the LORD of heaven: one with the Father known,
One with the Spirit through Him given from yonder glorious throne.
To Thee be endless praise, for Thou for us hast died;
Be Thou, O Lord, through endless days adored and magnified.

(by Matthew Bridges)

Begin your prayer time adoring the LORD.

THE LORD

I love the LORD, for he heard my voice; he heard my cry for mercy. Because he turned his ear to me I will call on him as long as I live.

Psalm 116:1 & 2 (NIV)

For the time is coming, says the LORD, when I will place a righteous Branch upon King David's throne. He shall be a king who shall rule with wisdom and justice and cause righteousness to prevail everywhere throughout the earth. And this is his name: The LORD Our Righteousness.

Jeremiah 23:6-8a (Paraphrased)

After he had washed their feet, Jesus put his outer garment back on and returned to his place at the table. "Do you understand what I have just done to you?" he asked. "You call me Teacher and LORD, and it is right that you do so, because I am. I am your LORD and Teacher, and I have just washed you feet. You then should wash each other's feet.

John 13:12-14 (Good News)

And Peter, having opened his mouth, said, Of a truth I am in the process of comprehending the fact that God does not show partiality to anyone because of his looks or circumstances, but in every nation he who fears Him and does uprightly is acceptable with Him. The word which He sent to the sons of Israel, proclaiming as good news peace through Jesus Christ, this One is LORD of all.

Acts 10:34 & 36 (Wuest)

Rejoice, the LORD is King!
Rejoice in glorious hope;
Your LORD and King adore,
Jesus the LORD shall come
Mortals, give thanks and sing,
And take His servants up
And triumph ever more;
To their eternal home.
Lift up your heart, lift up your voice
Rejoice, again I say, rejoice.

(by Charles Wesley)

Begin your prayer time adoring the LORD.

THE LORD

*T*hose who trust the LORD are like Mount Zion, which sits unmoved forever. As the mountains surround Jerusalem, the LORD surrounds his people now and forever.

Psalm 125:1 & 2 (NCV)

*T*he LORD God is my strength, and He has made my feet like hinds feet, and makes me walk on high places.

Habakkuk 3:19 (NAS)

*I*f you confess with your mouth, "Jesus is LORD," and believe in your heart that God raised him from the dead, you will be saved. For it is with your heart that you believe and are justified, and it is with the mouth that you confess and are saved.

Romans 10:9 & 10 (NIV)

*T*hey will wage war against the Lamb, and the Lamb will triumph over them, for He is LORD of lords and King of kings, and those with Him and on His side are chosen and called (elected) and loyal and faithful followers.

Revelation 17:14 (Amplified)

> *A*ll hail the power of Jesus name!
> Let angels prostrate fall;
> Bring forth the royal diadem,
> And crown Him LORD of all;
>
> Let every kindred every tribe,
> On this terrestrial ball,
> To Him all majesty ascribe,
> And crown Him LORD of all.
>
> *(by Edward Perronet)*

Begin your prayer time adoring the LORD.

THE LORD

And the LORD shall be king over all the earth: in that day there shall be one LORD and his name one.

Zechariah 14:9 (KJ)

Now my dear brothers, I want to clear up a wrong impression about spiritual gifts. You remember that, when you were pagans, whenever you felt irresistibly drawn, it was toward dumb idols? It is for that reason that I want you to understand that on the one hand no one can be speaking under the influence of the Holy Spirit and say "Curse Jesus", and on the other hand, no one can say "Jesus is LORD" unless he is under the influence of the Holy Spirit.

1 Corinthians 12:1-3 (NJB)

He (Jesus) humbled himself, and in obedience accepted death—even death on a cross. Therefore God raised him to the heights and bestowed on him the name above all names, that at the name of Jesus every knee should bow—in heaven, on earth, and in the depths—and every tongue confess, "Jesus is LORD", to the glory of God the Father.

Philippians 2:8b-11 (NEB)

Then I heard what sounded like the voice of a great crowd, like the roar of a mighty waterfall, like loud peals of thunder. I head them say: "Praise God! For the LORD, our Almighty God, is King!"

Revelation 19:6 (Good News)

Praise to the LORD, the Almighty, the King of creation!
O my soul praise Him, for He is thy health and salvation!
Come ye who hear, Now to His great throne draw near;
Join me in glad adoration!

Praise to the LORD, O let all that is in me adore Him!
All that hath life and breath, come now with praises before Him.
Let the Amen Sound from His people again,
Gladly for aye we adore Him.

(by Joachim Neander)

Yes, adore the LORD.

THE GOD OF MIGHT

⊞ MIGHT—from the root of magan, to be able. Ability to wield force, power of control. (Webster)

*O*ne age shall praise thy doings to another, uttering thy MIGHTY acts, dwelling on the glorious splendor of thy state, and on thy marvelous doings; they shall proclaim thy awful powers, and tell thy MIGHTY deeds; they shall spread the fame of thy great goodness, and sing songs of thy faithfulness.

Psalm 145:4-7 (Moffatt)

*L*ift your eyes and look to the heavens: Who created all these? He who brings out the starry host one by one, and calls then each by name. Because of his great power and MIGHTY strength, not one of them is missing.

Isaiah 40:26 (NIV)

I (John) indeed baptize you in (with) water because of repentance—that is, because of you changing your minds for better, heartily amending your ways with abhorrence to your past sins; but He Who is coming after me is MIGHTIER than I, Whose sandals I am not worthy or fit to take off or carry. He will baptize you with the Holy Spirit and with fire.

Matthew 3:11 (Amplified)

*T*he spacious firmament on high,
With all the blue ethereal sky,
And spangled heavens, a shining flame,
Their great Original proclaim:

The unwearied sun, from day to day,
Does his creator's power display;
And publishes to every land
The work of an ALMIGHTY hand.

(by Joseph Addison)

Begin your prayer time adoring the MIGHTY God.

THE GOD OF MIGHT

MIGHT—ALMIGHTY from eat-all; mihtig-might; possessing all might (Webster)

Who is this King of glory? The Lord strong and MIGHTY, The Lord MIGHTY in battle. Lift up your heads, O you gates! And lift them up, you everlasting doors! And the King of glory shall come in.

Psalm 24:8 & 9 (NAS)

They shall go into the holes of the rocks, And into the caves of the earth, From the terror of the Lord And the glory of His majesty, When He arises to shake the earth MIGHTILY.

Isaiah 2:19 (NKJ)

So everywhere we go we talk about Christ to all who will listen, warning them and teaching them as well as we know how. We want to be able to present each one to God, perfect because of what Christ has done for each of them. This is my work, and I can do it only because Christ's MIGHTY energy is at work within me.

Colossians 1:28 & 29 (Paraphrased)

God of our fathers, whose ALMIGHTY hand
Leads forth in beauty all the starry band
Of shining worlds in splendor through the skies,
Our grateful songs before Thy thrones arise.

Thy love divine hath led us in the past,
In this free land by Thee our lot is cast;
Be Thou our ruler, guardian, guide and stay,
Thy word our law, Thy paths our chosen way.

(by Daniel C. Roberts)

Begin your prayer time in adoration of the God of MIGHT.

THE GOD OF MIGHT

■ MIGHT—ALMIGHTY; used 57 times in Scripture for identification, invocation, description and praise. (Today's Dictionary of the Bible)

*R*emove not the old landmark, and enter not into the fields of the fatherless, For their Redeemer is MIGHTY; He will plead their cause against you.

Proverbs 23:10 & 11 (Amplified)

*E*ver since I heard about your faith in the Lord Jesus and your love for all the saints, I have not stopped giving thanks for you, remembering you in my prayers. I keep asking that the God of out Lord Jesus Christ, the glorious Father, may give you the Spirit of wisdom and revelation, so that you may know him better. I pray also that the eyes of your heart may be enlightened in order that you may know the hope to which he has called you, the riches of his glorious inheritance in the saints, and his incomparably great power for us who believe. That power is like the working of his MIGHTY strength.

Ephesians 1:15-19 (NIV)

*H*umble yourselves then, under God's MIGHTY hand, so that he will lift you up in his own good time.

1 Peter 5:6 (Good News)

*O*ur great High Priest is sitting at God's right hand above,
For us His hands uplifting, in sympathy and love;
While here below in weakness, we onward speed our way;
In sorrow oft and sickness, we sigh, and groan, and pray.

Through manifold temptation, my soul holds on its course,
Christ's MIGHTY intercession alone is my resource;
My gracious High Priest's pleadings, Who on the cross did bleed,
Bring down God's grace and blessings, help in each hour of need.

(by A.P. Cecil)

Begin your prayer time adoring the God of MIGHT.

THE GOD OF MIGHT

MIGHT—synonyms, strength, force, power, ability.

Great and MIGHTY God, whose name is Yahweh Sabaoth! Great in purpose, MIGHTY in execution, whose eyes are open on all the ways of men, rewarding each man as his ways and the results of his actions deserve!

Jeremiah 32:18b & 19 (NJB)

In conclusion be strong—not in yourselves but in the Lord, in the POWER of his boundless resource.

Ephesians 6:10 (Phillips)

After this I looked and saw a vast throng, which no one could count, from every nation, of all tribes, peoples and languages, standing in front of the throne and before the Lamb. They were robed in white and had palms in their hands, and they shouted together: "Victory to our God who sits on the throne and to the Lamb! And all the angels stood round the throne and the elders and the four living creatures, and they fell on their faces before the throne and worshipped God, crying: "Amen! praise and glory and wisdom, thanksgiving and honor, POWER and MIGHT, be to our God for ever and ever! Amen"

Revelation 7:9-12 (NEB)

Every day the Lord Himself is near me
With a special mercy for each hour;
All my cares He fain would bear and cheer me,
He whose name is Counselor and POWER.

The protection of His child and treasure
Is a charge that on Himself He laid;
"As thy days, thy strength shall be in measure,"
This the pledge to me He made.

(by Lina Sanddell Berg)

Begin your prayer time adoring the God of MIGHT.

THE GREAT NAMES OF GOD

■ NAME—That by which a thing or person is called or designated; in distinction of other persons or things. (Webster)

O LORD, how excellent, majestic and glorious is Your NAME in all the earth! You have set Your glory on and above the heavens'.

Psalm 8:1 (Paraphrased)

I am the LORD, that is my NAME; I will not give my glory to another, Nor my praise to graven images.

Isaiah 42:8 (NAS)

The NAME of the LORD is a strong tower; The righteous run to it and are safe.

Proverbs 18:10 (NKJ)

> "*Glory* to GOD on high!
> Peace on earth and joy,
> Good will to man."
> We who GOD'S blessings prove,
> His NAME all names above,
> Sing now the SAVIOUR'S love,
> Too vast to scan.

(by Thomas Kelley)

Begin your prayer time meditating on the NAMES of God and adore Him.

THE GREAT NAMES OF GOD

NAME—The name in Hebrew is sometimes used to signify the collected attributes or characteristics of the object named. The is particularly the case with the divine NAME. (Unger's)

*B*lessed be JEHOVAH GOD, the GOD of Israel, who only does wonderful things! Blessed be his glorious NAME forever! Let the whole earth be filled with his glory! Amen and Amen!

Psalm 72:18 & 19 (Paraphrased)

*A*bram was very rich in cattle, silver and gold; he traveled on from the Negeb to Bethel, to the site of the altar he had erected there at the first, and there he worshipped the ETERNAL.

Genesis 13:2-4 (Moffatt)

*T*herefore, as for you, in this manner be praying: Our FATHER, who is in heaven, let your NAME be praised.

Matthew 6:9 (Wuest)

> *J*ESUS is the NAME that charms us;
> He for conflict fits and arms us;
> Nothing moves and nothing harms us
> While we trust in Him.
>
> Keep us LORD, O keep us cleaving
> To Thyself and still believing,
> Till the hour of our receiving,
> Promised joys with Thee.
>
> *(by Thomas Kelly)*

Begin your prayer time meditating on the great NAMES of God and adore Him.

THE GREAT NAMES OF GOD

NAME—Giving one's name to another indicated the closeness or unity, a oneness, such as God giving his NAME to his people Israel. (Today's)

The LORD will make you his holy people, as he promised. But you must obey his commands and do what he wants you to do. Then everyone one earth will see that you are the LORD'S people, and they will be afraid of you.

Deuteronomy 28:9 & 10 (NCV)

In the past GOD spoke to our ancestors many times and in many ways through the prophets. But in these days he has spoken to us through his SON. GOD made him the owner of all things, and through him GOD created the universe. The SON OF GOD shines with the brightness of GOD'S glory; he is the exact likeness of GOD'S own being, and holds up the universe with his powerful word. After he had made men clean from their sins, he sat down in heaven at the right hand of GOD, the SUPREME POWER.

Hebrews 1:1-4 (Good News)

I write unto you, little children, because your sins are forgiven you for his NAME'S sake.

1 John 2:12 (KJ)

Great is Thy faithfulness, O GOD my FATHER,
There is no shadow of turning with Thee;
Thou changest not, Thy compassions, they fail not;
As Thou hast been Thou forever will be

Great is Thy faithfulness! Great is Thy faithfulness!
Morning by morning new mercies I see;
All I have needed Thy hand hath provided
Great is Thy faithfulness, LORD unto me!

(by Thomas O. Chisholm)

Begin your prayer time meditating on the great NAMES of God and adore Him.

THE GREAT NAMES OF GOD

*Y*ou shall not utter the NAME of YAHWEH your GOD to misuse it, For YAHWEH will not leave unpunished the man who utters his NAME to misuse it.

Exodus 20:7 (NJB)

*G*OD is known in Judah; His NAME is great in Israel.

Psalm 76:1 (NAS)

"*A*gain I tell you this: if two of you agree on earth about any request you have to make, that request will be granted by my heavenly FATHER. For where two or three have met together in my NAME, I am there among them."

Matthew 18:19 & 20 (NEB)

*A*s for the victor, I will make him a pillar in the temple of My GOD; he will leave it nevermore. And I will inscribe on him the NAME of the city of My GOD, the new Jerusalem that is coming down from heaven from My GOD— as well as My new NAME.

Revelation 3:12 (Berkeley)

*T*here have been names that I have loved to hear,
But never has there been a name so dear
To this heart of mine, as the name divine,
The precious, precious NAME of JESUS.

JESUS is the sweetest NAME I know,
And He's just the same as His lovely NAME
And that's the reason why I love Him so;
Oh, JESUS is the sweetest NAME I know.

(by Lela B. Lone)

Begin your prayer time meditating on the great NAMES of GOD and adore Him.

THE GREAT NAMES OF GOD

*T*hough Abraham may ignore us, though Israel regard us not, thou, O ETERNAL ONE, thou art our FATHER, our deliverer from old.

Isaiah 63:16

*G*lorify your NAME, not ours, O LORD! Cause everyone to praise your lovingkindness and your truth.

Psalm 115:1 (Paraphrased)

*B*ut as many as received Him (JESUS) to them He gave the right to become children of GOD, even to those who believe in His NAME.

John 1:12 (NKJ)

*L*et this same attitude and purpose and (humble) mind be in you which was in CHRIST JESUS—Let Him be your example in humility—Who, although being essentially one with GOD (possessing the fullness of the attributes which make GOD GOD, did not think this equality with GOD was a thing to be eagerly grasped or retained; But stripped Himself (of all privileges and rightful dignity) so as to assume the guise of a servant (slave) in that He became like man and was born a human being. And after He had appeared in human form He abased and humbled Himself (still further) and carried His obedience to the extreme of death, even death of (the) cross! Therefore (because He stooped so low), GOD has highly exalted Him and has freely bestowed on Him the NAME that is above every name.

Philippians 2:5-9 (Amplified)

I know of a NAME, a beautiful NAME,
That angels brought down to earth;
They whispered it low,
One night long ago,
To a maiden of lowly birth.

I know of a NAME, A beautiful NAME,
That unto a Babe was given;
The stars glittered bright
Through-out that glad night,
And angels praised GOD in heaven.

(by Jean Perry)

Begin your prayer time meditating on the NAMES of God and adoring Him.

THE GREAT NAMES OF GOD

*O*ur ancestors in Egypt never grasped the meaning of your marvels. They failed to appreciate your great love, they defied the MOST HIGH at the Sea of Reeds. For the sake of his NAME, he saved them to demonstrate his power.

Psalm 106:7 & 8 (NJB)

*T*hough all the peoples walk in the name of his god, As for us, we will walk in the NAME of the LORD our GOD forever and ever.

Micah 4:5 (NAS)

*U*pon the ground of our faith in His NAME, this man whom you are attentively gazing at with a critical, discerning eye and whom you positively identify as the person you know—His NAME made him strong, and the faith which is exercised through Him gave to him this entire soundness in the sight of all of you.

Acts 3:16 (Wuest)

*J*ESUS is the only One who can save people. His NAME is the only power in the world that has been given to save people. We must be saved through him.

Acts 4:12 (NCV)

> *T*ake the NAME of JESUS with you,
> Child of sorrow and of woe.
> It will joy and comfort give you,
> Take it, then, where ever you go
>
> At the NAME of Jesus bowing,
> Falling prostrate at His feet,
> KING of KINGS in heaven we'll crown Him,
> When our journey is complete.
>
> *(by Lydia Baxter)*

Begin your prayer time meditating on the great NAMES of God and adore Him.

THE GREAT NAMES OF GOD

*F*or from the rising of the sun to its setting My NAME shall be great among the nations, and in every place incense shall be offered to My NAME, and indeed a pure offering; for My NAME shall be great among the nations, says the LORD OF HOSTS.

Malachi 1:11 (Amplified)

*B*ut for you who revere my NAME, the SUN OF RIGHTEOUSNESS will rise with healing in its wings. And you will go out and leap like calves released from the stall.

Malachi 4:2 (NIV)

*E*verything you do or say, them should be done in the NAME of the LORD JESUS, as you give thanks through him to GOD the FATHER.

Colossians 3:17 (Good News)

*T*hey were singing the song of Moses, the servant of the Lord, and the song of the LAMB, as they chanted: "Great and marvelous are thy deeds, O LORD GOD, sovereign over all; just and true are thy ways, thou KING OF THE AGES. Who shall not revere thee, LORD, and do homage in thy NAME? For thou alone art holy. All nations shall come and worship in thy presence, for thy just dealing stand revealed.

Revelation 15:3 & 4 (NEB)

*T*he NAME of JESUS is so sweet,
I love its music to repeat;
It makes my joys full and complete,
The precious NAME of JESUS.

I love the NAME of Him whose heart
Knows all my griefs and bears a part;
Who bids all anxious fears depart
I love the NAME of JESUS.

(by W.C. Martin)

Begin your prayer time meditating on the NAMES of GOD and adore Him.

THE GOD WORTHY OF PRAISE

⊞ PRAISE—To commend, to applaud, to express approbation of. To extol in words or song; to magnify; to glorify. (Webster)

*P*RAISE the Lord! PRAISE, O servants of the Lord, PRAISE the name of the Lord! Blessed be the name of the Lord from this time forth and forevermore! From the rising of the sun to its going down the Lord's name is the be PRAISED.

Psalm 113:1-3 (NKJ)

*T*he Eternal is to be PRAISED!—I call to him, and I am rescued from my foes.

2 Samuel 22:4 (Moffatt)

"*H*ear, O kings, give ear, O rulers! I—to the Lord, I will sing, I will sing PRAISE to the Lord, the God if Israel

Judges 5:3 (NAS)

> *P*RAISE God, from whom all blessings flow;
> PRAISE Him, all creatures here below;
> PRAISE Him above, ye heavenly host;
> PRAISE Father, Son, and Holy Ghost!
>
> *(by Thomas Ken)*

Begin your prayer time adoring God through PRAISE.

THE GOD WORTHY OF PRAISE

Synonyms for PRAISE—Laudation, eulogy, applause, plaudit, commendation, extol, magnify, glorify. (Webster)

I PRAISE your greatness, my God the King; I will PRAISE you forever and ever. I will PRAISE you every day; I will PRAISE you forever and ever. The Lord is great and worthy of our PRAISE; no one can understand how great he is.

Psalm 145:1-3 (NCV)

"*At* the end of seven years I, Nebuchadnezzar, looked up to heaven, and my sanity returned, and I PRAISED and worshipped the Most High God and honored him who lives forever, whose rule is everlasting, his kingdom evermore.

Daniel 4:34 (Paraphrased)

*H*eal me, O Lord, and I shall be healed; save me and I shall be saved; for You are my PRAISE.

Jeremiah 17:14 (Amplified)

*P*RAISE the Saviour, ye who know Him!
Who can tell how much we owe Him?
Gladly let us render to Him
All we are and have.

Trust in Him, ye saints forever;
He is faithful, changing never;
Neither force nor guile can sever
Those He loves from Him.

(by Thomas Kelly)

Begin your prayer time adoring God through PRAISE.

THE GOD WORTHY OF PRAISE

PRAISE—PRAISE of God is the acknowledging of his perfections, works, and benefits. PRAISE and THANKSGIVING are generally considered synonymous. (Unger's)

My PRAISE shall be of thee in the great congregation: I will pay my vows before them that fear him.

Psalm 22:25 (KJ)

I will BLESS the Eternal at all times, his PRAISE shall be continually on my lips; my soul BOASTS openly of the Eternal, and as the humble hear it, they are glad.

Psalm 34:1 & 2 (Moffatt)

How lovely is your dwelling place, O Lord Almighty! My soul yearns, even faints for the courts of the Lord; my heart and my flesh cry out for the living God. Even the sparrow has found a home, and the swallow a nest for herself, where she may have her young—a place near your altar, O Lord Almighty, my King and my God. Blessed are those who dwell in your house; they are ever PRAISING you.

Psalm 84:1-4 (NIV)

Give to our God immortal PRAISE!
Mercy and truth are all His ways; Alleluia!
Alleluia! Wonders of grace to God belong,
Repeat His mercies in your song. Alleluia!

He sent His Son with power to save,
From guilt, and darkness and the grave; Alleluia!
Alleluia! Wonders of grace to God belong,
Repeat His mercies in your song. Alleluia!

(by Isaac Watts)

Begin your prayer time adoring God through PRAISE.

THE GOD WHO DESERVES PRAISE

"*You* shall fear the Lord your God: you shall serve Him, and to Him you shall hold fast, and take oaths in His name. He is your PRAISE, and He is your God, who has done for you these great and awesome things which your eyes have seen.

Deuteronomy 10:20 & 21 (NKJ)

I shall immortalize your name, nations will sing your PRAISES for ever and ever.

Psalm 45:17 (NJB)

The blind and crippled people came to Jesus in the Temple, and he healed them. The leading priests and teachers of the law saw that Jesus was doing wonderful things and that the children were PRAISING him in the Temple, saying, "PRAISE to the Son of David.

Matthew 21:14 & 15 (NCV)

We who first hoped in Christ—who first put our confidence in Him have been destined and appointed) to live for the PRAISE of His glory.

Ephesians 1:12 (Amplified)

> *P*RAISE my soul, the King of heaven,
> PRAISE Him, for His grace and favor
> To His feet thy TRIBUTE bring;
> To our fathers in distress;
> Ransomed, healed, restored, forgiven,
> PRAISE Him, still the same forever,
> Who like me, His praise should sing?
> Slow to chide, and swift to bless.
> Alleluia! Alleluia! Alleluia! Alleluia
> PRAISE the Everlasting King!
> Glorious in His faithfulness
>
> *(by Henry F. Lyte)*

Begin adoring God with PRAISES.

THE GOD WHO DESERVES PRAISE

*P*RAISE awaits you, O God, in Zion; to you our vows will be fulfilled. O you who hear prayer, to you all men will come. When we were overwhelmed by sins, you atoned for our transgressions. Blessed is the man you choose and bring near to live in your courts! We are filled with the good things of your house, of your holy temple. You answer us with awesome deeds of righteousness, O God our Saviour, the hope of all the ends of the earth and the farthest seas.

Psalm 65:1-5 (NIV)

*L*et the people PRAISE thee, O God; let all the people PRAISE thee,

Psalm 67:3 (KJ)

*A*nd suddenly there was with the angel a multitude of the army of heaven, PRAISING God and saying, Glory in the highest places to God, and upon earth peace among men of good will.

Luke 2:13 & 14 (Wuest)

*I*n Him we, too were made God's heritage, as foreordained according to His purpose, who works out everything in agreement with the design of His own will, so that we, foremost to put our hope in Christ, might bring PRAISE to His glory.

Ephesians 1:11 & 12 (Berkeley)

*T*he God of Abraham PRAISE, who reigns enthroned above;
Ancient of everlasting days, And Good of Love
Jehovah, great I AM, by earth and heaven confessed;
I bow and bless the sacred name, Forever blest.

The God of Abraham PRAISE, At whose supreme command
From earth I rise, and seek the joys At His right hand.
I all on earth forsake, Its wisdom, fame and power;
And Him my only portion make, My shield and tower.

(by Daniel ben Judah)

Begin your prayer time adoring God through PRAISE.

THE GOD WHO DESERVES PRAISES

There are ten Hebrew words for PRAISE, each with a different connotation. One means to extol in song, another to lift your hands, one more to jump for joy, one to extend a kiss heavenward, etc.

*P*RAISE Him, all heaven and earth! PRAISE Him, all the seas and everything in them.

Psalm 69:34 (Paraphrased)

*B*y Thee I have been sustained from my birth; Thou art He who took me from my mother's womb; My PRAISE is continually of Thee.

Psalm 71:6 (NAS)

*A*nd this is my prayer, that your love may grow richer and richer in knowledge and insight of every kind, and may thus bring you the gift of true discrimination. Then on the day of Christ you will be flawless and without blame, reaping the full harvest of righteousness that comes through Jesus Christ, to the glory and PRAISE of God.

Philippians 1:9-11 (NEB)

*L*et us, then, always offer PRAISE to Good our sacrifice through Jesus; that is, let us always give thanks to his name with our voices.

Hebrews 13:15 (Good News)

> *P*RAISE ye the Lord again, again.
> The Spirit strikes the chord;
> Nor touched He our hearts in vain;
> We PRAISE, we PRAISE the Lord.
>
> Forever be the glory given
> To Thee, O Lamb of God!
> Our every joy on earth, in heaven,
> We owe it to Thy blood.
>
> *(by Mary Bowley Peters)*

Begin your prayer time adoring God with PRAISES.

THE GOD WHO DESERVES PRAISE

The Lord is gracious, and full of compassion; slow to anger, and full of great mercy. The Lord is good to all; and his tender mercies are over all his works. All thy works shall PRAISE thee, O Lord; and thy saints shall bless thee.

Psalm 145:8-10 (KJ)

Alleluia! Let heaven PRAISE Yahweh: PRAISE him, heavenly heights, PRAISE him, all his angels, PRAISE him, all his armies! PRAISE him, sun and moon, PRAISE him, shining stars, PRAISE him, highest heavens, and waters above the heavens! Let them all PRAISE Yahweh, at whose command they were created; he has fixed them all in their place forever, by an unalterable statue. Let earth PRAISE Yahweh: sea-monsters, and all the deeps, fire and hail, snow and mist, gales that obey by decree, mountains and hills, orchards and forests, wild animals and farm animals, snakes and birds, all kings on earth and nations, princes, all rulers in the world, young men and girls, old people and children too! Let them all PRAISE the name of Yahweh, for his name and no other is sublime, transcending earth and heaven in majesty, raising the fortunes of his people, to the PRAISES of the devout, of Israel, the people dear to him.

Psalm 148:1-15 (NJB)

Our constant sacrifice to God should be the PRAISE of lips that give thanks to his name.

Hebrews 13:15 (Phillips)

But you are a chosen generation, a royal priesthood, a holy nation, His own special people, that you may proclaim the PRAISES of Him who called you out of darkness into His marvelous light.

Peter 2:9 (NKJ)

When I saw the cleansing fountain
Open wide for all my sin
I obeyed the Spirit's wooing,
When He said, Wilt thou be clean?

I will PRAISE Him! I will PRAISE Him!
PRAISE the Lamb for sinners slain;
Give Him glory, all ye people,
For His blood can wash away each stain

(by M. J. Harris)

Begin your prayer time adoring God through PRAISES.

THE GOD WHO DESERVES PRAISES

*H*allelujah! Yes, PRAISE the Lord! PRAISE him in his Temple, and in the heavens he made with mighty power. PRAISE him for his mighty works. PRAISE his unequaled greatness. PRAISE him with the trumpet and with lute and harp. PRAISE him with tambourines and processional. PRAISE him with stringed instruments and horns. PRAISE him with the cymbals, yes, loud clanging cymbals. Let everything alive give PRAISES to the Lord! You PRAISE him! Hallelujah!

Psalm 150:1-6 (Paraphrased)

*W*hen he had led them out to the vicinity of Bethany, he lifted up his hands and blessed them. While he was blessing them, he left them and was taken up to heaven. Then they worshipped him and returned to Jerusalem with great joy. And they stayed continually at the temple, PRAISING God.

Luke 24:50-53 (NIV)

*F*or it is fitting for Him, for whom are all things, and through whom are all things, in bringing many sons to glory, to perfect the author of their salvation through sufferings. For both He who sanctifies and those who are sanctified are all from one Father: for which reason He is not ashamed to call them brethren, saying, "I will proclaim Thy name to My brethren, In the midst of the congregation I will sing Thy PRAISE.

Hebrews 2:10-12 (NAS)

*A*nd the twenty-four elders and the four living beings fell down and worshipped God who is seated on the throne, saying, Amen. Hallelujah. And there came a voice from the throne saying, Be giving PRAISE to our God, all those who are His bondslaves, those who fear Him, those who are of a lowly station in life and those who are great.

Revelation 19:4 & 5 (Wuest)

*P*RAISE Him! PRAISE Him! Jesus, our blessed Redeemer!
Sing, O Earth, His wonderful love proclaim!
HAIL Him! HAIL Him! highest archangels in glory;
Strength and honor give to His holy name.

Like a shepherd Jesus will guard His children,
In His arms He carries them all day long:
PRAISE Him! PRAISE Him! tell of His excellent greatness;
PRAISE Him! PRAISE Him! ever in joyful song!

(by Fanny J. Crosby)

Begin your prayer time adoring God through PRAISES.

THE GOD OF POWER

POWER—Divinity—a celestial or invisible being or agent who has dominion over all of creation.

*G*od has spoken once, twice have I heard this, that POWER belongs to God.

Psalm 62:11 (Amplified)

*W*ith them He came down and stood on a level spot with a large throng of His disciples and a vast crowd of people from all over Judea and from Jerusalem and from the Tyre and Sydon coast, who came to hear Him and be cured of their diseases. Those troubled with unclean spirits, too, were healed. The whole concourse tried to touch Him because POWER issued from Him and healed everyone.

Luke 6:17-19 (Berkeley)

I am proud of the gospel; it is God's saving POWER for everyone who has faith; for the Jew first and for the Greek as well.

Romans 1:16 (Moffatt)

*A*ll hail the POWER of Jesus name!
Let angels prostrate fall;
Bring forth the royal diadem,
And crown Him Lord of all.

Let every kindred, every tribe,
On this terrestrial ball,
To Him all majesty ascribe,
And crown Him Lord of all.

(by Edward Perronet)

Begin your prayer time adoring a POWERFUL God.

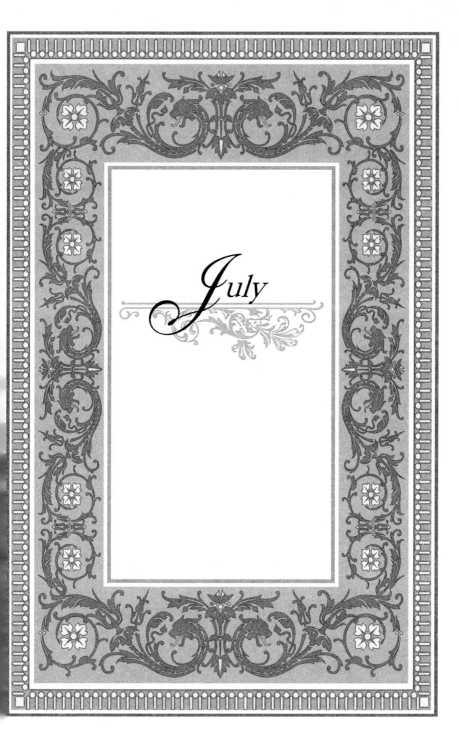

July

THE GOD OF POWER

▓ POWER—synonyms—faculty, capacity, efficacy, energy, capability, potentiality, force, might, ability, strength, susceptibility, influence, dominion, sway, command, government, agency, authority, rule, jurisdiction, effectiveness, caliber, cause. (Webster)

*Y*our right hand, Yahweh, shows majestic in POWER, your right hand, Yahweh, shatters the enemy.

Exodus 15:6 (NJB)

*A*nd Jesus seeing their faith, said to the paralytic, "Son be of good cheer; your sins are forgiven you." And at once some of the scribes said within themselves, "This man blasphemes!" But Jesus knowing their thoughts, said, "Why do you think evil in your hearts? For which is easier to say, Your sins are forgiven you, or to say, Arise and walk? But that you may know the Son of Man has POWER to forgive sins." Then he said to the paralytic, "Arise, take up your bed, and go to your house."

Matthew 2:2b-6 (NKJ)

*S*ince earliest times men have seen the earth and sky and all God made, and have known of his existence and great eternal POWER. So they will have no excuse (when they stand before God at Judgment Day).

Romans 1:20 (Paraphrased)

A MIGHTY fortress is our God, a bulwark never failing;
Our helper He, amid the flood, of mortal ills prevailing:
For still our ancient foe doth seek to work us woe;
His craft and power are great, and armed with cruel hate,
On earth is not his equal.

Did we in our own strength confide, our striving would be loosing;
Were not the right man on our side, the Man of God's own choosing:
Dost ask who that may be? Christ Jesus, it is He,
Lord Sabaoth, His name, from age to age the same
And He must win the battle.

(by Martin Luther)

Begin your prayer time adoring the God who has the POWER, the MIGHT to win battles.

THE GOD OF POWER

▓ POWER—or the ability of performing belongs essentially to God, who is ALL-POWERFUL, the OMNIPOTENT. (Unger's)

*L*ift your eyes and look to the heavens; Who created all these? He who brings out the starry host one by one, and calls them each by name. Because of his great POWER and mighty strength, not one of them is missing.

Isaiah 40:26 (NIV)

I am the good shepherd; I know my own and my own know me, just as the Father knows me and I know the Father; and I lay down my life for the sheep. And there are other sheep I have that are not of this fold, and these I have to lead as well. They too will listen to my voice, and there will be only one flock, and one shepherd. The Father loves me because I lay down my life in order to take it up again. No one takes it from me; I lay it down of my own free will, and as it is in my POWER to lay it down, so it is in my POWER to take it up again; and this is the commandment I have been given by my Father.

John 10:14-18 (TJB)

*I*n conclusion be strong—not in yourselves but in the Lord, in the POWER of his boundless resource.

Ephesians 6:10 (Phillips)

> *C*ome let us join our cheerful songs, and thus approach the throne,
> Had we but ten thousand tongues, Our theme of joy's but one;
> "Worthy the Lamb enthroned on high, to be exalted thus!"
> "Worthy the Lamb that died!" we cry, "For He was slain for us."
>
> Jesus is worthy to receive honor and POWER divine;
> And blessings more than we can give be, Lord, forever Thine,
> Soon shall the saints, exalted high, a glorious anthem raise;
> And all that dwell beneath the sky speak forth Thine endless praise.
>
> *(by Isaac Watts)*

Begin your prayer time adoring God for His mighty POWER.

July 3

THE GOD OF POWER

POWER—Power has the sense of: Ability, strength; Right privilege or dignity. (Unger's)

The Lord said to Moses, "Rise up early in the morning and stand before Pharaoh and say to him, "Thus says the Lord, the God of the Hebrews, Let my people go, that they may serve Me. For this time I will send all My plagues on you and your servants and your people, so that you may know there is no one like Me in all the earth. For if by now I had put forth My hand and struck you and your people with pestilence, you would then have been cut off from the earth. But, indeed, for this cause I have allowed you to remain, in order to show you My POWER, and in order to proclaim My name through all the earth.

Exodus 9:13-16 (NAS)

One day he (Jesus) was teaching, and Pharisees and teachers of the law were sitting around. People had come from every village of Galilee and from Judea and Jerusalem, and the POWER of God was with him to heal the sick.

Luke 5:17 (NEB)

For the Word that God speaks is alive and FULL OF POWER—making it active, operative, energizing and effective; it is sharper than any two-edged sword, penetrating to the dividing line of the breath of life (soul) and (the immortal) spirit, and of joints and marrow (that is, of the deepest parts of our nature) exposing and sifting and analyzing and judging the very thoughts and purposes of the heart.

Hebrews 4:12 (Amplified)

Crown the Saviour! Angels crown Him!
Rich the trophies Jesus brings;
In the seat of POWER enthrone Him,
While the vaults of heaven rings
Crown Him! Crown the Saviour King of Kings.

Hark! those bursts of acclamation!
Hark, those loud triumphant chords.
Jesus takes the highest station;
O what joy the sight affords!
Crown Him! King of kings and Lord of lords!

(by Thomas Kelly)

Begin your prayer time adoring God for His POWER.

THE GOD OF POWER

POWER—Greek—dunamis; ABSOLUTE AUTHORITY, or act of POWER. (Unger's)

The voice of the Lord is upon the waters: the God of glory thundereth: the Lord is upon many waters. The voice of the Lord is POWERFUL; the voice of the Lord is full of mercy.

Psalm 29:3 & 4 (KJ)

For the message about Christ's death on the cross is nonsense to those who are being lost; but for us who are being saved, it is God's POWER. As for us, we proclaim Christ on the cross, a message that is offensive to the Jews and nonsense to the Gentiles; but for those whom God has called, both Jews and Gentiles, this message is Christ, who is the POWER of God and the wisdom of God.

1 Corinthians 1:18,23 & 24 (GN)

And I saw, and I heard a voice of many angels who encircled the throne and a voice of the living beings and the elders—and their number was ten thousand times ten thousand and thousands of thousands—saying with a great voice, Worthy is the Lamb who has been slain to receive POWER and riches and wisdom and MIGHT and honor and glory and eulogy.

Revelation 5:11-13 (Wuest)

Join all the glorious names of wisdom, love and POWER,
That mortals ever knew, that angels ever bore;
All are too mean to speak His worth,
Too mean to set the Saviour forth

Thou art our Counselor, our Pattern, and our Guide,
And Thou our Shepherd art; Oh, keep us near Thy side.
Nor let our feet ever turn astray,
To wander in the crooked way.

(by Isaac Watts)

Begin your prayer time adoring the POWERFUL, MIGHTY God.

THE GOD OF POWER

The Lord does not become angry quickly, and his POWER is great. The Lord does not let the guilty go unpunished. Where the Lord goes there are whirlwinds and storms; and the clouds are the dust beneath his feet.

Nahum 1:3 (NCV)

Beginning from Jerusalem you are my witnesses of these things, and I will send out upon you the promise of My Father. But you wait here in the city (of Jerusalem) until you are clothed with POWER from on high.

Luke 24:48 & 49 (Berkeley)

Now to Him who is able to keep you from stumbling, and to present you faultless before the presence of His glory with exceeding joy, to God our Saviour, Who alone is wise, be glory and majesty, DOMINION and POWER, both now and forever.

Jude 24 & 25 (NKJ)

O Lord, you are worthy to receive the glory and honor and POWER, for you have created all things. They were created and called into being by your act of will.

Revelation 4:11 (Paraphrased)

Soldiers of Christ, arise, and put your armour on,
Strong in the strength which God supplies through His eternal son;
Strong in the Lord of hosts, and in His mighty POWER,
Who in the strength of Jesus trusts is more than conqueror.

Stand then in His great MIGHT, with all His strength endued,
And take, to arm you for the fight, the panoply of God;
That having all things done, and all your conflicts past,
Ye may overcome through Christ alone, and stand complete at last.

(by Charles Wesley)

Begin your prayer time adoring the God of POWER.

THE GOD OF POWER

*P*raise God for his MIGHT, whose sovereign sway is over Israel, whose might is in the skies. God who strikes awe from his sanctuary, the God of Israel who bestows prowess and POWER on people blessed by God.

Psalm 68:34 & 35 (Moffatt)

I do not cease to give thanks for you, making mention of you in my prayers. (For I always pray) the God of our Lord Jesus Christ, the Father of Glory, that He may grant you a spirit of wisdom and revelation—of insight into mysteries and secrets—in the (deep and intimate) knowledge of Him, by having the eyes of your heart flooded with light, so that you can know and understand the hope to which He has called you and how rich is His glorious inheritance in the saints—His set apart ones. And (so that you can know and understand) what is the immeasurable and unlimited and surpassing greatness of His POWER in and for us who believe, as demonstrated in the working of His mighty strength,

Ephesians 1:16-19 (Amplified)

*I*n the past God spoke to our forefathers through the prophets at many times and in various ways, but in these last days he has spoken to us by his Son, whom he appointed heir of all things, and through whom he made the universe. The Son is the radiance of God's glory and the exact representation of his being, sustaining all things by his POWERFUL word.

Hebrews 1:1-3 (NIV)

*T*hank God, the God and Father of our Lord Jesus Christ, that in his great mercy we have been born again into a life full of hope, through Christ's rising again from the dead! You can now hope for a perfect inheritance beyond the reach of change and decay, "reserved" in Heaven for you. And in the meantime you are guarded by the POWER of God operating through your faith,

1 Peter 1-3 (Phillips)

*W*ould you be free from the burden of sin? There is POWER, POWER
There's power in the blood; Wonder-working POWER
Would you over evil a victory win? In the blood of the Lamb
There's wonderful POWER in the blood. There is POWER, POWER
Wonder-working POWER In the precious blood of the lamb

(by Lewis E. Jones)

Begin your prayer time adoring the God of all POWER.

THE GOD WHO PREACHES

⬛ PREACH—to proclaim; to publish; to declare publicly. A religious discourse. (Webster)

*A*nd the word of the Lord came unto Jonah the second time saying, Arise, go unto Nineveh, that great city, and PREACH unto it the PREACHING that I bid thee.

Jonah 3:1 & 2 (KJ)

*W*hat I say to you in the dark, TELL in the light; and what you hear whispered in the ear, PROCLAIM upon the housetops.

Matthew 10:27 (Amplified)

*F*or indeed Jews ask for signs, and Greeks search for wisdom; but we PREACH Christ crucified, to the Jews a stumbling block, and to Gentiles foolishness; but to those who are called, both Jews and Greeks, Christ the power of God and the wisdom of God.

1 Corinthians 1:22-24 (NAS)

*T*ELL me the old, old story, of unseen things above,
Of Jesus and His glory, Of Jesus and His love;
TELL me the story simply, as to a little child,
For I am weak and weary, and helpless and defiled.

TELL me the story slowly, That I may take it in—
That wonderful redemption, God's remedy for sin;
TELL me the story often, For I forget so soon,
The "early dew" of morning has passed away at noon.

(by Catherine Hankey)

Begin you prayer time for the method He uses to PREACH the truth.

THE GOD WHO USES PREACHING

PREACHING—by preaching is generally understood the delivering of a religious discourse based upon a text of Scripture. (Unger's)

But He said to him. Let the dead bury their own dead; you go and PREACH the kingdom of God.

Luke 9:60 (Berkeley)

For if I PREACH the gospel, I have nothing to boast of, for necessity is laid upon me; yes, woe is me if I do not PREACH the gospel! For if I do this willingly, I have a reward; but if against my will, I have been entrusted with a stewardship. What is my reward then? That when I PREACH the gospel, I may present the gospel of Christ without charge, that I may not abuse my authority in the gospel.

1 Corinthians 9:18-18 (NKJ)

I solemnly call upon you in the presence of God and of Jesus Christ, who will judge all men, living and dead: because of his coming and of his Kingdom, I command you to PREACH the message, to insist upon TELLING it, whether the time is right or not; to convince, reproach, and encourage, teaching with all patience.

2 Timothy 4:1 & 2 (Good News)

*T*ELL me the story softly, with earnest tones and grave;
Remember I'm the sinner whom Jesus came to save;
TELL me the story always, if you would really be,
In any time or trouble a comforter to me.

TELL me the same old story, When you have cause to fear
That this world's empty glory Is costing me too dear;
Yes, and when that world's glory is dawning on my soul,
TELL me the old, old story "Christ Jesus makes thee whole."

(by A. Catherine Hankey)

Begin your prayer time by adoring God for His method of TELLING the Gospel.

THE GOD WHO USES PREACHING

PREACH, TO—Hebrew, 1. basar, to bring glad tidings 2. kara, to call. (Smith's)

*F*rom then on, Jesus began to PREACH, "Turn from sin, and turn to God, for the Kingdom of heaven is near."

Matthew 4:17 (Paraphrased)

*N*ow, brothers, I want to remind you of the gospel I PREACHED to you, which you received and on which you have taken your stand. by this gospel you are saved, if you hold firmly to the word I PREACHED to you.

1 Corinthians 15:1 & 2 (NIV)

*T*here is only one God, and only one intermediary between God and men, the Man Christ Jesus. He gave himself as a ransom for us all—an act of redemption which happened once, but which stands for all times as a witness to what he is. I was appointed PROCLAIMER and messenger of this great act of his, to teach (as incredible as it may sound) the gentile world to believe and know the truth.

1 Timothy 2:5-7 (Phillips)

> *G*od speed the day, when those of every nation
> "Glory to God!" triumphantly shall sing;
> Ransomed, redeemed, rejoicing in salvation,
> Shout Hallelujah, for the Lord is King
>
> "All power is given unto Me,
> Go ye into all the world
> And PREACH the gospel,
> And lo, I am with you always."
>
> *(by James McGranshan)*

Begin your prayer time adoring God for allowing you to hear His truth through PREACHING.

THE GOD WHO USES PREACHING

PREACH—Greek 1. Dianggello—to announce fully. 2. Dialegomai—to discourse 3. Evanggellizo—good news. 4. Kerisso—to proclaim. 5. Laleo—to speak. 6. Prokeousso—beforehand. (Smith's)

*T*he Spirit of the Lord is upon me: for he has consecrated me to PREACH the gospel to the poor, he has set me to PROCLAIM release for captives and recovery of sight for the blind, to set free the oppressed, to PROCLAIM the Lord's year of favor.

Luke 4:18 & 19 (Moffatt)

*B*efore God and before Christ Jesus who is to be the judge of the living and the dead, I put this duty to you, in the name of his Appearing and of his kingdom: PROCLAIM the message and, welcome or unwelcome, insist on it.

2 Timothy 4:1 (TJB)

*T*o Him who has power to make your standing sure, according to the Gospel I brought you and the PROCLAMATION of Jesus Christ, according to the revelation of that divine secret kept in silence for long ages but now disclosed, and through prophetic scriptures by eternal God's command made known to all nations, to bring them to faith and obedience—to God who alone is wise, through Jesus Christ, be glory for endless ages!

Romans 16:25-27 (NEB)

> *O* Christian haste, thy mission high fulfilling,
> To TELL to all the world that God is Light;
> That He who made all nations is not willing
> One soul should perish, lost in shades of night.
>
> PROCLAIM to every people, tongue and nation
> That God in whom they live and move is love:
> TELL how he stooped to save His lost creation,
> And died on earth that man might live above.
>
> *(by Mary A. Thomson)*

Begin your prayer time adoring God for the gift of PREACHING.

THE GOD WHO USES PREACHING

PREACH—Greek 7. Proeuanggellizomai—to announce glad tidings beforehand 8. Parrhesiazomai—to be free (in speech or action) 9. Plero—to fulfill 10. Akoe—the hearing. (Smith's)

So then the Lord Jesus, after He had spoken to them, was received up into heaven, and sat on the right hand of God. And those having gone forth, PREACHED everywhere, the Lord working with them, and confirming the Word through the attesting miracles which accompanied them.

Mark 16:19 & 20 (Wuest)

He said to them, "It is written that the Christ would suffer and rise from the dead on the third day and that a change of hearts and lives and forgiveness of sins would be PREACHED in his name to all nations starting at Jerusalem.

Luke 24:46 & 47 (NCV)

Some indeed PREACH Christ even from envy and strife, and some also from good will: The former PREACH Christ from selfish ambition, and not sincerely, supposing to add affliction to my chains; but the latter out of love, knowing that I am appointed for the defense of the gospel. What then? Only that in every way, whether in pretense or in truth, Christ is PREACHED; and in this I rejoice, yes, and will rejoice.

Philippians 1:15-18 (NKJ)

TELL me the stories of Jesus I love to hear;
Things I would ask Him to tell me if He were here:
Scenes by the wayside, tales of the sea,
Stories of Jesus, TELL them to me.

Show me the scene in the garden, of bitter pain.
Show me the cross where my Saviour for me was slain.
Sad ones or bright ones. so that they be
Stories of Jesus, TELL them to me.

(by William H. Parker)

Begin your prayer time adoring God for the method of PREACHING.

GOD OUR REFUGE

REFUGE—Shelter or protection from danger or distress. (Webster)

The eternal God is thy REFUGE , and underneath are the everlasting arms; and he shall thrust out the enemy from before thee; and shall say, Destroy them.

Deuteronomy 33:27 (KJ)

God is our REFUGE and strength, A very present help in trouble. Therefore we will not fear, though the earth should change, And though the mountains should slip in to the heart of the sea; Though its waters roar and foam, Though the mountains quake at its swelling pride.

Psalm 46:1-3 (NAS)

In the fear of the Lord there is strong confidence, and His children will have a place of REFUGE.

Proverbs 14:26 (NKJ)

The Lord's our rock, in Him we hide,
A SHELTER in the time of storm;
Secure whatever ill betide,
A SHELTER in the time of storm.

A shade by day, defense by night,
A SHELTER in the time of storm.
No fears alarm, no foes affright,
A SHELTER in the time of storm.

(by Vernon J. Charlesworth)

Begin your prayer time adoring God for being your REFUGE.

GOD OUR REFUGE

*J*ehovah is my rock, my fortress and my Savior. I will hide in God, who is my rock and my REFUGE. He is my shield and my salvation, my REFUGE and high tower. Thank you, O my Savior, for saving me from all my enemies.

2 Samuel 22:2 & 3 (Paraphrased)

*H*ave mercy on me, O God, have mercy on me, for in you my soul takes REFUGE. I will take REFUGE in the shadow of your wings until the disaster has passed.

Psalm 57:1 (NIV)

*T*rust, lean on, rely on and have confidence in Him at all times, you people; pour out your heart before Him. God is a REFUGE for us—a fortress and a high tower.

Psalm 62:8 (Amplified)

*Y*ahweh, my strength, my stronghold, my REFUGE in the day of distress! To you the nations will come from the confines of the earth and say, "Our fathers inherited nothing but delusion, nothing void of all power. Can man make his own gods? If so, these are not gods!" "Now listen, I am going to make them acknowledge, this time I am going to make them acknowledge my hand and my might; and then they will know that Yahweh is my name.

Jeremiah 16:19-21 (TJB)

*T*he raging storms may round us beat,
A SHELTER in the time of storm;
For Jesus lives, our safe retreat,
A SHELTER in the time of storm

O Rock divine, O REFUGE dear,
A SHELTER in the time of storm;
Be Thou our helper ever near
A SHELTER in the time of storm.

O Jesus is a Rock in a weary land
A SHELTER in the time of storm.

(by Vernon J. Charlesworth)

Begin your prayer time adoring God for His SHELTERING care.

GOD OUR REFUGE

*Y*ou who respect the Lord should trust him; he is your helper and your PROTECTION.

Psalm 115:11 (NCV)

*N*o one gives me a passing thought. No one will help me; no one cares a bit what happens to me. Then I prayed to Jehovah. "Lord" I pled, "you are my only place of REFUGE. Only you can keep me safe."

Psalm 142:4 & 5 (Paraphrased)

"*T*o hapless men thou art a strength, a strength to the forlorn in woe; a SHELTER from the storm, a shade in heat, silencing proud men as they shout, and humbling tyrants."

Isaiah 25:4 (Moffatt)

*W*hen God made his promise to Abraham, he swore by himself, because he had no one greater to swear by: "I vow I will bless you abundantly and multiply your descendants." Thus it was that Abraham, after patient waiting, attained the promise. Men swear by a greater than themselves, and the oath provides a confirmation to end all dispute: and so, God, desiring to show even more clearly to the heirs of his promise how unchanging was his promise, how unchanging was his purpose, guaranteed it by oath. Here, then, are two irrevocable acts in which God could not possibly play false, to give powerful encouragement to us, who have claimed his PROTECTION by grasping the hope set before us. That hope we hold. It is like an anchor for our lives, an anchor safe and sure.

Hebrews 6:13-18 (NEB)

*U*nder His wings I am safely abiding;
Though the night deepens and tempests are wild,
Still I can trust Him; I know He will keep me;
He has redeemed me, and I am His child.

Under His wings, what a REFUGE in sorrow!
How the heart yearningly turn to His rest!
Often when earth has no balm for my healing,
There I find comfort, and there I am blest.

(by William O. Cushing)

Begin your prayer time adoring the God who is your REFUGE.

THE GOD IN WHOM WE REJOICE

REJOICE—To experience joy and gladness in a high degree; to be exhilarated with lively and pleasurable sensations; to exult. (Webster)

*N*ow therefore arise, O Lord God, into thy resting place, thou, ark of thy strength: let thy priests, O Lord God, be clothed with salvation, and let thy saints REJOICE in goodness.

2 Chronicles 6:41 (KJ)

*B*ut let the righteous be GLAD; let them EXULT before God; Yes, let them REJOICE with GLADNESS.

Psalm 68:3 (NAS)

*A*lways be REJOICING. Be praying unceasingly. In everything be giving thanks, for this is the will of God in Christ Jesus for you.

1 Thessalonians 5:16 (Wuest)

*T*o God be the glory, great things He hath done,
So loved He the world that He gave us His Sin,
Who yielded His life an atonement for sin,
And opened the Lifegate that all may go in.

Praise the Lord, Praise the Lord, Let the earth hear His voice!
Praise the Lord, praise the Lord, Let the people REJOICE!
O come to the Father through Jesus the Son,
And give Him the glory, great things He hath done.

(by Fanny J. Crosby)

Begin your prayer time adoring God through REJOICING.

THE GOD IN WHOM WE REJOICE

REJOICE synonyms—Delight, glory, exult, joy, triumph, gladden, revel, be glad, cheer, please, enliven, gratify. (Webster)

The Lord reigns; let the earth REJOICE; let the multitude of isles and coastlands BE GLAD.

Psalm 97:1 (Amplified)

This is the day made memorable by Yahweh, what immense JOY for us.

Psalm 118:24 (TJB)

Philip began to speak; starting from this very passage of scripture (Isaiah 53:7 & 8), he told him the Good News about Jesus. As they traveled down the road they came to a place where there was some water, and the (Ethiopian) official said, "Here is some water. What is to keep me from being baptized?" Philip said to him, "You may be baptized if you believe with all your heart." "I do," he answered; I believe that Jesus Christ is the Son of God." The official ordered the carriage to stop; and both of them, Philip and the official went down into the water, and Philip baptized him. When they came out of the water the Spirit of the Lord took Philip away. The official did not see him again, but continued on his way full of JOY.

Acts 8:35-38 (Good News)

"Hosanna in the highest!"
That ancient song we sing,
For Christ is our Redeemer
The Lord of heaven, our King.

O may we ever praise Him
With heart and life and voice,
And in His blissful presence
Eternally REJOICE!

(by Jeanette Trelfall)

Begin your prayer time adoring God through REJOICING in who He is.

THE GOD IN WHOM WE REJOICE

I will praise the Lord, who counsels me; even at night my heart instructs me. I have set the Lord always before me. Because he is at my right hand, I will not be shaken. Therefore my heart is glad and my tongue REJOICES; my body also will rest secure.

Psalm 16:7-9 (NIV)

Then I was beside Him, as a master craftsman; And I was daily His delight, REJOICING always before Him, REJOICING in His inhabited world, and my delight was with the sons of men.

Proverbs 8:30 & 31 (NKJ)

Now you are going through pain, but I shall see you again and your hearts will thrill with JOY—the JOY that no one can take away from you.

John 16:22 (Phillips)

(Share others' JOY), REJOICING with those who REJOICE; and (share others grief), weeping with those who weep.

Romans 12:15 (Amplified)

*R*EJOICE and be glad!
The Redeemer has come!
Go look on His cradle,
His cross and His tomb.

REJOICE and be glad!
Now the pardon is free!
The Just for the unjust
Has died on the tree.

(by Horatius Bonar)

Begin your prayer time adoring and REJOICING in God.

THE GOD IN WHOM WE REJOICE

*L*et them thank the Eternal for his kindness, and for the wonders he does for men; let them offer the sacrifice of thanksgiving, and JOYFULLY recount what he has done.

Psalm 107:21 & 22 (Moffatt)

*Y*es, and REJOICE I will, well knowing that the issue of it all will be my deliverance, because you are praying for me and the Spirit of Jesus Christ is given me for support.

Philippians 1:19 (NEB)

*M*ary responded, "Oh, how I praise the Lord. How I REJOICE in God my Savior!"

Luke 1:46 & 47 (Paraphrased)

*F*or who except you is our hope or happiness or prided crown in the presence of our Lord Jesus at His coming? For you are our glory and JOY.

1 Thessalonians 2:19 & 20 (Berkeley)

REJOICE and be glad!
Now the pardon is free!
The Just for the unjust
Has died on the tree.

REJOICE and be glad!
For the Lamb that was slain
O'er death is triumphant,
And liveth again.

(by Horatius Bonar)

Begin your prayer time adoring God with REJOICING.

THE GOD IN WHOM WE REJOICE

The Lord is my strength and song, and He has become my salvation. The sound of JOYFUL shouting and salvation is in the tent of the righteous; the right hand of the Lord does valiantly.

Psalm 118:14 & 15 (NAS)

May the Lord give you JOY always. I say it again: REJOICE!

Philippians 4:4 (Good News)

At that very hour He (Jesus) REJOICED exceedingly, this REJOICING being energized by the Holy Spirit, and said, I give praise to you, openly and from the heart, Father, Lord of heaven and earth, because you hid these things from the wise and the learned, and uncovered them to the untaught.

Luke 10:21 (Wuest)

But I REJOICED in the Lord greatly, and now at the last your care of me hath flourished again;

Philippians 4:10 (KJ)

REJOICE, ye pure in heart,
REJOICE, give thanks, and sing;
Your festal banner wave on high,
The cross of Christ your King.

With all the angel choirs,
With all the saints on earth,
Pour out the strains of JOY and bliss,
True rapture, noblest mirth!

REJOICE, REJOICE
REJOICE, give thanks, and sing.

(by Edward H. Plumptre)

Begin your prayer time with JOYFUL adoration.

THE GOD IN WHOM WE REJOICE

*B*ut let all who take refuge in you BE GLAD; let them sing for JOY. Spread your protection over them, that those who love your name may REJOICE in you.

Psalm 5:11 (NIV)

*R*EJOICE in the Lord, O you righteous! For praise from the upright is beautiful.

Psalm 33:1 (NKJ)

*Y*our laws are my JOYOUS treasure forever.

Psalm 119:111 (Paraphrased)

*L*ove endures long and is patient and kind; love never is envious nor boils over with jealousy; is not boastful or vainglorious, does not display itself haughtily. It is not conceited—arrogant and inflated with pride; it is not rude (unmannerly) and does not act unbecomingly. Love (God's love in us) does not insist on its own rights or its own way, for it is not self-seeking; it is not touchy or fretful or resentful; it takes no account of the evil done to it—pays no attention to suffering wrong. It does not rejoice at injustice and unrighteousness, but REJOICES when right and truth prevail.

1 Corinthians 13:4-6 (amplified)

*Y*es, on through life's long path,
Still chanting as we go;
From youth to age, by night and day,
In GLADNESS and in woe.

Then on, ye pure in heart,
REJOICE, give thanks and sing;
Your festal banner wave on high,
The cross of Christ your king.

REJOICE, REJOICE,
REJOICE give thanks, and sing.

(Author unknown)

Begin your prayer time adoring God for the JOY He gives.

July 21

THE GOD WHO LISTENS TO PRAYER

PRAYER—The act of praying, asking or begging a favor earnestly; an earnest petition, suit or supplication; an entreaty. (Webster)

I for myself, APPEAL to God and Yahweh saves me; evening, morning, noon, I complain, I groan; he will HEAR ME CALLING.

Psalm 55:16 & 17 (TJB)

*B*ut you, when you pray, enter your inner room and with your door closed PRAY to your Father, the Invisible, and your Father who sees in secret will reward you (openly).

Matthew 6:6 (Berkeley)

*I*n the same way the Spirit comes to the aid of our weakness. We do not even know how we ought to PRAY, but through our inarticulate groans the Spirit himself is PLEADING for us, and God who searches our inmost being knows what the Spirit means, because he PLEADS for God's own people in God's way; and in everything, as we know, he co-operated for good with those who love God and are called according to his purpose.

Romans 8:26-28 (NEB)

> *E*re you left your room this morning
> When you met with great temptation
> Did you think to PRAY?
> Did you think to PRAY?
> In the name of Christ our Saviour,
> by His dying love and merit
> Did you sue for loving favor,
> Did you claim the Holy Spirit
> As a shield today?
> As you guide and stay?
> Oh, how praying rests the weary
> Prayer will change the night to day;
> So in sorrow or in gladness,
> Don't forget to PRAY.
>
> *(by Mary Ann Kider)*

Begin your prayer time adoring God for the gift of PRAYER.

THE GOD WHO LISTENS TO OUR PRAYERS

PRAYER is conversation with God; the contact of the soul with God, not in contemplation or meditation, but in direct address to Him. (Today's)

O thou Eternal, I cry for help in the day-time, and at night I moan before thee; let my PRAYER reach thy presence, bend an ear to my cry.

Psalm 88:1 & 2 (Moffatt)

After saying goodbye to the disciples, he (Jesus) went away to a hill to PRAY.

Matthew 6:46 (Good News)

Be happy in your faith at all times. Never stop PRAYING. Be thankful, whatever the circumstances may be. If you follow this advice you will be working out the will of God expressed to you in Christ Jesus.

Thessalonians 5:16-18 (Phillips)

> *When* your heart was filled with anger,
> Did you think to pray?
> Did you plead for grace my brother,
> That you might forgive another
> O how praying rests the weary!
> Who had crossed your way?
> Prayer will change the night to day;
> So in sorrow and in gladness,
> When sore trials came upon you,
> Don't forget to PRAY.
> Did you think to PRAY?
> When your soul was bowed in sorrow,
> Balm of Gilead did you borrow
> At the gates of day?

> *(by Mary Ann Kider)*

Begin your prayer time adoring the God who listens to your PRAYERS.

THE GOD WHO LISTENS TO OUR PRAYERS

PRAYER history—PRAYER, constituting as it does the most direct expression of religious feeling and consciousness, has, been, from the very first, the principal means by which men, created in the image of God, have evinced their attitude toward him, and from the earliest times, ever since the days of Enoch men began to call upon the name of the Lord, it has formed an integral part of the worship of God. (Unger's)

The Lord will command His lovingkindness in the daytime; And His song will be with me in the night, A PRAYER to the God of my life.

Psalm 42:8 (NAS)

*O*ne time Jesus was PRAYING in a certain place. When he finished, one of his followers said to him, "Lord, teach us to PRAY as John taught his followers." Jesus said to them, "When you PRAY, say: "Father, may your name always be kept holy. May your kingdom come. Give us the food we need for each day. Forgive us for our sins, because we forgive everyone who has done wrong to us. And do not cause us to be tempted."

Luke 11:1-4 (NCV)

*S*o I want men everywhere to PRAY with holy hands lifted up to God, free from sin and anger and resentment.

1 Timothy 2:8 (Paraphrased)

Still, still with Thee, when purple morning breaketh,
When the bird waketh, and the shadows flee;
Fairer than morning, lovelier than the daylight,
Dawns the sweet consciousness, I am with Thee.

When sinks the soul, subdued by toil, to slumber,
Its closing eyes look up to Thee in PRAYER;
Sweet the repose beneath Thy wings o'ershading,
But sweeter still to wake and find Thee there.

(by Harriet Beecher Stowe)

Begin your PRAYER time in adoration to the God who gave us this way to communicate with Him.

THE GOD WHO LISTENS TO OUR PRAYERS

PRAYER—synonyms—request, petition, suit, entreaty, supplication. (Webster)

The sacrifice of the wicked is an abomination to the Lord; but the PRAYER of the upright is his delight.

Proverbs 15:8 (KJ)

And He (Jesus) was giving them an illustration which had for its teaching point that it is a necessity in the nature of the case for them at all times to be PRAYING and not to be loosing courage.

Luke 18:1 (Wuest)

PRAY at all times—on every occasion, in every season—in the Spirit, with all (manner) PRAYER and ENTREATY. To that end keep alert and watch with strong purpose and perseverance, interceding in behalf of the saints (God's consecrated people).

Ephesians 6:18 (Amplified)

> Sweet hour of PRAYER, sweet hour of PRAYER
> That calls me from a world of care,
> And bids me at my Father's throne,
> Make all my wants and wishes known.
>
> In seasons of distress and grief
> My soul has often found relief;
> And oft escaped the tempter's snare,
> by thy return, sweet hour of PRAYER.
>
> *(by W.W. Walford)*

Begin your prayer time adoring the God who hears your PRAYERS.

THE GOD WHO LISTENS TO OUR PRAYERS

PRAYER—is the free utterance of the soul's wants to God the Father, asking benefits in the name of our Saviour, and interceding for the good of others also. Faith is quickened by prayer; and it may be said that prayer is an indication of the spiritual condition of the soul—it being to the soul what breath is to the body. (Today's Dictionary of the Bible)

And it was so, that when Solomon had made an end of PRAYING all this PRAYER and SUPPLICATION unto the Lord, he arose from before the altar of the Lord, from kneeling on his knees with his hands spread up to heaven. And he stood and blessed all the congregation with a loud voice.

1 Kings 8:54 & 55 (KJ)

You have heard that it was said, "Love your neighbor and hate your enemy. But I (Jesus) say to you, Love you enemy and PRAY for your persecutors.

Matthew 5:43 & 44 (Berkeley)

For everything God created is good, and nothing is to be rejected if it is received with thanksgiving, because it is consecrated by the word of God and PRAYER.

1 Timothy 4:4 & 5 (NIV)

Sweet hour of PRAYER! sweet hour of PRAYER
The joy I feel, the bliss I share,
Of those whose anxious spirits burn
With strong desires for Thy return!

With such I hasten to the place
Where God, my Saviour, shows His face
And gladly take my station there,
And wait for thee, sweet hour of PRAYER.

(by W.W. Walford)

Begin your prayer time adoring God for giving us the avenue of PRAYER.

THE GOD WHO LISTENS TO OUR PRAYERS

*M*oreover, as for me, far be it from me that I should sin against the Lord in ceasing to PRAY for you; but I will teach you the good and right way.

1 Samuel 12:23 (NKJ)

*D*o not fret or have any anxiety about anything, but in every circumstance and in everything by PRAYER and PETITION (definite requests) with thanksgiving continue to make your wants known to God.

Philippians 4:6 (Amplified)

*T*he PRAYER offered in faith will save the sick man, the Lord will raise him from his bed, and any sins he may have committed will be forgiven.

James 5:15 (NEB)

*F*or the Lord keeps his eyes on the righteous and always listens to their PRAYERS; but he turns against those who do evil.

1 Peter 3:12 (Good News)

*S*weet hour of PRAYER, sweet hour of PRAYER,
Thy wings shall my PETITION bear
To Him whose truth and faithfulness
Engage the waiting soul to bless;

And since He bids me seek His face,
Believe His word, and trust His grace,
I'll cast on Him my every care,
And wait for thee, sweet hour of PRAYER.

(by W.W. Walford)

Begin your prayer time adoring the God to whom you always have the avenue of PRAYER.

THE GOD WHO ANSWERS OUR PRAYERS

*W*hen the Lord builds up Zion, He will appear in His glory; He will regard the plea of the destitute, and will not despise their PRAYER.

Psalm 102:16 & 17 (Amplified)

*A*nd I (Jesus) will PRAY the Father, and he shall give you another Comforter, that he may abide with you forever.

John 14:16 (KJ)

I want men everywhere to lift up holy hands in PRAYER, without anger or disputing.

1 Timothy 2:8 (RSV)

*W*e are near the end of all things now, and you should therefore be calm, self-controlled men of PRAYER.

1 Peter 4:7 (Phillips)

'*T*is the blessed hour of PRAYER,
When our hearts lowly bend,
And we gather to Jesus,
Our Saviour and Friend;

If we come to him in faith,
His protection to share,
What a balm for the weary!
O how sweet to be there.

(by Fanny J. Crosby)

Adore God for the balm of PRAYER.

THE GOD WHO ANSWERS OUR PRAYERS

Then if my people who bear my name humble themselves, and PRAY and seek my presence and turn from their wicked ways, I myself will hear from heaven and forgive their sins and restore their land.

2 Chronicles 7:14 (TJB)

Anyone who is having troubles should PRAY. Anyone who is happy should sing praises.

James 15:3 (NCV)

Beloved, I PRAY you may prosper in every way and keep well.

3 John 3 (Moffatt)

He stepped forward and took the scroll from the right hand of the one sitting on the throne. And as he took the scroll, the twenty-four Elders fell down before the Lamb, each with a harp and golden vials filled with incense—the PRAYERS of God's people!

Revelation 5:7 & 8 (Paraphrased)

'Tis the blessed hour of PRAYER,
When the Saviour draws near,
With a tender compassion
His children to hear;

When He tells us we may cast
At His feet every care,
What a balm for the weary!
O how sweet to be there!

(by Fanny J. Crosby)

Adore God for hearing and answering our PRAYERS.

GOD THE PROMISE KEEPER

PROMISE—in a general sense, a declaration written or verbal made by one person to another, which binds the person who made it, either in honor, conscience, or law, to do or forbear a certain act specified; a declaration which gives to the person to whom it is made a right to expect or to claim the performance of the act. (Webster)

*B*lessed be the Lord, who has given rest to His people Israel, according to all that He PROMISED; not one word has failed of all His good PROMISE, which He PROMISED through Moses His servant.

1 Kings 8:56 (NAS)

As for you, you are those who, having seen these things, are to testify concerning them. And behold! As for myself, I am sending forth the PROMISE of my Father upon you. And as for you, you take up residence in the city until you are endowed with power from on high.

Luke 25:48 & 49 (Wuest)

And this is the PROMISE that He has PROMISED us eternal life.

1 John 2:25 (NKJ)

Standing on the PROMISES of Christ my King,
Through eternal ages let His praises ring;
Glory in the highest, I will shout and sing
Standing on the PROMISES of God.

Standing on the PROMISES that cannot fail,
When the howling storms of doubt and fear assail,
by the living word of God I shall prevail,
Standing on the PROMISES of God.

(by R. Kelso Carter)

Begin your prayer time adoring God for kept PROMISES.

GOD THE PROMISE KEEPER

PROMISE—Latin promiseum, from promittere, to send before or forward; pro, forth, and mittere, to send. (Webster)

The Lord your God hath multiplied you, and behold, ye are this day as the stars of heaven for multitude. (The Lord God of your fathers make you a thousand times so many more as ye are, and bless you, as he hath PROMISED you.)

Deuteronomy 1:10 & 11 (KJ)

And we are here to bring the Good News to you; what God PROMISED our ancestors he would do, he has now done for us, who are their descendants, by raising Jesus to life.

Acts 13:32 (Good News)

It is our deep desire, however, that each of you shall evidence the same earnestness all the way through, to enjoy the full assurance of your hope to the limit, so you may not grow disinterested, but behave as those who through faith and patience inherit the PROMISES.

Hebrews 6:11 & 12 (Berkeley)

Standing on the PROMISES of Christ the Lord,
Bound to Him eternally by loves strong cord,
Overcoming daily with the Spirit's sword,
Standing on the PROMISES of God.

Standing on the PROMISES I cannot fall,
Listening every moment to the Spirit's call,
Resting in my Saviour as my all in all,
Standing on the PROMISES of God.

(by R. Kelso Carter)

Begin your prayer time adoring God for kept PROMISES.

GOD THE PROMISE KEEPER

PROMISE—synonyms—assurance, engagement, word, contract, pledge, covenant, arrangement. (Webster)

The Lord spread a cloud for covering (by day), and a fire to give light in the night. The Israelites asked, and He brought quails, and satisfied them with the bread of heaven. He opened the rock, and waters gushed out; they ran in the dry places like a river. For He (earnestly) remembered His holy word and PROMISE, and Abraham His servant.

Psalm 105:39-42 (Amplified)

For no matter how many PROMISES God has made, they are "Yes" in Christ. And so through him the "Amen" is spoken by us to the glory of God.

2 Corinthians 1:20 (NIV)

For in making a PROMISE to Abraham God swore by himself (since he should swear by non greater).

Hebrews 6:13 (Moffatt)

> Precious PROMISE God hath given
> To the weary passer-by,
> On the way from earth to heaven,
> "I will guide thee with My eye."
>
> When the shades of life are falling,
> And the hour has come to die,
> Hear the trusty Pilot calling,
> "I will guide thee with Mine eye."
>
> *(by Nathaniel Niles)*

Begin your prayer time with adoration for the God of kept PROMISES.

August

GOD THE PROMISE KEEPER

"*B*lessed be Yahweh" he said, "who has granted rest to his people Israel, keeping all of his PROMISES; of all the PROMISES of good that he made through Moses his servant, not one has failed."

1 Kings 8:56 (TJB)

*E*ven today I stand here on trial because of a hope that I hold in a PROMISE that God made to our forefathers—a PROMISE for which our twelve tribes serve God zealously day and night,, hoping to see it fulfilled.

Acts 26:5 & 6 (Phillips)

(*R*esting) in the hope of eternal life, (life) which the ever truthful God Who cannot deceive, PROMISED before the world or the ages of time began.

Titus 1:2 (Amplified)

*J*esus has the power of God, by which he has given us everything we need to live and to serve him. Jesus called us by his glory and goodness. Through these he gave the very great and precious PROMISES. With these gifts you can share in being like God, and the world will not ruin you with its evil desires.

2 Peter 1:3 & 4 (NCV)

*P*eace with God is Christ in glory,
God is just and God is love;
Jesus died to tell the story,
Foes to bring to God above.

Now, free access to the Father,
Through the Christ of God we have;
by the Spirit here abiding,
PROMISE of the Father's love.

(Author unknown)

Adore God for His kept PROMISES.

THE GOD FROM WHOM WE RECEIVE

RECEIVE—To be a receiver; to obtain possession of something from an outside source. To take, get, or obtain, as a thing due, offered, sent, paid, given, or communicated. (Webster)

He who has clean hands and a pure heart, Who has not lifted up his soul to an idol, Nor sworn deceitfully. He shall RECEIVE blessing from the Lord, And righteousness from the God of his salvation.

Psalm 24:4 & 5 (NKJ)

But to as many as did RECEIVE and welcome Him, He gave the authority (power, privilege, right) to become the children of God, that is, to those who believe in—adhere to, trust in and rely on His name.

John 1:12 (Amplified)

In the same manor, therefore, as you RECEIVED the Christ, Jesus, the Lord, in Him be constantly ordering your behavior, having been rooted with the present result that you are firmly established, and constantly being built up in Him and constantly being established with reference to the Faith, even as you were instructed, abounding in it in the sphere of thanksgiving.

Colossians 2:6 & 7 (Wuest)

Naught have I gotten but what I RECEIVED;
Grace hath bestowed it since I have believed;
Boasting excluded, pride I abase;
I'm only a sinner saved by grace!

Tears unavailing, no merit had I;
Mercy had saved me, or else I must die;
Sin had alarmed me, fearing God's face;
But now I'm a sinner saved by grace!

(by James M. Gray)

Begin your prayer time adoring the God from whom you RECEIVE all things.

August 3

THE GOD FROM WHOM WE RECEIVE

🔲 RECEIVE synonyms—accept, admit, obtain, take, hold. (Webster)

*U*ntil now you have asked for nothing in My name; ask, and you will receive, that your joy may be made full.

John 16:24 (NAS)

*W*hoever RECEIVES you receives ME and whoever RECEIVES Me RECEIVES Him who sent me.

Matthew 10:40 (Berkeley)

*F*or we have not followed cunningly devised fables, when we made known unto you the power and coming of our Lord Jesus Christ, but were eyewitnesses of his majesty. For we RECEIVED from God the Father honor and glory, when there came such a voice to him from the excellent glory, This is my beloved Son, in whom I am well pleased. And this voice which came from heaven we heard, when we were with him in the holy mount.

2 Peter 1:16-18 (KJ)

> *O* what a wonderful, wonderful day—day I will never forget;
> After I'd wondered in darkness away, Jesus my Saviour I met.
> O what a tender, compassionate friend—He met the need of my heart;
> Shadows dispelling, With joy I am telling, He made all the darkness depart!
>
> Now, I've a hope that will surely endure after the passing of time;
> I have a future in heaven for sure, there in those mansions sublime.
> And it's because of that wonderful day when at the cross I believed;
> Riches eternal and blessings supernal from His precious hand I RECEIVED.
>
> *(by John W. Peterson)*

Begin your prayer time with adoration over all you have RECEIVED.

THE GOD FROM WHO WE RECEIVE

*A*nd if you have faith, everything you ask for in prayer you will RECEIVE.

Matthew 21:22 (TJB)

*J*esus repeated, 'Peace be with you!', and then he said, "As the Father sent me so I send you." He then breathed on them, saying, "RECEIVE the Holy Spirit."

John 20:21 & 22 (NEB)

*I*n our work together with God, then, we beg of you: you have RECEIVED God's grace, and you must not let it be wasted. Hear what God says: "I heard you in the hour of my favor, I helped you in the day of salvation." Listen! This is the hour to RECEIVE God's favor, today is the day to be saved!

2 Corinthians 6:1 & 2 (GN)

*T*hen he took a little child, set it among them, and putting his arms round it said to them, Whoever receives one of these little ones in my name RECEIVES me, and whoever RECEIVES me RECEIVES not me but him who sent me.

Mark 9:36 & 37 (Moffatt)

*O*nly a step to Jesus!
A step from sin to grace;
What hast thy heart decided?
The moments fly apace.

Only a step, only a step;
Come, He waits for thee;
Come, and, thy sin confessing,
Thou shalt RECEIVE blessing;
Do not reject the mercy
He freely offers thee.

(by Fanny J. Crosby)

Begin prayer adoring God for each gift of mercy you have RECEIVED.

THE GOD FROM WHOM WE RECEIVE

*L*et me ask you this one question: Did you RECEIVE the Holy Spirit by trying to keep the Jewish laws? Of course not, for the Holy Spirit came upon you only after you heard about Christ and trusted him to save you.

Galatians 3:2 (Paraphrased)

*D*ear friends, if our hearts do not condemn us, we have confidence before God and RECEIVE from him anything we ask, because we obey his commands and do what pleases him.

1 John 21 & 22 (NIV)

*T*he teaching I gave you is the same teaching I RECEIVED from the Lord: On the night when the Lord Jesus was handed over to be killed, he took bread and gave thanks for it. Then he broke the bread and said, "This is my body; it is for you. Do this to remember me." In the same way, after they ate, Jesus took the cup. He said, "This cup is the new agreement that is sealed with the blood of my death. When you drink this, do it to remember me."

1 Corinthians 11:23-26 (NCV)

*T*herefore, since we are RECEIVING a kingdom which cannot be shaken, let us have grace, by which we may serve God acceptably with reverence and godly fear.

Hebrews 12:18 (NKJ)

*I*n the world you've failed to find
Ought of peace for troubled mind;
Come to Christ, on Him believe,
Peace and joy you shall RECEIVE.

Come to Christ, confession make;
Come to Christ, and pardon TAKE;
Trust in Him from day to day,
He will keep you all the way.

(by Daniel W. Whittle)

Begin praying with adoration for all you have RECEIVED from God.

THE GOD WHO RECEIVES US

"*L*et not your heart be troubled; believe in God, believe also in Me. In My Father's house are many dwelling places; if it were not so I would have told you; for I go to prepare a place for you. And if I go and prepare a place for you, I will come again, and RECEIVE you to Myself; that where I am, there you may be also."

John 14:1-3 (NAS)

*S*inners Jesus will RECEIVE;
Sound this word of grace to all
Who the heavenly pathway leave,
All who linger, all who fall.

Come and He will give you rest;
Trust Him, for His word is plain;
He will take the sinfulest;
Christ RECEIVETH sinful men.

Now my heart condemns me not,
Pure before the law I stand;
He who cleansed me from all spot,
Satisfied its last demand.

Christ RECEIVETH sinful men,
Even me with all my sin;
Purged from every spot and stain,
Heaven with Him I enter in.

Sing it o'er and o'er again;
Christ RECEIVETH sinful men;
Make the message clear and plain:
Christ RECEIVETH sinful men.

(by Erdmann Neumeister)

Begin your prayers with adoration and praise to the God who RECEIVES you to Himself.

THE GOD TO WHOM WE MUST GIVE AN ACCOUNT

ACCOUNT—1. A computation of debts and credits. 2. A computation of reckoning. 3. Narrative; relation; statement of facts, recital of particular events. (Webster)

*B*ut I tell you, on the day of judgment men will have to give an ACCOUNT for every idle (inoperative, non-working) word they speak.

Matthew 12:36 (Amplified)

"*A*s I live," saith the Lord, "to Me every knee shall bow and every tongue shall render acknowledgment to God." Accordingly, every one of us shall give ACCOUNT of himself to God.

Romans 14:11 & 12 (Berkeley)

*T*herefore He who supplies the Spirit to you and works miracles among you, does He do it by the works of the law, or by the hearing of faith?—just as Abraham "believed God, and it was ACCOUNTED to him for righteousness."

Galatians 3:5 & 6 (NKJ)

*T*he old ACCOUNT of sin
Was settled long ago
When Christ to
Calvary's tree did go

You can be free of
Your sin's ACCOUNT
With faith in the God Who
Died on the Mount.

(Author unknown)

Adore the Son Who willingly paid your ACCOUNT.

THE GOD WE MUST ACKNOWLEDGE

ACKNOWLEDGE—To own, avow, or admit to be true, by a declaration of assent; as, to acknowledge God. (Webster)

I ACKNOWLEDGE my sin to Thee, and my iniquity I did not hide; I said, "I will confess my transgressions to the Lord;" And Thou didst forgive the guilt of my sin.

Psalm 32:5 (NAS)

In all your ways know, recognize and ACKNOWLEDGE Him, and He will direct and make straight and plain your paths.

Proverbs 3:6 (Amplified)

No one who denies the Son has the Father; whoever ACKNOWLEDGES the Son has the Father also.

1 John 2:23b (NIV)

Dying with Jesus, by death reckoned mine;
Living with Jesus, a new life divine;
Looking to Jesus till glory doth shine,
Moment by moment, O LORD, I AM THINE.

Moment by moment I'm kept in His love;
Moment by moment I've life from above;
Looking to Jesus till glory doth shine;
Moment by moment, O LORD, I AM THINE.

(by Daniel D. Whittle)

Adore God for allowing us to ACKNOWLEDGE Him as Saviour.

THE GOD WHO LED IN BAPTISM

🔲 BAPTISM—The application of water to a person, as a sacrament or religious ceremony, by which he is initiated into the visible church of Christ. (Webster)

*T*hen Jesus came on the scene from Galilee to be BAPTIZED by John at the Jordan. John tried to prevent him; "I need to be BAPTIZED by you," he said, "and you come to me!" But Jesus answered him, "Come now, this is how we should fulfill all our duty to God." Then John gave in to him. Now when Jesus had been BAPTIZED, the moment he rose out of the water, the heavens opened and he saw the Spirit of God coming down like a dove upon him. And a voice from heaven said, "This is my Son, the Beloved, in him is my delight."

Matthew 3:13-17 (Moffatt)

"*Y*ou then, are to go and make disciples of all nations and BAPTIZE them in the name of the Father and of the Son, and of the Holy Spirit. Teach them to observe all that I have commanded you and, remember I am with you always, even to the end of the world.

Matthew 28:19 & 20 (Phillips)

*H*ave you forgotten that when we were BAPTIZED into union with Christ we were BAPTIZED into his death? by BAPTISM we were buried with him, and lay dead, in order that, as Christ raised from the dead in the splendor of the Father, so also we might set our feet upon the new path of life.

Romans 6:3 & 4 (NEB)

*L*ord Jesus, we remember
The travail of Thy soul,
When in love's deep pity
The waves did over Thee roll.

BAPTIZED in death's cold waters
For us Thy blood was shed,
For us Thou, Lord of glory
Wast numbered with the dead.

(by James G. Deck)

Adore God, for taking His stand in BAPTISM.

THE GOD WHO LED IN BAPTISM

*J*ohn was BAPTIZING in the desert and preaching a BAPTISM of changed hearts and lives for the forgiveness of sins.

Mark 1:4 (NCV)

*F*or Christ is like a single body, which has many parts; it is still one body, even though it is made up of different parts. In the same way, all of us, Jews and Gentiles, slaves and free men, have been BAPTIZED into the one body by the same Spirit, and we have all been given the one Spirit to drink.

1 Corinthians 12:12 & 13 (GN)

*Y*ou have one Master, one faith, one BAPTISM, one God and Father of all, who rules over all, works through all, and is present in all.

Ephesians 4:4 & 5 (Message)

*Y*ou have been buried with him, when you were BAPTIZED, and by BAPTISM, too, you have been raised up with him through your belief in the power of God who raised him from the dead.

Colossians 2:12 (NJB)

*B*eside this emblematic grave,
We seek Thy blessing Lord,
On those who are to be BAPTIZED,
In keeping with Thy word.

Thou didst this ordinance ordain,
That all who trust in Thee
Might, in this way, confess to all
Their union, Lord, with Thee.

(by Alfred P. Gibbs)

Adore God for giving us the sacrament of BAPTISM.

THE GOD WHO CHASTENS

▦ CHASTEN—To correct by punishment; to punish; to inflict pain in order to reclaim; to discipline. (Webster)

O Israel, thou hast sinned from the days of Gibeah... It is my desire that I should CHASTISE them; and the people shall be gathered against them.

Hosea 10:9a & 10a (KJ)

The Lord has PUNISHED me, but not handed me over to death.

Psalm 118:18 (Paraphrased)

Son of mine, stop making light of the Lord's DISCIPLINE, CORRECTION, and guidance. Stop fainting when you are effectually rebuked by Him. For the one whom the Lord loves, He DISCIPLINES, CORRECTS, and guides, and He SCOURGES every son whom He receives and cherishes.

Hebrews 12:5b & 6 (Wuest)

There's a wideness in God's mercy,
Like the wideness of the sea;
There's a kindness in His JUSTICE,
Which is more than liberty.

For the love of God is broader
Than the measure of man's mind;
And the heart of the Eternal
Is most wonderfully kind.

(by Frederick W. Faber)

Adore God because He CHASTENS in love.

THE GOD WHO CHASTENS

CHASTEN—synonyms—Chastise, discipline, correct, punish, purify. (Webster)

"*H*ow enviable the man whom God CORRECTS! Oh, do not despise the CHASTENING of the Lord when you sin."

Job 5:17 (Paraphrased)

*L*ord, in trouble they have visited You, They poured out a prayer when Your CHASTENING was upon them.

Isaiah 26:19 (NKJ)

*Y*ou must endure for the sake of CORRECTION; God is treating you as sons. For what sort of a son is it whom the Father does not DISCIPLINE?

Hebrews 12:7 (Berkeley)

*T*hose whom I love I REBUKE and DISCIPLINE. So be earnest and repent.

Revelation 3:19 (NIV)

*D*own to the depths of woe
Christ came to set me free;
He bared His breast, received the blow,
Which JUSTICE aimed at me!

There JUSTICE met my sin,
On the accursed tree;
To prove His love, my heart to win,
Christ gave Himself for me!

(by G.W. Frazer)

Adore God for the price He paid to keep us from eternal PUNISHMENT.

GOD OUR CONFIDENCE

CONFIDENCE—An assurance of mind or firm belief in the trustworthiness of another, or in the truth and reality of a fact; trust, reliance. (Webster)

By awesome deeds Thou dost answer us in righteousness, O God of our salvation. Thou art the TRUST of all the ends of the earth and of the farthest sea.

Psalm 65:5 (NAS)

But Christ was faithful as a son in the household of his own Father. And we are members of this household if we maintain our TRUST and joyful hope steadfast to the end.

Hebrews 3:6 (Phillips)

And now, little children, abide (love, remain permanently) in Him, so that when He is made visible, we may have and enjoy perfect CONFIDENCE (boldness, assurance) and not be ashamed and shrink from Him at His coming.

1 John 2:28 (Amplified)

Simply TRUSTING every day,
TRUSTING through a stormy way;
Even when my faith is small,
TRUSTING Jesus, that is all.

TRUSTING as the moments fly,
TRUSTING as the days go by;
TRUSTING Him what-ever befalls,
TRUSTING Jesus, that is all.

(by Edgar P. Stites)

Adore the God in Whom you have CONFIDENCE.

GOD DECLARED

🔲 DECLARE—To clear; To make known; To assert positively; To avow; To announce the existence of. (Webster)

*T*he heavens DECLARE the glory of God, the vault of heaven PROCLAIM his handiwork.

Psalm 19:1 (NJB)

*C*ome and hear, all ye that fear God, and I will DECLARE what he hath done for my soul.

Psalm 66:16 (KJ)

*G*od gave the law through Moses; but grace and truth came through Jesus Christ. No one has ever seen God. The only One, who is what God is, and who is near the Father's side, has MADE HIM KNOWN.

John 1:17 & 18 (GN)

"*I* (Jesus) will PROCLAIM thy name to my brothers, in the midst of the church I will sing of thee," and again, "I will put my trust in him," and again, "Here am I and the children God has given me."

Hebrews 2:12 & 13 (Moffatt)

> *T*he spacious firmament on high,
> With all the blue, ethereal sky,
> And spangled heavens, a shining frame,
> Their great Original PROCLAIM:
>
> The unwearied sun, from day to day,
> Does his creator's power display;
> And PUBLISHES to every land
> The work of an Almighty hand.
>
> *(by Joseph Addison)*

Adore the DECLARED God.

THE GOD WHO SAID, "DO'

▦ DO—To perform; to execute; to carry into effect; to exert labor or power upon to bring anything to the state desired or to completion. (Webster)

*D*o to others what you want them to do to you. This is the meaning of the law of Moses and the teaching of the prophets.

Matthew 7:12 (NCV)

*A*nd He (Jesus) said to him, In the law what has been written and is on record? In what way do you read it? And answering he said, You shall love the Lord your God with your whole heart and with your whole soul and with your whole strength and with your whole mind, and your neighbor as yourself. And He said to him, You answered correctly. BE DOING this and you shall live.

Luke 10:26-28 (Wuest)

*J*esus gave this answer: "I tell you the truth, the Son can DO nothing by himself; he can DO only what he sees his Father DOING; because whatever the Father DOES the Son also DOES.

John 5:19 (NIV)

> *T*here's surely somewhere a lowly place
> In earth's harvest fields so wide,
> Where I may labor through life's short day
> For Jesus the crucified.
>
> So trusting my all unto Thy care,
> I know Thou lovest me!
> I'll DO Thy will with a heart sincere,
> I'll be what you want me to be.
>
> *(by Charles H. Gabriel)*

Adore God for what He is able to DO.

THE GOD WHO SAID, "DO"

DO—synonyms—Accomplish, achieve, execute, effect, perform. (Webster)

"I am the vine, you are the branches. He who abides in Me and I in him, bears much fruit; for without Me you can DO nothing.

John 15:5 (NKJ)

So, whether you eat or drink or whatever you do, DO it all to the glory of God.

1 Corinthians 10:31 (Berkeley)

For all who have sinned without the Law will also perish without the Law; and all who have sinned under the Law will be judged by the Law; for not the hearers of the Law are just before God, but the DOERS of the law will be justified.

Romans 2:12 & 13 (NAS)

Don't forget to DO good and to share what you have with those in need, for such sacrifices are very pleasing to him.

Hebrews 16:13 (Paraphrased)

Go, labor on; spend and be spent,
Thy joy to DO the Father's will;
It is the way the Master went;
Should not the servant tread it still?

Toil on, faint not, keep watch and pray;
Be wise the erring soul to win;
Go forth into the world's highway,
Compel the wonderer to come in.

(by Horatius Bonar)

Adore God for what He allows you to DO.

GOD OF REST

🔲 REST—to pause, to cease, be quiet, to stop, to end, to lean, to depend, to rely, to satisfy, to sleep, to slumber. (Webster)

*A*nd on the seventh day God ended His work which He had done, and He RESTED on the seventh day from all His work which He had done.

Genesis 2:2 (NKJ)

*W*ork six days only, and REST the seventh; this is to give your oxen and donkeys a REST, as well as the people of your household—your slaves and visitors.

Exodus 23:12 (Paraphrased)

*C*ome here to me, all you who are growing weary to the point of exhaustion, and who have been loaded with burdens and are bending beneath their weight, and I alone will cause you to CEASE from your labor and take away your burdens and thus refresh you with REST.

Matthew 11:28 (Wuest)

"*C*ome unto Me," It is the Saviour's voice,
The lord of life, who bids the heart rejoice;
O weary heart, with heavy cares opprest,
"Come unto Me," and I will give you REST.

Life, REST, and peace, the flowers of deathless bloom,
The Saviour gives us—not beyond the tomb—
But here, and now: on earth some glimpse is given
Of joys which wait us through the gates of heaven.

(by Nathanael Norton)

Adore God for the gift of REST.

THE GOD OF REST

*R*EST in the Lord and wait patiently for Him.

Psalm 37:7a (NAS)

*T*hus says the Lord, Stand by the roads and look, and ask for the eternal paths, where is the good, old way; then walk in it, and you will find REST for your souls.

Jeremiah 6:16a (Amplified)

*T*herefore, as the Spirit says, "Today if you will hear His voice, do not harden your hearts in that provoking situation at the time of the desert ordeal, where your fathers for forty years tried Me by putting Me to the proof and saw what I did. So I became sorely displeased with that generation and said, 'Their hearts are always off the track; they have not recognized My paths.' So in my indignity I swore, "They shall not enter into My REST."

Hebrews 3:7-11 (Berkeley)

*T*hen I heard a voice from heaven, saying, 'Write this! From henceforth happy are the dead who die in the Lord!" "Happy indeed," says the Spirit, "for they REST from their labors and their deeds go with them!"

Revelation 14:14 (Phillips)

O REST in the Lord,
Wait patiently for Him,
And He shall give thee
Thy heart's desires

Commit thy ways unto Him,
And trust in Him;
And fret not thyself
Because of evil doers.

O REST in the Lord,
Wait patiently for Him;

*(by Felix Mendelssohn
based on Psalm 37)*

Adore God for allowing you to REST in Him.

THE GOD OF REST

*D*uring the night I had a vision and there before me was a man riding a red horse! He was standing among the myrtle trees in a ravine. Behind him were red, brown and white horses. I asked, "What are these my Lord?" The angel who was talking with me answered, "I will show you what they are." Then the man standing among the myrtle trees explained, "They are the ones the Lord has sent to go throughout the earth." And they reported to the angel of the Lord who was standing among the myrtle trees, "We have gone throughout the earth and found the whole world at REST and in peace."

Zechariah 1:8-11 (NIV)

*N*ow, since God has left us the promise that we may enter his REST, let us be very careful so none of you will fail to enter. The Good News was preached to us just as it was to them. But the teaching they heard did not help them, because they heard it but did not accept it with faith. We who have believed are able to enter God's REST.

Hebrews 4:1-3a (NCV)

*O*ut of the old life, into the new;
Out of the unrest, into the peace,
Out of the false strife, into the true;
Out of the tempest, into calm seas

Out of darkness, into the light,
Out of night's shadows, into the light,
Father, Father, O take me.
Father, O Father take me.

Out of the weariness, into the REST;
Out of the bitterness, into the blest;
Out of the mortal, to the Eternal,
Father, Father, O take me!

(by Myron V. Freese)

Adore God for the promise of eternal REST.

THE GOD WHO RESTORES

🔲 RESTORE—To bring back to a former and better state; to renew, to recover. (Webster)

*R*ESTORE unto me the joy of thy salvation; and uphold me with thy free spirit.

Psalm 51:12 (KJ)

I will RESTORE your judges as of old, your counselors as in bygone days. Then you will be called City of Integrity, Faithful City.

Isaiah 1:26 (TJB)

*O*n another occasion when he went to synagogue, there was a man in the congregation who had a withered arm; and they were watching to see whether Jesus would cure him on the Sabbath, so that they could bring a charge against him. He said to the man with the withered arm, "Come and stand out here." Then he turned to them; "Is it permitted to do good or to do evil on the Sabbath, to save life or to kill?" They had nothing to say; and, looking around at them with anger and sorrow at their obstinate stupidity, he said to the man, "Stretch out your arm." He stretched it out and his arm was RESTORED.

Mark 5:3-5 (NEB)

*I*t's dark as a dungeon and the sun seldom shines
And I question, Lord, why must this be
But He tells me there's strength in my sorrow,
And there's victory in trials for me.

He leads me beside still waters
Somewhere in the valley below;
He draws me aside to be tested and tried,
But in the valley He RESTORETH my soul.

(by Dottie Rambo)
Copyright 1970 by Heart Warming Music

Adore God for RESTORATION.

THE GOD WHO RESTORES

RESTORE synonyms—repay, return, give up, replace, renew, refund, repair, recover, heal. (Webster)

The Lord is my shepherd; I shall not want. He maketh me to lie down in green pastures: he leadeth me beside still waters. He RESTORETH my soul; he leadeth me in the paths of righteousness for his names sake.

Psalm 23:1-3 (KJ)

Therefore all who devour you shall be devoured, and all your adversaries, every one of them, shall go into captivity, and they who despoil you shall become a spoil, and all who pray upon you will I give for a prey. For I will RESTORE health to you, and I will HEAL your wounds, says the Lord.

Jeremiah 30:16 & 17a (Amp)

Brethren, if, however, a man be overtaken in a sin, as for you who are the spiritual ones, be RESTORING such a one in the spirit of meekness, taking heed to yourself lest you also be tempted.

Galatians 6:1 (Wuest)

A wonderful Saviour is Jesus my Lord,
He TAKETH MY BURDEN AWAY;
He holdeth me up, and I shall not be moved,
He GIVETH ME STRENGTH as my day.

With numberless blessings each moment He crowns,
And filled with His fullness divine,
I sing in my rapture, Oh, glory to God
For such a Redeemer as mine!

(by Fanny J. Crosby)

Adore God for RESTORATION.

THE GOD WHO RESTORES

*B*e glad then, you children of Zion, And rejoice in the Lord your God: for He has continually given you the former rain faithfully, And He will cause the rain to come down for you the former rain, and the latter rain in the first month. The threshing floors shall be full of wheat, and the vats shall overflow with wine and oil. "So I will RESTORE to you the years that the swarming locust has eaten, the crawling locust, the consuming locust, and the chewing locust, my great army which I sent among you. You shall eat in plenty and be satisfied, and praise the name of the Lord your God, Who has dealt wondrously with you; and my people shall never be put to shame. Then you shall know that I am in the midst of Israel, and that I am the Lord your God and there is no other.

Joel 2:23-27 (NKJ)

*T*hen they reached Bethsaida. A blind man was brought to him (Jesus), with the request that he would touch him. So he took the blind man by the hand and led him outside the village; then, after spitting on his eyes, he laid his hands on him and asked him, "Do you see anything?" He began to see and said, "I can make out people, for I see them as large as trees moving." At this he laid his hands once more on his eyes, and the man stared in front of him; he was quite RESTORED, he saw everything distinctly.

Mark 8:22-25 (Moffatt)

> *D*own in the human heart,
> Crushed by the tempter,
> Feelings lie buried
> That grace can RESTORE;
>
> Touched by a loving heart,
> Wakened by kindness,
> Chords that were broken
> Will VIBRATE ONCE MORE.
>
> *(by Fanny J. Crosby)*

Adore the God who RESTORES.

THE REVEALING GOD

▦ REVEAL—To disclose; to show; to make known (that which would be unknown without divine or supernatural instruction). (Webster)

*T*he secret things belong to the Lord our God, but the things REVEALED belong to us and to our children forever, that we may follow all the words of this law.

Deuteronomy 29:29 (NIV)

"*B*ehold, I will bring to it health and healing, and I will heal them; I will REVEAL to them an abundance of peace and truth.

Jeremiah 33:6 (NAS)

*M*y Father has given me all things. No one knows the Son except the Father, and no one knows the Father except the Son, and those to whom the Son wants to REVEAL Him.

Matthew 11:27 (Good News)

*W*e thank Thee, Lord, for weary days
When desert springs were dry,
And first we KNEW what depth of need
Thy love could satisfy,

The sweet companionship of One
Who once the desert trod:
The glorious fellowship with One
Upon the throne of God.

(Author unknown)

Adore God for all He has REVEALED to you.

THE REVEALING GOD

REVEAL synonyms—Divulge, unveil, disclose, show, impart, discover. (Webster)

*O*he voice of him that crieth in the wilderness, Prepare ye the way of the Lord, make straight in the desert a highway for our Lord. Every valley shall be exalted, and every mountain and hill shall be made low: and the crooked shall be made straight, and the rough places plain: and the glory of the Lord shall be REVEALED, and all flesh shall see it together: for the mouth of the Lord hath spoken it.

Isaiah 40:3-5 (KJ)

I consider that the sufferings of this present time (this present life) are not worth being compared with the glory that is about to be REVEALED to us and in us and for us, and conferred on us!

Roman 8:18 (Amplified)

*B*ut as it is written, "What no eye has seen, what no ear has heard, neither has it come up in the human heart, that has God made ready for those who love Him." Through the Spirit, however, God has REVEALED to us; for the spirit examines everything, even the deep things of God.

1 Corinthian 2:9 & 19 (Berkeley)

"*W*ith-in the Veil:" Be this, beloved thy portion.
With-in the secret of thy Lord to dwell;
Beholding Him, until thy face His glory,
Thy life His love, thy lips His praise shall tell.

"With-in the Veil:" for any as thou gazest
Upon the matchless beauty of His face,
Canst thou become a living REVELATION
Of His great heart of love, His untold grace.

(by Freda H. Allen)

Adore God for all He has REVEALED.

THE REVEALING GOD

REVELATION—(Gr. apokalapsis, an answering, or unveiling.) a term expressive of the fact that God has made known to men truths and realities which men could not discover for themselves. (Unger's)

During the night God EXPLAINED the secret to Daniel in a vision. Then Daniel praised the God of heaven. Daniel said: Praise God forever and ever, because he has wisdom and power. He changes the times and the seasons of the year. He takes away the power of kings and gives their power to new kings. He gives wisdom to those who are wise and knowledge to those who understand. He MAKES KNOWN secrets that are deep and hidden; he knows what is hidden in darkness and light is all around him.

Daniel 2:19-22 (NCV)

The gospel I preach to you is no human invention. No man gave it to me, no man taught it to me; it came to me as a direct REVELATION from Jesus Christ.

Galatians 1:15-17 (Phillips)

Praise be to the God and Father of our Lord Jesus Christ, who in his mercy gave us new birth into a living hope by the resurrection of Jesus Christ from the dead! The inheritance to which we are born is one that nothing can destroy or spoil or wither. It is kept for you in heaven, and you, because you put your faith in God, are under the protection of his power until salvation comes the salvation which is even now in readiness and will be REVEALED at the end time.

1 Peter 1:3-5 (NEV)

O Father of all eternal love, REVEAL to me my task, I pray;
Help me, O Lord, to do the things that should be done today.
The plan of life for me UNFOLD, Thy will I wish to do,
To follow Thee each hour I live, and stand forever true.

O Father hear my humble cry, help me to gladly give
My service, love and sacrifice, and praise Thee while I live.
Help me to build with-in my soul for all eternity,
The Temple of the living God, and there to worship Thee.

(by Rev. B.V. Tippett)

Adore God for REVEALING the plan of salvation.

THE REVEALING GOD

▦ REVELATION—An example of supernaturally given knowledge is the fact that Christ was conceived by the Holy Ghost. So we may say then, that the explanation of her conception was REVEALED to the Virgin Mary. (Today's)

Surely the Lord will do nothing, without REVEALING His secret to His servants the prophets.

Amos 3:7 (Amplified)

Just as it was in Noah's days, so also shall it be in the days of the Son of Man. They were eating, they were drinking, they were marrying, they were being given in marriage, until the day when Noah entered the ark. And there came the deluge and destroyed all. Likewise, it was so in Lot's days. They were eating, they were drinking, they were buying, they were selling, they were planting, they were building. But the day on which Lot went out of Sodom, it rained fire and brimstone from heaven and destroyed all the inhabitants. According to the same pattern shall it be on the day when the Son of Man is being REVEALED.

Luke 17:26-30 (Wuest)

Beloved, now we are children of God; and it has not yet been REVEALED what we shall be, but we know that when He is REVEALED, we shall be like Him, for we shall see Him as He is.

1 John 3:2 (NKJ)

More about Jesus would I KNOW,
More of His grace to others show;
More of His saving fullness see,
More of His love who died for me.

More about Jesus let me learn,
More of His holy will discern;
Spirit of God my teacher be,
SHOWING the things of Christ to me.

(by Eliza E. Hewitt)

Adore God for His REVELATION of Christ.

THE REVEALING GOD

"*Truly*," said the king to Daniel, "your God is God of gods and Lord of kings and a REVEALER of mysteries, since you have been able to REVEAL this mystery.

Daniel 2:47 (Moffatt)

God's wrath is REVEALED coming down from heaven upon all the sin and evil of men, whose evil ways prevent the truth from being known.

Romans 1:18 (GN)

Of this church I was made a minister according to the stewardship from God bestowed on me for your benefit, that I might fully carry out the preaching of the word of God, that is, the mystery which has been hidden from the past ages; but has now been manifested to His saints, to whom God willed to MAKE KNOWN what is the riches of the glory of this mystery among the Gentiles, which is Christ in you, the hope of glory.

Colossians 1:25 & 27 (NAS)

I press toward the goal for the prize of the upward call of God in Christ Jesus. Therefore let us, as many as are mature, have this mind; and if in anything you think otherwise, God will REVEAL even this to you.

Philippians 3:14 & 15 (NKJ)

> *It* passeth knowledge,
> That dear love of Thine,
> Lord Jesus, Saviour;
> Yet this soul of mine
> Would of Thy love
> In all its breath and length,
> Its height and depth,
> Its everlasting strength,
> KNOW more and more.
>
> *(by Mary Shekleton)*

Adore God for His willingness to REVEAL mysteries.

THE REVEALING GOD

*T*hen Daniel praised the God of heaven and said, "Praise be the name of God for ever and ever; wisdom and power are his. He changes times and seasons; he sets up kings and deposes them. He gives wisdom to the wise and KNOWLEDGE to the discerning. He REVEALS deep and hidden things; he KNOWS what lies in darkness, and light dwells with him. I thank and praise you, O God of my fathers:"

Daniel 2:20b-22 (NIV)

I entreat you, then I, Paul, who in the cause of you Gentiles am now a prisoner of Christ Jesus for surely you have heard how God has assigned the gift of his grace to me for your benefit. It was by a REVELATION that his secret was made known to me. I have already written a brief account of this, and by reading it may perceive that I understand the secret of Christ. In former generations this was not disclosed to the human race; but now it has been REVEALED by inspiration to his dedicated apostles and prophets, that through the Gospel the Gentiles are joint heirs with the Jews, part of the same body, sharers together in the promise made in Christ Jesus.

Ephesians 3:1-6 (NEB)

*W*hen my life work is ended and I cross the swelling tide,
When the bright and glorious morning I shall see:
I shall KNOW my Redeemer when I reach the other side,
And His smile will be the first to welcome me.

I shall KNOW him, I shall KNOW him,
When redeemed by His side I shall stand;
I shall KNOW Him, I shall KNOW Him,
by the print of the nails in His hand.

(by Fanny Crosby)

Adore God for the redeeming REVELATION.

GOD USES SIGNS TO REVEAL TRUTH

SIGN—That by which anything us shown, made known, or represented; that which furnishes evidence of the existence or approach of anything; a mark, a token; an indication. (Webster)

*A*nd God said, Let there be lights in the firmament of the heaven to divide the day from the night; and let them be for SIGNS, and for seasons, and for days, and years;

Genesis 1:14 (KJ)

*A*nd the angel said to them, "Have no fear, for observe, I announce to you the good news of great joy that shall be for all people; for today there was born for you in the city of David a Savior, who is Christ the Lord. And this shall be a TOKEN for you: you shall find the babe wrapped in swaddling clothes and lying in a manger."

Luke 2:10-12 (Berkeley)

*O*ne night Nicodemus, a leading Jew and a Pharisee, came to Jesus. "Master," he began, "we realize that you are a teacher who has come from God. Obviously no one could show the SIGNS that you show unless God were with him."

John 3:1 & 2 (Phillips)

> *B*reak Thou the bread of life, dear Lord, to me,
> As Thou didst break the loaves beside the sea.
> With-in the sacred page I seek Thee Lord;
> My spirit pants for Thee, O living Word!
>
> Open Thy word of truth, that I may SEE
> Thy message written clear and plain for me;
> Then in sweet fellowship walking with Thee,
> Thine image on my life engraved will be.
>
> *(by Mary A. Lathbury)*

Adore God for the SIGNS He has given in Scripture.

GOD USES SIGNS TO REVEAL TRUTH

SIGN synonym—Symbol, indication, token, mark, omen, presage, emblem, manifestation, symptom, note, index, signal, prognostic. (Webster)

Show me a SIGN of (Your evident) goodwill and favor, that those who hate me may see it and be put to shame because You, Lord, (will show Your approval of me when you) help and comfort me.

Psalm 86:17 (Amplified)

The officer pleaded with him, "Sir, come down before my boy dies." Then Jesus said, "Return home and your son will live." The man believed what Jesus said and started for home. When he was on his way down his servants met him with the news, "Your boy is going to live." So he asked them what time it was when he got better. They said, "Yesterday at one in the afternoon the fever left him," The father noted that this was the exact time when Jesus said to him, "Your son will live", and he and all his household became believers. This was now the second SIGN which Jesus performed after coming down from Judea into Galilee.

John 4:49-54 (NEB)

Many another SIGN did Jesus perform in presence of his disciples, which is not recorded in this book; but these SIGNS are recorded so that you may believe that Jesus is the Christ, the Son of God, and believing may have life through his Name.

John 20:30 & 31 (Moffatt)

O God of Light, Thy Word, a lamp unfailing,
Shines through the darkness of our earthly way,
O'er fear and doubt, o'er black despair prevailing,
Guiding our steps to Thine eternal day.

From days of old through swiftly rolling ages,
Thou hast REVEALED Thy will to mortal men,
Speaking to saints, to prophets, kings and sages,
Who wrote the message with immortal pen.

(by Sarah E. Taylor)

Adore God for using SIGNS to guide us.

GOD USES SIGNS TO REVEAL TRUTH

SIGN—the rendering of several Hebrew and Greek words, which usually denote a miraculous, or, at least, divine or extraordinary token of some (generally) future event. (Unger's)

"Therefore the Lord Himself will give you a SIGN: Behold the virgin shall conceive and bear a Son, and shall call His name Immanuel."

Isaiah 7:14 (NKJ)

And Simeon blessed them, and said to Mary His mother, "Behold, this Child is appointed for the fall and rise of many in Israel, and for a SIGN to be opposed and a sword will pierce even your own soul to the end that thoughts from many hearts may be REVEALED.

Luke 2:34 & 35 (NAS)

Now the Pharisees and Sadducees came to Jesus and they asked Him to show them a SIGN (spectacular miracle) from heaven attesting to His divine authority. He replied to them, When it is evening you say, it will be fair weather, for the sky is red. And in the morning, It will be stormy today, for the sky is red and has a gloomy and threatening look, You know how to interpret the appearance of the sky, but you cannot interpret the SIGNS of the times.

Matthew 16:1-3 (Amplified)

Undimmed by time, the Word is still REVEALING
To sinful men Thy justice and Thy grace;
And questing hearts that long for peace and healing
See Thy compassion in the Saviour's face.

To all the world the message Thou art sending,
To every land, to every race and clan,
And myriad tongues, in one great anthem blending,
Acclaim with joy Thy wondrous gift to man.

(by Sarah E. Taylor)

Adore God for the SIGN of a Saviour's coming and the SIGNS he wrought on earth.

September

GOD USES SIGNS TO REVEAL TRUTH

You will go out in joy and be led forth in peace; the mountains and hills will burst into song before you, and all the trees of the field will clap their hands. Instead of the thorn bush will grow a pine tree, and instead of briers the myrtle will grow. This will be for the Lord's renown, for an everlasting SIGN, which will not be destroyed.

Isaiah 55:12 & 13 (NIV)

I thought it good to show the SIGNS and wonders that the high God hath wrought toward me. How great are his SIGNS! and how mighty are his wonders! His kingdom is an everlasting kingdom, and his dominion is from generation to generation.

Daniel 4:2 & 3 (KJ)

And so the Lord Jesus, after he had spoken to them, was taken up into heaven: there at the right hand of God he took his place, while they, going out, preached everywhere, the Lord working with them and confirming the word by the SIGNS that accompanied it.

Mark 16:19 & 20 (TJB)

I will not venture to speak of anything but what Christ has wrought through me toward persuading Gentiles by word and deed, by the power of SIGNS and wonders, and all by the power of the Holy Spirit, so that out from Jerusalem and all around as far as Illyricum, I have in fullness preached the Gospel of Christ.

Romans 15:18 & 19 (Berkeley)

Father, we worship Thee,
Through Thy beloved Son;
And, by the Spirit, now draw near
Before Thy holy throne.

We bless Thee most of all
For Him Who Thee unveiled;
Whose precious blood redemption wrought,
And thus Thy heart REVEALED.

(by Alfred P. Gibbs)

Adore God for the REVELATION of His Son.

THE GOD WHO SPEAKS

SPEAK—To utter words or articulate sounds; to express thoughts by words. (Webster)

Then God SAID, Let there be light and there was light.
God CALLED the light Day, and the darkness He CALLED night.
Then God SAID, Let there be a firmament...let it divide the waters.
God CALLED the firmament Heaven.
Then God SAID.... let the dry land appear.
And God CALLED the dry land Earth.
Then God SAID (vegetation)
Then God SAID (light)
Then God SAID (animals)
Then God SAID (each thing was to produce after its own kind)
Then God SAID (let us make man)
Then God SAID (everything is good)

Genesis 1:3, 5-6, 8-11, 14, 20, 24, 26 & 29-31(NKJ)

God, after He SPOKE long ago to the fathers in the prophets in many portions and in many ways, in these last days has SPOKEN to us in His Son, whom He appointed heir of all things, through whom also He made the world.

Hebrews 1:1 & 2 (NAS)

> SPEAK, Lord, in the stillness,
> While I wait on Thee;
> Hushed my heart to listen
> In expectancy.
>
> SPEAK, O blessed Master,
> In this quiet hour,
> Let me see Thy face Lord,
> Feel Thy touch of power.
>
> *(by E. May Grimes)*

Adore God for what He has SPOKEN.

THE GOD WHO SPEAKS

SPEAK synonyms—Talk, discourse, utter, tell, say, converse (Webster)

The Eternal SPOKE to you face to face, out of the fire at the hill, while I stood between the Eternal and you, in order to report what the Eternal SAID for you were terrified at the fire and would not ascend the hill. He SAID: "I am the Eternal your God, who brought you from the land of Egypt, that slave-pen."

Deuteronomy 5:4-6 (Moffatt)

"*Therefore* My people shall know what my name is and what it means; therefore they shall know in that day that I am He Who SPEAKS; behold, I Am!"

Isaiah 52:6 (Amplified)

Whoever does accept His testimony definitely certifies that God is true; for He whom God has sent SPEAKS the words of God, who grants the Spirit in unlimited measure.

John 3:33 & 34 (Berkeley)

For the words Thou SPEAKEST,
"They are life" indeed;
Living Bread from heaven,
Now my spirit feed!

All to Thee is yielded,
I am not my own;
Blissful, glad surrender
I am Thine alone.

(by E. May Grimes)

Adore God for His willingness to SPEAK to us.

THE GOD WHO SPEAKS

The heavens declare the glory of God; and the firmament sheweth his handiwork.

Day unto day uttereth SPEECH, and night unto night sheweth knowledge. There is no speech or language where their voice is not heard.

Psalm 19:1-3 (KJ)

So I also choose harsh treatment for them and will bring upon them what they dread. For when I CALLED, no one answered, when I SPOKE, no one listened. They did evil in my sight and chose what displeases me.

Isaiah 66:4 (NIV)

The woman answered, "I know that Messiah" (that is Christ) "is coming. When he comes he will TELL us everything." Jesus SAID, "I am he, I who am SPEAKING to you now.

John 4:24 & 25 (NEB)

"If God were really your Father," REPLIED Jesus, "you would have loved me. For I came from God: and I am here. I did not come of my own accord—he sent me, and I am here. Why do you not understand my WORDS?

John 8:43 (Phillips)

SPEAK, Thy servant heareth!
Be not silent, Lord;
Waits my soul upon Thee
For the quickening WORD!

Fill me with the knowledge
Of Thy glorious will;
All Thine own good pleasure
In Thy child fulfill.

(by E. May Grimes)

Adore God for the many avenues He uses to SPEAK to you.

THE GOD WHO SPEAKS

God has SPOKEN once, twice I have heard this: it is for you God to be strong, for you, Lord, to be loving; and you yourself repay man as his works deserve.

Psalm 62:11 (TJB)

I publicly PROCLAIM bold promises; I do not whisper obscurities in some dark corner so that no one can know what I mean. And I don't TELL Israel to ask me for what I didn't plan to give! No, for I, Jehovah, SPEAK only truth and righteousness.

Isaiah 45:19 (Paraphrased)

For no prophecy ever originated because some man willed it (to do so) it never came by human impulse—but men SPOKE from God who were borne along (moved and impelled) by the Holy Spirit.

2 Peter 2:21 (Amplified)

Jesus got into the boat, and his disciples went with him. Suddenly a fierce storm hit the lake, so that the waves covered the boat. But Jesus was asleep. The disciples went to him and woke him up. "Save us, Lord!" they said. "We are about to die!" Why are you so frightened?" Jesus ANSWERED. "How little faith you have!" Then he got up and gave a COMMAND to the winds and to the waves, and there was a great calm.

Matthew 8:23-26 (GN)

Lord, SPEAK to me, that I may speak
In living echoes of Thy tone;
As Thou hast sought, so let me seek
Thy erring children lost and lone.

O fill me with Thy fullness, Lord,
Until my very heart over flows
In kindling thought and glowing word,
Thy love to TELL, Thy praise to show.

(by Frances R. Havergal)

Begin your prayer time with adoration to the God who SPEAKS to you.

GOD IS OUR STRENGTH

STRENGTH—The state, property, or quality of being strong; force; power; energy; vigor. (Webster)

I will love You, O Lord, my STRENGTH. The Lord is my rock and my DELIVERER;
my God, my STRENGTH, in whom I will trust; My shield and the horn of my salvation, my stronghold.

Psalm 18:1 & 2 (NKJ)

And Moses said to the people, Remember this day, in which ye came out from Egypt, out of the house of bondage; for by STRENGTH of hand the Lord brought you out from this place:

Exodus 13:3 (KJ)

And His mercy is to those who fear Him to generations and generations. He brought about STRENGTH with His arm.

Luke 1:50 & 51a (Wuest)

> *All* hail the POWER of Jesus name!
> Let angels prostrate fall;
> Bring forth the royal diadem,
> And crown Him Lord of all.
>
> Ye chosen seed of Israel's race,
> Ye ransomed from the fall,
> Hail Him who saves you by His grace,
> And crown Him Lord of all.
>
> *(by Edward Perronet)*

Adore God for His STRENGTH.

GOD IS OUR STRENGTH

STRENGTH synonyms—Force, power, robustness, toughness, lustiness, firmness, solidity, puissance, efficiency, energy, vehemence, potency, vigor.

The salvation of the righteous comes from the Lord; he is their STRONGHOLD in time of trouble.

Psalm 37:39 (NIV)

The Lord is my rock and my fortress and my deliverer; My God, my rock, in whom I take refuge; My shield and the horn of my salvation, my STRONGHOLD and my refuge; My Savior, Thou dost save me from violence.

2 Samuel 22:2 & 3 (NAS)

Thrice I invoked the Lord about this, to have it removed from me, and He told me, "my grace is sufficient for you, for My STRENGTH comes to perfection where there is weakness."

2 Corinthians 12:8 & 9 (Berkeley)

Would you be free from the burden of sin?
There's POWER in the blood,
Would you over evil a victory win?
There's wonderful POWER in the blood.

Would you be free from your passion and pride?
There's POWER in the blood,
Come for a cleansing to Calvary's tide;
There's wonderful POWER in the blood.

(by Lewis E. Jones)

Adore God for His STRENGTH over everything.

GOD IS OUR STRENGTH

My body and my mind may become weak, but God is my STRENGTH. He is mine forever.

Psalm 73:26 (NCV)

But true wisdom and POWER are God's. He alone knows what we should do; he understands.

Job 12:13 (Paraphrased)

I beg you, then, not to lose heart over my sufferings for you; indeed, they are your glory. With this in mind, then, I kneel in prayer to the Father, from whom every family in heaven and on earth takes its name, that out of the treasures of his glory he may grant you STRENGTH and POWER through his Spirit in your inner being, that through faith Christ may dwell in your hearts in love.

Ephesians 3:13-16 (NEB)

The first time I had to defend myself no one was on my side—they all deserted me, God forgave them. Yet the Lord himself stood by me and gave me the STRENGTH to proclaim the message clearly and fully, so that the gentiles could hear it, and I was rescued from "the lion's mouth."

2 Timothy 4:16 & 17 (Phillips)

> *Would* you be whiter, much whiter than snow?
> There's POWER in the blood;
> Sin stains are lost in its life-giving flow;
> There's wonderful POWER in the blood.
>
> Would you do service for Jesus your King?
> There's POWER in the blood;
> Would you live daily His praises to sing?
> There's wonderful POWER in the blood.

(by Lewis E. Jones)

Adore God for His STRENGTH and POWER.

GOD IS OUR STRENGTH

Yahweh, our Lord, how great your name throughout the earth! Above the heavens is your majesty chanted by the mouths of children, babes in arms, You set your STRONGHOLD firm against your foes to subdue enemies and rebels.

Psalm 8:1 & 2 (TJB)

The way of the Lord is STRENGTH to the upright: but destruction shall be to the workers of iniquity.

Proverbs 10:29 (KJ)

I have STRENGTH for all things in Christ Who EMPOWERS me—I am ready for anything and equal to anything through Him Who infuses inner STRENGTH into me, (that is, I am self-sufficient in Christ's sufficiency).

Philippians 4:13 (Amplified)

But after you have suffered for a little while, the God of all grace, who calls you to share his eternal glory in union with Christ, will himself perfect you, and give you firmness, STRENGTH, and a sure foundation.

1 Peter 5:10 (GN)

Eternal Father, STRONG to save,
Whose arm doth bind the restless wave,
Who bidest the mighty ocean deep
Its own appointed limits keep;
O hear us when we cry to Thee
For those in peril on the sea.

O Saviour, whose almighty word
The winds and waves submissive heard,
Who walkest on the foaming deep
And calm amid its rage didst sleep
O hear us when we cry to Thee
For those in peril on the sea.

(by William Whiting)

Adore God for the STRENGTH He gives.

GOD IS OUR STRENGTH

*V*indicate me, O God, and plead my cause against an ungodly nation; Oh deliver me from the deceitful and unjust man! For you are the God of my STRENGTH.

Psalm 43:1 & 2a (NKJ)

I will come in the POWER of Yahweh to commemorate your righteousness, yours alone.

Psalm 71:16 (TJB)

O Lord, You are my God; I will exalt You, I will praise your name; for You have done wonderful things, even purposes planned of old and fulfilled in faithfulness and truth... For You have been a STRONGHOLD to the poor, a STRONGHOLD to the needy in his distress, a shelter from the storm, a shade from the heat;

Isaiah 25:1 & 4a (Amplified)

O Lord, my STRENGTH and my STRONGHOLD, and my refuge in the day of distress.

Jeremiah 16:19a (NAS)

> *O* Trinity of love and POWER,
> Our brethren shield in danger's hour;
> From rock and tempest, fire, and foe,
> Protect them where-so-ever they go;
> And ever let there rise to Thee
> Glad hymns of praise from land and sea.
>
> *(by William Whiting)*

Adore God for being a STRONGHOLD in your life.

GOD IS OUR STRENGTH

*G*od is our shelter and STRONGHOLD for us, we shall find him very near.

Psalm 46:1 (Moffatt)

*W*hen I pray, you answer me, and encourage me by giving me the STRENGTH I need.

Psalm 138:3 (Paraphrased)

*T*hen I looked, and I heard the voices of many angels around the throne, and the four living creatures, and the elders. There were thousands and thousands of angels, saying in a loud voice: "The Lamb who was killed is worthy to receive POWER, wealth, wisdom, and STRENGTH, honor, glory, and praise!" Then I heard all creatures in heaven and on earth and under the earth and in the sea saying: "To the One who sits on the throne and to the Lamb be praise and honor and glory and POWER forever and ever." The four living creatures said, "Amen," and the elders bowed down and worshipped.

Revelation 5:11-14 (NCV)

*T*hen I heard a voice from heaven proclaiming aloud: 'This is the hour of victory for our God, the hour of his sovereignty and POWER, when his Christ comes to his rightful rule.

Revelation 12:10 (TEB)

> *G*uide us, O Thou great Jehovah,
> Pilgrims through this barren land;
> We are week, but Thou art mighty;
> Hold us by Thy POWERFUL hand;
> Bread of heaven feed us now and evermore.
>
> Open wide the living fountain,
> Whence the healing waters flow;
> Be Thyself our cloudy pillar
> All the dreary desert through;
> STRONG Deliverer, be
> Thou still our STRENGTH and shield.
>
> *(by William Williams)*

Praise and adore God for His STRENGTH.

THE GOD TO BE THANKED

🔲 THANK—To express gratitude to, as for a favor; to make acknowledgments to, as for kindness bestowed. (Webster)

*E*nter into His gates with THANKSGIVING, and with a THANK offering, and into His courts with praise! Be THANKFUL and say so to Him, bless and affectionately praise His name.

Psalm 100:4 (Amplified)

*A*s they were eating, Jesus took bread, blessed and broke it and gave it to the disciples, saying, Take, eat, this is my body. He also took the cup, and after giving THANKS, He gave it to them.

Matthew 26:26 & 27 (Berkeley)

*D*on't worry over anything whatever; tell God every detail of your needs in earnest and THANKFUL prayer, and the peace of God, which transcends human understanding, will keep constant guard over your hearts and minds as they rest in Christ Jesus.

Philippians 4:6 & 7 (Phillips)

*N*ow THANK we all our God
With heart and hands and voices,
Who wondrous things hath done,
In whom His world rejoices;

Who, from our mother's arms
Hath blessed us on our way
With countless gifts of love,
And still is ours today.

(by Martin Rinkart)

Give your adoring THANKS to God.

THE GOD TO BE THANKED

*W*hat I want from you is your true THANKS; I want your promises fulfilled. I want you to trust me in your times of trouble, so I can rescue you, and you can give me glory.

Psalm 40:14 & 15 (Amplified)

I THANK thee, and praise thee, O Thou God of my fathers, who hast given me wisdom and might, and hast made known unto me now what we desired of thee:

Daniel 2:23 (KJ)

*A*t that time Jesus spoke these words: 'I THANK thee, Father, Lord of heaven and earth, for hiding these things from the learned and wise, and revealing them to the simple.

Matthew 11:25 (NEB)

*F*irst, I am constantly THANKING my God through Jesus Christ concerning all of you because your faith is constantly being spread abroad in the whole world;

Romans 1:8 (Wuest)

*A*ll praise and THANKS to God
The Father now be given,
The Son, Who rose and lives,
And sits in highest heaven,

Our God eternal is
Whom earth and heaven adore;
Now we by grace are His
And shall be evermore.

(Author unknown)

Adore God through your THANKFULNESS.

THE GOD TO BE THANKED

*O*h come let us sing to the Eternal, let us sing loudly to our saving Strength, let us come before him with THANKSGIVING , shouting to Him songs of praise!

Psalm 95:1 & 2 (Moffatt)

*T*hen Jesus took the loaves of bread, THANKED God for them, and gave them to the people who were sitting there. He did the same with the fish, giving as much as the people wanted.

John 6:11 (NCV)

*O*ne person esteems one day above the another; another esteems every day alike. Let each be fully convinced in his own mind. He who observes the day, observes it to the Lord; and he who does not observe the day, to the Lord he does not observe it. He who eats, eats to the Lord, for he gives God THANKS; and he who does not eat, to the Lord he does not eat, and gives God THANKS.

Romans 14:5 & 6 (NKJ)

*N*ow THANKS be to God for His Gift, (precious) beyond telling—His indescribable, inexpressible, free Gift!

2 Corinthians 9:15 (Amplified)

*C*ome, ye THANKFUL people come
Raise the song of harvest home:
All is safely gathered in
Ere the winter storms begin.

God, our Maker, doth provide
For our wants to be supplied;
Come, ye THANKFUL people, come
Raise the song of harvest home

(by Henry Alford)

Adore God for in everything be THANKFUL.

❄ *277* ❄

THE GOD TO BE THANKED

*L*et them give THANKS to the Lord for His lovingkindness, and for His wonders to the sons of men. Let them also offer sacrifices of THANKSGIVING, and tell of His works with joyful singing.

Psalm 107:21 & 22 (NAS)

*G*ive THANKS to Yahweh, call his name aloud, proclaim his deeds to the peoples. Sing to him, play to him, tell over all his marvels. Glory in his holy name, let the hearts that seek Yahweh rejoice!

1 Chronicles 16:8-10 (TJB)

*B*e persistent in prayer, and keep alert as you pray, with THANKS to God.

Colossians 4:2 (Good News)

*A*nd the twenty-four elders, who were seated on their thrones before God, fell on their faces and worshipped God, saying: "We give THANKS to you, Lord God Almighty, who is and who was, because you have taken your great power and have begun to reign.

Revelation 11:16 & 17 (NIV)

*T*HANK you, Lord,
For saving my soul,
THANK you, Lord,
For making me whole

THANK you, Lord,
For giving to me
Thy great salvation
So rich and free.

(by Seth Sykes)

Adore God for the privilege of THANKING Him now and through eternity.

THE GOD WHO QUENCHES THIRST

THIRST—a want and eager desire after anything. (Webster)

*T*hus says the Lord who made you and formed you from the womb, who will help you: For "I will pour water on him who is THIRSTY, and floods on the dry ground; I will pour My Spirit on your descendants, and My blessings on your offspring;"

Isaiah 44:2a & 3 (NKJ)

*H*ow blest are those who hunger and THIRST to see right prevail; they shall be satisfied.

Matthew 5:6 (NEB)

*O*n the last day, the climax of the holiday, Jesus shouted to the crowds, "If anyone is THIRSTY, let him come to me and drink. For the Scriptures declare that rivers of living water shall flow from the inmost being of anyone who believes in me."

John 7:37 & 38 (Good News)

> *C*ome, ye THIRSTY, to the living waters,
> Hungry, come and on His bounty feed;
> Not thy fitness is the plea to bring Him,
> But thy pressing utmost need.
>
> Coming humbly, daily to this Saviour,
> Breathing all the heart to Him in prayer;
> Coming some day to the heavenly mansions,
> He will give thee welcome there.
>
> *(by Eliza E. Hewitt)*

Adore God for quenching your THIRST.

THE GOD WHO QUENCHES THIRST

As the hart pants and longs for the water brooks, so I pant and long for You, O God. My inner self THIRSTS for God, for the Living God. When shall I come and behold the face of God?

Psalm 42:1 & 2 (Amplified)

Ho, everyone that THIRSTETH, come ye to the waters, and he that hath no money, come ye, buy, and eat; yea come buy wine and milk without money and without price.

Isaiah 55:1 (KJ)

For this reason they are before God's throne, and night and day they serve Him in His temple, while He, who sits on the throne, spreads His tent over them. They shall nevermore either hunger or THIRST, nor shall the sun or any heat whatever beat upon them; for the Lamb, who has ascended the center of the throne, shall shepherd them and shall lead them to the springs of living water. And God shall wipe away all tears from their eyes.

Revelation 7:15-17 (Berkeley)

Then he said to me, It is done! I am the Alpha and Omega the beginning and the end. I will give the THIRSTY water without price from the fountain of life. The victorious shall inherit these things, and I will be God to him and he will be son to me.

Revelation 21:5-7 (Phillips)

Come, Thou FOUNT of every blessing,
Tune my heart to sing Thy grace;
Streams of mercy never ceasing,
Call for songs of loudest praise.

Teach me, Lord, some rapturous measure,
Meet for blood-bought hosts above;
While I sing the countless treasure
Of my God's unchanging love.

(by Robert Robinson)

Adore the Fount who quenches your deepest THIRST.

GOD'S THRONE

⊞ THRONE—1. A seat occupied by one having power or authority. 2. A place identified with power or grandeur, or made especially subject to respect or reverence by association; a shrine. 3. Sovereign power and dignity; also, the wielder of that power. (Webster)

In heaven has the Eternal fixed his THRONE, and his dominion covers all the world.

Psalm 193:19 (Moffatt)

*M*icaiah continued, "Therefore hear the word of the Lord: I saw the Lord sitting on his THRONE with all the host of heaven standing around him on his right and on his left."

1 Kings 22:19 (NIV)

And behold: you shall conceive in your womb and shall give birth to a son, and you shall call His name Jesus. This one shall be great, and Son of the Most High shall He be called, and God, the Lord, shall give Him the THRONE of David His father, and He shall reign as King over the house of Jacob forever and of His kingdom there shall not be an end.

Luke 1:31-33 (Wuest)

> *G*reat are the offices He bears,
> And soon the happy day shall come
> And bright His character appears,
> When we shall reach our destined home,
> Exalted on the THRONE;
> And see Him face to face;
> In song of sweet untiring praise,
> Then with our Saviour, Master, Friend,
> We would, to everlasting days,
> The glad eternity we'll spend,
> Make all His glories known
> And celebrate His grace.
>
> *(by Samuel Medley)*

Adore God on His THRONE.

GOD'S THRONE

THRONE—Jehovah's THRONE is described as "high and lifted up."
(Unger's)

*I*n the year of King Uzziah's death, I saw the Lord sitting on a THRONE,
lofty and exalted, with the train of His robe filling the temple.

Isaiah 6:1 (NAS)

*S*ee, Yahweh is ENTHRONED for ever, he sets up his THRONE for judgment;
he is going to judge the world with justice, and pronounce a true verdict on
the nations.

Psalm 9:7 & 8 (NJB)

*B*ut now I tell you: do not use any vow when you make a promise; do not
swear by heaven, because it is God's THRONE; nor by earth, because it is
the resting place for his feet; nor by Jerusalem, because it is the city of the
great king.

Matthew 5:34 (GN)

*T*hy name is holy, O our God!
Before Thy THRONE we bow;
Thy bosom is Thy saints abode,
We call Thee Father now!

ENTHRONED with Thee, now sits the Lord,
And in Thy bosom dwells
Justice, that smote Him with the sword,
Our perfect pardon seals.

(by Robert C. Chapman)

Adore our God on a lofty THRONE, who stooped to die for you.

September 20

GOD'S THRONE

*H*eaven is my THRONE and the earth is my footstool: what temple can you build for me as good as that?

Isaiah 66:1 (TLB)

I watched till THRONES were put in place, And the Ancient of Days was seated: His garment was white as snow, And the hair of His head was like pure wool. His THRONE was a fiery flame, Its wheels a burning fire.

Daniel 7:9 (NKJ)

*A*t that time they shall call Jerusalem the THRONE of the Lord: and all the nations shall be gathered into it, to the name of the Lord, to Jerusalem; neither shall they walk any more after the imagination of their evil heart.

Jeremiah 3:17 (KJ)

"*T*hy THRONE, O God, is for ever and ever, And the sceptre of justice is the sceptre of his kingdom. Thou hast loved right and hated wrong; Therefore, O God, (the Son) thy God (the Father) has set thee above thy fellows, by anointing with the oil of exultation.

Hebrews 1:8 & 9 (NEB)

*B*ehold the glories of the Lamb
Amidst the Father's THRONE!
Prepare new honors for His name,
And songs before unknown!

To Thee, O Lamb, To Thee, once slain,
Be endless blessings paid!
Salvation, glory, joy, remain
Forever on Thy head!

(by Isaac Watts)

Adore God on His THRONE.

THE GOD OF TIME

TIME—The general idea of successive existence; the measure of duration. Time is absolute or relative; absolute time is considered without any relation to bodies and their motion. Relative time is the sensible measure of any portion of duration, often marked by particular phenomena, as the apparent movement of celestial bodies. (Webster)

There is a TIME for everything, and a season for every activity under heaven:
a TIME to be born, and a TIME to die.
a TIME to plant and a TIME to uproot,
a TIME to kill and a TIME to heal,
a TIME to tear down and a TIME to build,
a TIME to weep and a TIME to laugh,
a TIME to mourn and a TIME to dance,
a TIME to scatter stones and a TIME to gather them,
a TIME to embrace and a TIME to refrain,
a TIME to search and a TIME to give up,
a TIME to keep and a TIME to throw away,
a TIME to tear and a TIME to mend,
a TIME to be silent and a TIME to speak,
a TIME to love and a TIME to hate,
a TIME for war and a TIME for peace.

Ecclesiastics 3:1-8 (NIV)

In TIMES like these you need a Saviour,
In TIMES like these you need an anchor;
Be very sure, be very sure,
Your anchor holds and grips the Solid Rock!

This Rock is Jesus, Yes, He's the One,
This Rock is Jesus,—The only one;
Be very sure, be very sure
Your anchor holds and grips the Solid Rock!

(by Ruth Caye Jones)

Adore God for the TIMES and seasons He has given us.

THE GOD OF TIME

TIME—the rendering of several Hebrew and Greek terms (Unger's) 1. Yam, Hebrew—used both in the particular sense of a natural day, and in the sense of a set TIME or particular TIME. 2. Zeman, Hebrew—an appointed TIME 3. Mo'ed, Hebrew—a set TIME 4. Mahar, Hebrew—a set TIME.

*F*or in the TIME of trouble he shall hide me in his pavilion: in the secret of his tabernacle shall he hide me; he shall set me upon a rock.

Psalm 27:5 (KJ)

I will ratify my compact with Isaac, whom Sarah will bear to you when the TIME comes round next year.

Genesis 17:21 (Moffatt)

*I*n the past God spoke to our ancestors through the prophets many TIMES and in many different ways. But now in these last days God has spoken to us through his Son. God has chosen his Son to own all things, and through him he made the world.

Hebrews 1:1 & 2 (NCV)

*I*n TIMES like these you need the Bible,
In TIMES like these, oh, be not idle;
Be very sure, be very sure,
Your anchor holds and grips the Solid Rock!

In TIMES like these I have a Saviour,
In TIMES like these, I have an anchor;
I'm very sure, I'm very sure
My anchor holds and grips the Solid Rock.

(by Ruth Caye Jones)

Adore God for His care through all TIME.

THE GOD OF TIME

TIME—set out in biblical times by sunrise and sunset, as it is today among the Bedouin people of Arabia. (Today's)

My TIMES are in Your hand; deliver me from the hand of my foes and those who pursue me and persecute me.

Psalm 31:15 (Amplified)

And the Lord set a definite TIME, saying, "Tomorrow the Lord will do this thing in the land."

Exodus 9:5 (NAS)

So, when they were all together, they asked him, "Lord, is this the TIME you are to establish once again the sovereignty of Israel?" He answered, "It is not for you to know about dates or TIMES, which the Father has set within his own control."

Acts 1:6 & 7 (NAS)

Take TIME to be holy,
Speak oft with thy Lord;
Abide in Him always,
And feed on His word.

Make friends of God's children;
Help those who are weak;
Forgetting in nothing,
His blessing to seek.

(by William D. Longstaff)

Adore God for His control of TIME.

THE GOD OF TIME

TIME—Beside the ordinary uses of this word, the Bible some times employs it to denote a year, or a prophetic year, consisting 390 natural years. (Smith's)

*P*raise the Lord! Praise, O servants of the Lord, Praise the name of the Lord! Blessed be the name of the Lord from this TIME forth and forevermore!

Psalm 113:1 & 2 (NKJ)

*Y*ahweh, have pity on us, we hope in you. Be our strong arm each morning, our Salvation, in TIME of distress.

Isaiah 33:3 (NJB)

*K*now this, though, that in the last days there are troublesome TIMES pending.

2 Timothy 3:1 (Berkeley)

*T*ake TIME to be holy,
The world rushes on;
Spend much TIME in secret
With Jesus alone,

by looking to Jesus,
Like Him thou shalt be;
Thy friends in thy conduct
His likeness shall see.

(by William D. Longstaff)

Adore God in His provision of TIME.

THE GOD OF TIME

Plant the good seed of righteousness and you will reap a heart of love: Plow the hard ground of your hearts, for now is the TIME to seek the Lord, that He may come and shower salvation upon you.

Hosea 10:12 (LB)

The Lord is a refuge for the oppressed, a stronghold in TIMES of trouble

Psalm 9:9 (NIV)

On the first day of unleavened bread the disciples came to Jesus with the question, "Where do you want us to make the preparations for you to eat the Passover?" "Go into the city," Jesus replied, "to a certain man there and say to him, 'the Master says,' My TIME is near, I am going to keep the Passover with my disciples at your house.

Matthew 26:1 & 2 (Phillips)

When you see the armies all around Jerusalem, you will know it will soon be destroyed. At that TIME, the people in Judea should run away to the mountains. The people in Jerusalem must get out and those who are near the city should not go in. These are the days of punishment to bring about all that is written in Scripture.

Luke 21:20-22 (NCV)

Take TIME to be holy,
Let Him be thy guide,
And run not before Him,
What ever betide;

In joy or in sorrow,
Still follow Thy Lord,
And looking to Jesus,
Still trust in His word.

(by William D. Longstaff)

Adore God, because all of His predictions of TIME will come true.

THE GOD OF TIME

In God is my salvation and my glory: the rock of my strength, and my refuge is in God. Trust in Him at all TIMES; ye people, pour out your heart before him: God is a refuge for us. Selah.

Psalm 62:7 & 8 (KJ)

Remember the former things which I did of old; for I am God, and there is none else; I am God, and there is none like Me. Declaring the end and the result from the beginning and from ancient TIMES the things that are not yet done, saying, My counsel shall stand, and I will do all My pleasure and purpose.

Isaiah 46:9 & 10 (Amplified)

Yes, it is eternal life that God, who cannot lie, promised ages ago, and now in his own good TIME he has openly declared himself in the proclamation which was entrusted to me by ordinance of God our Saviour.

Titus 1:2 & 3 (NEB)

Happy is the one who reads this book, and happy are those who listen to the words of this prophetic message and obey what is written in this book! For the TIME is near when all this will happen.

Revelation 1:3 (GN)

Take TIME to be holy,
Be calm in thy soul;
Each thought and each motive
Beneath His control;

Thus led by His Spirit
To fountains of love,
Thou soon shall be fitted
For service above.

(by William D. Longstaff)

Adore God for His TIME plan.

THE GOD WHO UNDERSTANDS

UNDERSTAND—literally, to stand under or among, hence, to understand. (Webster)

*W*ith Him are wisdom and might; to Him belong counsel and UNDERSTANDING.

Job 12:13 (NAS)

*H*ear this, all you peoples; Give ear, all you inhabitants of the world, Both low and high, Rich and poor together. My mouth shall speak wisdom, And the meditation of my heart shall bring UNDERSTANDING.

Psalm 49:1-3 (NKJ)

*A*nd we (have seen and) know positively that the Son of God has (actually) come to this world and has given us UNDERSTANDING and insight progressively to perceive (recognize) and come to know better and more clearly Him who is true; and we are in Him Who is true, in His Son Jesus Christ, the Messiah. He is the true God and Life eternal.

1 John 5:20 (Amplified)

*G*od UNDERSTANDS your sorrow,
He sees the falling tear,
And whispers, "I am with thee,"
Then falter not nor fear.

He UNDERSTANDS your longing,
Your deepest grief He shares;
Then let Him bear your burden,
He UNDERSTANDS and cares.

(by Oswald J. Smith)

Adore God for His UNDERSTANDING.

THE GOD WHO UNDERSTANDS

UNDERSTAND—To apprehend or comprehend fully; to know or apprehend the meaning, import, intention, or meaning of. (Webster)

The Royal Line of David will be cut off, chopped down like a tree; but from the stump will grow a Shoot—yes, a new Branch from the old root. And the Spirit of the Lord shall rest on him, the Spirit of wisdom, UNDERSTANDING, counsel and might; the Spirit of knowledge and fear of the Lord.

Isaiah 11:1 & 2 (TLB)

Wisdom begins with respect for the Lord, and UNDERSTANDING begins with knowing the Holy One.

Proverbs 9:10 (NCV)

We are asking God that you may see all things, as it were, from his point of view by being given spiritual insight and UNDERSTANDING.

Colossians 1:9 (Phillips)

God UNDERSTANDS your heartache,
He knows the bitter pain;
O, trust Him in the darkness,
You cannot trust in vein.

God UNDERSTANDS your weakness,
He knows the tempter's power;
And He will walk beside you
However dark the hour.

(by Oswald Smith)

Adore God for the UNDERSTANDING He gives us.

THE GOD WHO UNDERSTANDS

*G*reat is our Lord and mighty in power; his UNDERSTANDING has no limit.

Psalm 147:5 (NIV)

*H*e hath made the earth by his power, he hath established the world by his wisdom, and hath stretched out the heaven by his UNDERSTANDING.

Jeremiah 51:15 (KJ)

*H*e then spoke to them, These are my teachings, which I spoke to you while I was still with you, that everything written in the law of Moses and in the Prophets and Psalms about Me must come true. He then opened their minds to UNDERSTAND the Scriptures.

Luke 24:44 & 45 (Berkeley)

*T*hink about what I am saying, because the Lord will give you the ability to UNDERSTAND everything.

2 Timothy 2:7 (NCV)

*N*o one UNDERSTANDS like Jesus,
He's a friend beyond compare,
Meet Him at the throne of mercy,
He is waiting for you there.

No one UNDERSTANDS like Jesus,
When the days are dark and grim;
No one is so near, so dear as Jesus,
Cast your every care on Him.

(by John Peterson)

Adore God for His ability to UNDERSTAND human beings.

THE GOD WHO UNDERSTANDS

*F*rom Thy precepts I get UNDERSTANDING; therefore I hate every false way.

Psalm 119:104 (NAS)

*A*s for these four youths, God gave them knowledge and skill in all learning and wisdom; and Daniel had UNDERSTANDING in all visions and dreams.

Daniel 1:17 (Amplified)

"*B*ut the seed that fell into good soil is the man who hears the word and UNDERSTANDS it, who accordingly bears fruit, and yields a hundredfold, or, it may be, sixtyfold or thirtyfold."

Matthew 13:23 (NEB)

*Y*es, I want you to know that I do have to struggle for you, and for those in Laodicea, and for so many others who have never seen me face to face. It is all to bind you together in love and stir your minds, so that your UNDERSTANDING may come to full development, until you really know God's secret in which all the jewels of wisdom and knowledge are hidden.

Colossians 2:1 & 2 (NJB)

*N*o one UNDERSTANDS like Jesus,
Every woe He sees and fields;
Tenderly He whispers comfort,
And the broken heart He heals.

No one UNDERSTANDS like Jesus,
When the foes of life assail;
You should never be discouraged,
Jesus cares and will not fail.

(by John Peterson.)

Adore God for His unfailing UNDERSTANDING.

October

THE GOD WHO UNDERSTANDS

*G*reat is our Lord, and abundant in strength: His UNDERSTANDING is infinite.

Psalm 147:5 (KJ)

*T*he Lord says: Let not the wise man bask in his wisdom, nor the mighty man in his might, nor the rich man in his riches. Let them boast in this alone: That they truly know me, and UNDERSTAND that I am the Lord of justice and of righteousness whose love is steadfast; and that I love to be this way.

Jeremiah 9:23 & 24 (TLB)

I will pray with my spirit—by the Holy Spirit that is within me; but I will also pray intelligently with my mind and UNDERSTANDING; I will sing with my spirit by the Holy Spirit that is within me; but I will sing (intelligently) with my mind and UNDERSTANDING also.

1 Corinthians 15:15 (Amplified)

*H*ere is wisdom. He who has UNDERSTANDING, let him calculate at once the number of the Wild Beast, for the number is that of man. And his number is six hundred sixty six.

Revelation 13:18 (Wuest)

*N*o one UNDERSTANDS like Jesus
When you falter on the way;
Though you fail him, sadly fail Him,
He will pardon you today.

No one UNDERSTANDS like Jesus,
When the days are dark and grim;
No one is so near, so dear as Jesus.
Cast your every care on Him.

(by John Peterson)

Adore God because He is complete UNDERSTANDING, and adore Him for the UNDERSTANDING He imparts to us.

THE GOD WHO IS UPRIGHT

UPRIGHT—Conformable to moral rectitude; honest, just, adhering to rectitude in all social intercourse; as, an upright man; upright conduct. (Webster)

I proclaim the name of Yahweh, Oh, tell the greatness of our God! 'He is the Rock, his work is perfect, for all his ways are EQUITY. A God faithful, without unfairness, UPRIGHTNESS itself and Justice.'

Deuteronomy 32:3 & 4 (TJB)

*G*ood and UPRIGHT is the Lord; Therefore He teaches sinners in the way.

Psalm 25:8 (NKJ)

*H*ere is all I have been able to discover: God made the race of men UPRIGHT, but many a cunning wile have they contrived.

Ecclesiastics 7:29 (Moffatt)

*J*esus, Thy blood and UPRIGHTNESS
My beauty are, my glorious dress;
Midst flaming worlds, in these arrayed,
With joy shall I lift up my head.

Lord, I believe were sinners more
Than sands upon the ocean shore,
Thou hast for all a ransom paid,
For all a full atonement made.

(by Nicolaus L. von Zinzendorf)

Adore God, because He is UPRIGHT.

THE GOD WHO IS UPRIGHT

 UPRIGHT synonyms—honest, honorable, pure, principled, conscientious, just, fair, equitable. (Webster)

The way of the (consistently) righteous—those living in religious and moral rectitude in every area and relationship of their lives is level and straight; You O Lord, Who are UPRIGHT direct and level the path of the (uncompromisingly) just and righteous.

Isaiah 26:7 (Amplified)

Teach me to do thy will; for thou art my God: thy spirit is good; lead me into the land of UPRIGHTNESS.

Psalm 143:10 (KJ)

In conclusion, my brothers, fill your minds with those things which are good and deserve praise; things that are true, noble, right, PURE, lovely, and HONORABLE,

Philippians 4:8 (GN)

Holy, Holy, Holy! Lord God Almighty!
Early in the morning our song shall rise to Thee;
Holy, Holy, Holy! Merciful and mighty!
God in Three Persons, blessed Trinity.

Holy, Holy, Holy! Though the darkness hide Thee,
Though the eye of sinful man Thy glory may not see,
Only Thou art Holy; there is none beside Thee
Perfect in power, in love, and PURITY.

(by Reginald Heber)

Adore God because He is UPRIGHT.

THE GOD WHO IS UPRIGHT

*G*od is a JUST judge, And God is angry with the wicked every day.

Psalm 7:11

I will extol the Lord with all my heart in the council of the UPRIGHT and in the assembly. Great are the works of the Lord; they are pondered by all who delight in them.

Psalm 111:1 & 2 (NIV)

*B*ut the wisdom that comes from God is first of all PURE, then peaceful, gentle, and easy to please. This wisdom is always ready to help those who are troubled and to do good for others. It is always FAIR and HONEST.

James 7:17 (NCV)

*B*ehold what manner of love the Father has bestowed on us, that we should be called children of God! Therefore the world does not know us, because it did not know Him.
Beloved, now are we children of God; and it has not yet been revealed what we shall be, but we know that when He is revealed, we shall be like Him, for we shall see Him as He is. And everyone who has this hope in Him PURIFIES himself, just as He is PURE.

1 John 3:2 & 3 (NKJ)

> *F*ather, we worship Thee,
> Through Thy beloved Son;
> And by the Spirit now draw near
> Before Thy holy throne.
>
> We bless Thee Thou art Light,
> UPRIGHT and true art Thou;
> Holy and reverend Thy name,
> Our hearts before Thee bow.
>
> *(by Alfred P. Gibbs)*

Adore God for His UPRIGHTNESS.

GOD OUR VISION

⊞ VISION—Hebrew, hazah, to perceive, Greek harao, to see, a supernatural presentation of certain scenery or circumstances to the mind of a person while awake. (Unger's)

*A*fterwards Jehovah spoke to Abraham in a VISION, and this is what he told him, "Don't be fearful, Abram, for I will defend you. And I will give you great blessings.

Genesis 15:1 (TLB)

*T*his is the message of a man who hears the word of God. I see a VISION from the Almighty, and my eyes are open as I fall before him.

Numbers 24:4 (NCV)

*A*nd a VISION appeared to Paul during the night. A certain man, a Macedonian, was standing and begging him and saying. Come over into Macedonia at once and give us aid. And when he had seen the VISION, immediately we endeavored to go forth into Macedonia, concluding that God had called us to tell them the good news.

Acts 16:9 & 10 (Wuest)

I've SEEN the face of Jesus
He smiled in love on me;
It filled my heart with rapture,
My soul with ecstasy.

The scars of deepest anguish
Were lost in glory bright;
I've SEEN the face of Jesus,
It was a wondrous sight.

(by W. Spencer Walton)

Adore God because He shares Himself through VISIONS.

📄

GOD OUR VISION

VISION—a supernatural, prophetic or imaginary appearance; something seen in a dream, ecstasy, trance, or the like. (Webster)

And afterward I will pour out My Spirit upon all flesh, and your sons and your daughters shall prophesy, your old men shall dream dreams, your young men shall see VISIONS.

Joel 2:28 (Amplified)

Once Thou didst speak in VISION to Thy Godly ones, And didst say, "I have given help to one who is mighty; I have exalted one chosen from the people."

Psalm 89:19 (NAS)

Now there was in Damascus a disciple by the name of Ananias, to whom the Lord said in a VISION, Ananias! He said "Here am I Lord!"

Acts 9:10 (Berkeley)

Be Thou my VISION,
O Lord of my heart
Naught be all else to me,
Save that Thou art;

Thou my best thought,
by day or by night
Waking or sleeping,
Thy presence my light.

(8th Century Irish hymn)

Adore God for touching us through VISIONS.

GOD OUR VISION

VISION—a vivid apparition, not a dream. (Today's)

*G*od speaks first in one way, and then in another, but no one notices. He speaks by dreams, and VISIONS that come in the night.

Job 33:14 & 15a (TJB)

*I*n a VISION by night the mystery was revealed to Daniel. And Daniel blessed the God of Heaven.

Daniel 2:19 (Moffatt)

*P*eter began by laying before them the facts as they had happened. "I was in the city of Joppa', he said, 'at prayer; and while in a trance I had a VISION: a thing was coming down that looked like a great sheet of sail-cloth, slung by the four corners, and lowered from the sky till it reached me. I looked intently to make out what was in it and I saw four-footed creatures of the earth, wild beasts, and things that crawl or fly. Then I heard a voice saying to me, "Up' Peter, kill and eat." But I said, "No, Lord, no: nothing unclean has ever entered my mouth. A voice from heaven answered a second time, "It is not for you to call profane what God counts clean."

Acts 11:4-10 (NEB)

Since I've SEEN His beauty
All else I count but loss,
The world, its fame and pleasure,
Is now to me but dross.

His light dispelled my darkness,
His smile was, oh so sweet!
I've SEEN the face of Jesus,
I can but kiss his feet.

(by W. Spencer Walton)

Adore God for speaking through VISIONS.

GOD OUR VISION

$\mathcal{I}$ will stand upon my watch, and set me upon the tower, and will watch to see what he will say unto me, and what I will answer when I am reproved. And the Lord answered me, and said, Write the VISION, and make it plain upon tables, that he may run that readeth it.

Habakkuk 2:1 & 2 (KJ)

$\mathcal{W}$here there is no VISION, the people are unrestrained. But happy is he who keeps the law.

Proverbs 29:18 (NAS)

$\mathcal{A}$nd moreover, some women of our company astounded us. They were at the tomb early (in the morning), But they did not find His body; and they returned saying that they had (even) seen a VISION of angels who said that He was alive.

Luke 24:22 & 23 (Amplified)

$\mathcal{I}$ was told the number of mounted troops; it was two hundred million. And in my VISION I saw the horses and riders: they had breastplates red as fire, blue as sapphire, and yellow as sulfur.

Revelation 9:16 & 17 (GN)

$\mathcal{U}$pon that cross of Jesus
Mine eyes at times can SEE
The very dying form of One
Who suffered there for me;

And from my smitten heart with tears
Two wonders I confess
The wonders of redeeming love
And my unworthiness.

(by Elizabeth C. Clephane)

Adore God for the VISION he has given of Himself through Scripture.

THE VOICE OF GOD

VOICE—To give utterance to; to announce; to rumor; to report. (Webster)

*T*hen the Lord called to Adam and said to him, "Where are you?" So he said, "I heard your VOICE in the garden, and I was afraid because I was naked: and I hid myself.

Genesis 3:9 & 10 (NKJ)

*N*ations tremble and kingdoms shake. God SHOUTS and the earth crumbles. The Lord All-Powerful is with us; the God of Jacob is our defender.

Psalm 46:6 & 7 (NCV)

*N*ow when all the people had been baptized, and when Jesus had been baptized and was praying, heaven opened and the Holy Spirit descended in bodily form like a dove upon him: then came a VOICE from heaven, "Thou art my son, the Beloved, today have I become thy father."

Luke 3:21 & 22 (Moffatt)

> *I* heard the VOICE of Jesus say,
> "Come unto me and rest;
> Lay down, thou weary one,
> Lay down thy head upon my breast."
>
> I came to Jesus as I was,
> Weary, and worn, and sad;
> I found in Him a resting place,
> And He has made me glad.
>
> *(by Horatius Bonar)*

Adore the powerful speaking VOICE of God.

THE VOICE OF GOD

Sing praises to Him Who rides upon the heavens; lo, He sends forth His VOICE, His mighty VOICE.

Psalm 68:33 (Amplified)

"Go out and stand before me on the mountain," the Lord told him. And as Elijah stood there the Lord passed by, and a mighty windstorm hit the mountain; it was such a terrible blast that the rocks were torn loose, but the Lord was not in the wind. After the wind, there was an earthquake, but the Lord was not in the earthquake. And after the earthquake, there was a fire, but the Lord was not in the fire. And after the fire, there was the sound of a gentle WHISPER. When Elijah heart it, he wrapped his face in a scarf and went out and stood at the entrance of the cave. And a VOICE said, "Why are you here Elijah?"

1 Kings 19:11-13 (TLB)

Wherefore, as the Holy Spirit says: Today, if His VOICE you will hear, do not go on hardening your hearts as in the rebellion.

Hebrews 3:7 & 8 (Wuest)

I heard the VOICE of Jesus say,
"Behold, I freely give
The living water; thirsty one,
Stoop down, and drink, and live."

I came to Jesus, and I drank
Of that life-giving stream;
My thirst was quenched, my soul revived,
And now I live in Him.

(by Horatius Bonar)

Adore God because His VOICE speaks to you.

THE VOICE OF GOD

*H*as your arm the strength of God's, can your VOICE thunder as loud?

Job 40:9 (NJB)

*H*ear the word of the Lord, you who tremble at His word: "Your brothers who hate you, who exclude you for my name's sake have said, 'Let the Lord be glorified, that we may see your joy.' But they will be put to shame. A VOICE of uproar from the city, a VOICE from the temple, the VOICE of the Lord who is rendering recompense to His enemies.

Isaiah 66:5 & 6 (NAS)

*T*he man who goes in by the door is the shepherd of the sheep. The gatekeeper opens the gate for him; the sheep hear his VOICE as he calls his own sheep by name, and he leads them out. When he has brought them out, he goes ahead of them, and the sheep follow him, because they know his VOICE.

John 10:2-4 (GN)

'*N*ow my soul is in turmoil, and what am I to say? Father, save me from this hour. No, it was for this that I came to this hour. Father, glorify thy name. 'A VOICE sounded from heaven: 'I have glorified it, and I will glorify it again.' The crowd standing by said it was thunder, while others said, 'An angel has spoken to him.' Jesus replied, This VOICE spoke for your sake, not mine.

John 12:27-29 (NEB)

> *I* heard the VOICE of Jesus say,
> "I am this dark world's Light;
> Look unto Me, thy morn shall rise,
> And all thy day be bright."
>
> I looked to Jesus, and I found
> In Him my star, my sun;
> And in that Light of life I'll walk,
> Till traveling days are done.
>
> *(by Horatius Bonar)*

Adore God for the power in His VOICE.

THE VOICE OF GOD

The VOICE of the Lord is upon the waters: the God of glory THUNDERETH: the Lord is upon many waters. The VOICE of the Lord is powerful; the VOICE of the Lord is full of majesty.

Psalm 29:3 & 4 (KJ)

As the king was walking on the roof of the royal palace of Babylon, he said, "Is not this the great Babylon I have built as a royal residence, by my mighty power and for the glory of my majesty?" The words were still on his lips when a VOICE came from heaven, "This is what is decreed for you, King Nebuchadnezzar: Your royal authority has been taken from you."

Daniel 4:29-31 (NIV)

It was forty years later in the desert of mount Sinai that an angel appeared to him in the flames of a burning bush, and the sight filled Moses with wonder. As he approached to look at it more closely the VOICE of the Lord spoke to him, saying, I am the God of thy fathers, the God of Abraham, and the God of Isaac, and the God of Jacob. Then Moses trembled and was afraid to look any more.

Acts 7:30-32 (Phillips)

Behold, I stand at the door and knock; if anyone hears and listens and heeds My VOICE and opens the door, I will come into him and will eat with him, and he (shall eat) with Me.

Revelation 3:20 (Amplified)

Jesus CALLS us; o'er the tumult
Of our life's wild, restless sea,
Day by day His sweet VOICE soundeth,
SAYING "Christian, follow me."

Jesus CALLS us from the worship
Of the vain world's golden store,
From each idol that would keep us,
SAYING, "Christian, love me more."

(by Cecil F. Alexander)

Adore God for the sweetness of His VOICE.

THE VOICE OF GOD

*C*ome, let us worship and bow down, kneeling to him who made us; the Eternal is our God, and we the people whom he shepherds. If you would only listen to my VOICE today.

Psalm 95:6 & 7 (Moffatt)

*N*ow Zerubbabel son of Shealtiel, Joshua son of Jehozadak, the high priest, and all the remnant of the people, paid attention to the VOICE of Yahweh their God and to the words of the prophet Haggai, Yahweh having sent him to them.

Haggai 1:12 (TJB)

"*T*oday, if you hear His VOICE, do not harden your hearts.

Hebrews 4:7b (Berkeley)

*T*hen a VOICE came from the throne, saying: "Praise our God, all you who serve him, both small and great!"

Revelation 19:5 (NCV)

O Master, when thou CALLEST,
No voice may say Thee nay,
For blest are they that follow
Where Thou doest lead the way.

In freshest prime of morning,
Or fullest glow of noon,
The note of heavenly warning,
Can never come too soon.

(by Sarah G. Stock)

Adore God for His majestic VOICE.

THE VOICE OF GOD

As the trumpet blast blew louder and louder, Moses spoke and God THUNDERED his reply.

Exodus 19:19 (TLB)

Sing unto God, ye kingdoms of the earth; O sing praises unto the Lord; To him that rideth upon the heaven of heavens, which were of old; lo, he doth send out his VOICE, and that a mighty VOICE.

Psalm 68:32 & 33 (KJ)

After baptism Jesus came up out of the water at once, and at that moment heaven opened; he saw the Spirit of God descending like a dove to alight upon him; and a VOICE from heaven was heard saying, "This is my Son, my Beloved, on whom my favor rests.

Matthew 3:16 & 17 (TEB)

And I heard a loud VOICE from the throne, saying, "Now God's presence is with people, and he will live with them, and they will be his people. God himself will be with them and will be their God."

Revelation 21:3 (NCV)

> *I* HEAR THE WORDS of love,
> I gaze upon the blood,
> I see the mighty sacrifice,
> And I have peace with God.
>
> I know He liveth now
> At God's right hand above;
> I know the throne on which He sits,
> I know His truth and love!
>
> *(by Horatius Bonar)*

Adore God for the powerful love in His VOICE.

THE VOICE OF GOD

*T*o Him who rides upon the highest heavens, which are from ancient times; Behold, He speaks forth with His VOICE a mighty VOICE.

Psalm 68:33 (NAS)

*E*ven those who are far away shall come and build the temple of the Lord. Then you shall know the Lord of hosts has sent Me to you. And this shall come to pass if you diligently obey the VOICE of the Lord your God.

Zechariah 6:15 (NKJ)

I tell you the truth: the time is coming—the time has already come—when the dead will hear the VOICE of the Son of God, and those who hear it will live.

John 5:25 (GN)

*M*oreover, I heard a VOICE from heaven, saying, 'Write this: "Happy are the dead who die in the faith of Christ! Henceforth," SAYS the Spirit, "they may rest from their labors; for they take with them the record of their deeds."

Revelation 14:13 (NEB)

*H*ark, the VOICE of Jesus CALLING,
"Who will go and work today?
Fields are white, and harvests waiting,
Who will bear the sheaves away?

Loud and long the Master CALLETH,
Rich reward He offers thee;
Who will answer, gladly saying,
"Hear am I; send me, send me"?

(by Daniel March)

Adore God since His VOICE CALLED to you.

THE GOD WHO IS THE WAY

WAY—A track or path along or over which one passes, progresses, or journeys; a place for passing; a path, a route, road, street, or passage of any kind. (Webster)

When the men got up to leave, they looked down upon Sodom, and Abraham walked along with them to see them on their way. Then the Lord said, "Shall I hide from Abraham what I am about to do? Abraham will surely become a great and powerful nation, and all nations on earth will be blessed through him. For I have chosen him, so that he will direct his children and his household after him to keep the WAY of the Lord by doing what is right and just, so that the Lord will bring about for Abraham what he has promised him."

Genesis 18:16-19 (NIV)

For the Lord knows the WAY of the righteous: but the way of the ungodly shall perish.

Psalm 1:6 (KJ)

Go in by the narrow gate. For the wide gate has a broad road which leads to disaster and there are many people going that way. The narrow gate and the hard ROAD lead out into life and only a few are finding it.

Matthew 7:14 (Phillips)

I must needs go home by the WAY of the cross,
There's no other WAY but this;
I shall never get sight of the gates of light,
If the WAY of the cross I miss.

The WAY of the cross leads home,
The WAY of the cross leads home;
It is sweet to know as I onward go
The WAY of the cross leads home.

(by Jessie B. Pounds)

Adore God for being THE WAY.

THE GOD WHO IS THE WAY

WAY—1. A path or road. 2. A route. 3. Moral conduct. 4. Way of life, customs, manners. 5. Way of Salvation. (Today's)

*L*ord, teach me your WAYS, and guide me to do what is right because I have enemies.

Psalm 27:11 (NCV)

*F*or my part, far be it from me that I should sin against Yahweh by ceasing to plead for you or to instruct you in the good and right WAY.

1 Samuel 12:23 (TJB)

*J*esus said to him, I am the WAY and the Truth and the Life; no one comes to the Father except by (through) Me.

John 14:6 (Amplified)

I must needs go on in the blood-sprinkled WAY,
The path that the Saviour trod,
If I ever climb to the heights sublime,
Where the soul is at home with God.

Then I bid farewell to the way of the world,
To walk in it nevermore:
For my Lord says, "Come," and I seek my home,
Where He waits at the open door.

(by Jessie B. Pounds)

Adore God for being the Way.

THE GOD WHO IS THE WAY, AND WHO LEADS OUR WAY

WAY synonym—Road, street, avenue, passage, path, trail, alley, channel, course, route, thoroughfare, highway.

God be merciful to us and bless us, And cause His face to shine upon us. That your WAY may be known in all the earth, Your salvation among all nations.

Psalm 67:1 & 2 (NKJ)

The Eternal deals with me as I am upright, he recompenses me for my clean life; for I have kept the Eternal's ROAD, and never sinned by swearing from my God.

2 Samuel 22:21 & 22 (Moffatt)

And a certain Jew named Apollos, a native of the city of Alexandria, a learned and eloquent man, came down to Ephesus, being a powerful man in the scriptures. This man had been instructed in the WAY of the Lord, and being fervent in his spirit was speaking and teaching accurately the things concerning Jesus.

Acts 18:24 & 25 (Wuest)

> All the WAY my Saviour leads me;
> What have I to ask beside?
> Can I doubt His tender mercy,
> Who through life has been my guide?
>
> Heavenly peace, divinest comfort,
> Here by faith in Him to dwell!
> For I know what ever befall me,
> Jesus doeth all things well.
>
> *(by Fanny J. Crosby)*

Adore the God of our WAY.

THE GOD WHO IS THE WAY, AND WHO LEADS OUR WAY

WAY—Hebrew, Derech; Greek, hodos. A road, a track, path, or highway. (Today's Dictionary of the Bible)

I am the Lord, your Holy One, the creator of Israel, your King. Thus says the Lord, Who makes a WAY in the sea and a path in the mighty waters.

Isaiah 43:15 & 16 (Amplified)

*S*earch me, O God, and know my heart; test my thoughts. Point out anything you find in me that makes you sad, and lead me along the PATH of everlasting life.

Psalm 139:23 & 24 (TLB)

*W*hen the messengers were on their way back, Jesus began to speak to the people about John; 'What was the spectacle that drew you to the wilderness? A reed-bed swept by the wind? No? Then what did you go out to see? A man dressed in silks and satins? Surely you must look in palaces for that. But why did you go out? To see a prophet? Yes indeed, and far more than a prophet. He is the man of whom Scripture says, "Here is my herald, whom I send on ahead of you, And he will prepare the WAY before you."

Matthew 11:7-10 (NEB)

> *A*ll the WAY my Saviour leads me,
> Cheers each winding path I tread.
> Gives me grace for every trial,
> Feeds me with the living bread.
>
> Though my weary steps may falter,
> And my soul athirst may be,
> Gushing from the Rock before me,
> Lo! a spring of joy I see.
>
> *(by Fanny J. Crosby)*

Adore the One who is the only WAY.

THE GOD WHO IS THE WAY,
AND WHO LEADS OUR WAY

O God, your WAYS are holy. Where is there any other as mighty as you? You are the God of miracles and wonders! You still demonstrate your awesome power. You have redeemed us who are the sons of Jacob and Joseph by your might. When the Red Sea saw you, how it feared! It trembled to its depths! The clouds poured down their rain, and the thunder rolled and crackled in the sky. Your lightning flashed. There was thunder in the whirlwind; the lightening lighted up the world! The earth trembled and shook. Your ROAD led by a PATHWAY no one knew was there! You led your people along the ROAD like a flock of sheep, with Moses and Aaron as shepherds.

Psalm 77:13-20 (TLB)

*M*aster, we know that you are an honest man who teaches the WAY of God faithfully and that you are not swayed by men's opinion of you.

Matthew 22:16 (Phillips)

*S*he followed Paul and us, shouting loudly, "These men are servants of the Most High God: they are announcing to you the WAY of salvation."

Acts 16:17 (Berkeley)

> *A*ll the WAY my Saviour leads me;
> O the fullness of His love!
> Perfect rest to me is promised
> In my Fathers house above.
>
> When my spirit, clothed immortal,
> Wings its flight to realms of day,
> This my song through endless ages:
> Jesus led me all the WAY.
>
> *(by Fanny J. Crosby)*

Adore God, the WAY.

THE GOD WHO IS THE WAY, AND WHO LEADS OUR WAY

*B*ut He knows the WAY I take; When He has tried me, I shall come forth as gold. My foot has held fast to His PATH; I have kept His WAY and not turned aside.

Job 23:10 & 11 (NAS)

*T*he Lord is slow to anger and great in power; the Lord will not leave the guilty unpunished. His WAY is in the whirlwind and the storm, and clouds are the dust of his feet.

Nahum 1:3 (NIV)

*W*e have, then, brothers, complete freedom to go into the Most Holy Place by means of the death of Jesus. He opened for us a new WAY, a living WAY, through the curtain—that is, through his own body. We have a great high priest in charge of the house of God. Let us come near to God, then, with a sincere heart and a sure faith, with hearts that have been made clean from a guilty conscience, and bodies washed with pure water.

Hebrews 10:19-22 (GN)

*I*s your life a CHANNEL of blessing?
Is the love of God flowing through you?
Are you telling the lost of the Saviour?
Are you ready His service to do?

Is you life a CHANNEL of blessing?
Are you burdened for those who are lost?
Have you urged upon those who are straying
The Saviour who died on the cross?

(by Harper G. Smith)

Adore God for showing you the WAY to eternal life.

THE GOD WHO IS THE WAY, AND WHO LEADS OUR WAY

*Y*ahweh, make you WAYS known to me, teach me your PATHS. Set me in the WAY of your truth, and teach me, for you are the God who saves me.

Psalm 25:4 & 5 (NJB)

*A*nd they shall be my people, and I will be their God: And I will give them one heart, and one WAY, that they may fear me forever, for the good of them, and of their children after them.

Jeremiah 32:38 & 39 (KJ)

O the depth of the riches and wisdom and knowledge of God! How unfathomable (inscrutable, unsearchable) are His judgments—His decisions! And how untraceable (Mysterious, undiscoverable) are His WAYS—His methods, His PATHS.

Romans 11:33 (Amplified)

*A*nd they sing the song of Moses, the servant of God, and the song of the Lamb, saying: "Great and marvelous are Your works, Lord God Almighty! Just and true are your WAYS, O King of the saints!"

Revelation 15:3 (NKJ)

*I*s your life a CHANNEL of blessing?
Is it daily telling of Him?
Have you spoken the word of salvation
To those who are dying in sin?

Make me a CHANNEL of blessing today,
Make me a CHANNEL of blessing I pray:
My life possessing, my service blessing,
Make me a CHANNEL of blessing today.

(by Harper G. Smith)

Adore God for the CHANNELS of blessing in your life.

THE GOD WHO IS THE WAY,
AND WHO LEADS OUR WAY.

*H*e is the Rock, his work is perfect, for all his WAYS are Equity. A God faithful, without unfairness, Uprightness itself and Justice.

Deuteronomy 32:4 (TJB)

*G*ive me back the joy of your salvation. Keep me strong by giving me a willing spirit. Then I will teach your WAYS to those who do wrong, and sinners will turn back to you.

Psalm 51:12 & 13 (NCV)

*B*ut God is faithful who will not permit you to be tested nor tempted above that with which you are able to cope, but will, along with the testing time or temptation, also make a WAY out in order that you may be able to bear up under it.

1 Corinthians 10:13 (Wuest)

*F*or David says of him: "I foresaw that the presence of the Lord would be with me always, for he is at my right hand so that I may not be shaken; therefore my heart was glad and my tongue spoke my joy; moreover, my flesh shall dwell in hope, for thou wilt not abandon my soul to Hades, nor let thy loyal servant suffer corruption. Thou hast shown me the WAYS of life, Thou wilt fill me with gladness by thy presence."

Acts 2:25-28 (NEB)

*H*ave Thine own WAY, Lord! Have Thine own WAY!
Thou art the Potter; I am the clay.
Mould me and make me after Thy will,
While I am waiting, yielded and still.

Have Thine own WAY, Lord! Have Thine own WAY!
Search me and try me, Master today!
Whiter than snow, Lord, wash me just now,
As in Thy presence humbly I bow.

(by Adelaide A. Pollard)

Adore God for being THE WAY.

THE GOD WHO IS THE WAY

O that My people would listen to Me, that Israel would walk in my WAYS.

Psalm 81:13 (Amplified)

*Y*et the Lord pleads with you still: Ask where the good ROAD is, the godly PATHS you used to walk in, in the days of long ago. Travel there and you will find rest for your souls.

Jeremiah 6:16 (TLB)

A prayer of Habakkuk the prophet, On shigionoth. Lord, I have heard of your fame; I stand in awe of your deeds, O Lord. Renew them in our day, in our time make them known; in wrath remember mercy. God came from Teman, the Holy One from Mount Paran. His glory covered the heavens and his praise filled the earth. His splendor was like the sunrise; rays flashed from his hand, where his power was hidden. Plague went before him; pestilence followed his steps. He stood, and shook the earth; he looked and made the mountains tremble. The ancient mountains crumbled and the age-old hills collapsed. His WAYS are eternal.

Habakkuk 3:1-6 (NIV)

*H*ave Thine own WAY, Lord! Have Thine own WAY!
Wounded and weary, Help me I pray!
Power all power surely is Thine!
Touch me and heal me, Saviour divine!

Have Thine own WAY, Lord! Have Thine own WAY!
Hold o'er my being absolute sway!
Fill with Thy Spirit till all shall see
Christ only, always, living in me!

(by Adelaide A. Pollard)

Adore God for being THE WAY.

THE WILL OF GOD

WILL—1. To form a volition; to exercise an act of the will. 2. To desire; to wish. 3. To resolve; to determine; to decree. (Webster)

The Lord WILL give strength to His people; The Lord WILL bless His people with peace.

Psalm 29:11 (NAS)

Surely God WILL never do wickedly, Nor WILL the Almighty pervert justice.

Job 34:12 (NKJ)

May your Kingdom come, May your WILL be done on earth as it is in heaven.

Matthew 6:7 (GN)

> *Is* it Thy WILL that I should be
> Buried in symbol, Lord, with Thee:
> Owning Thee by this solemn sign,
> Telling the world that I am Thine?
>
> Forth from Thy burial, Lord, I come
> For Thou hast triumphed o'er the tomb;
> Thy resurrection life I share
> My portion is no longer here
>
> *(Author unknown)*

Adore God for His perfect WILL.

THE WILL OF GOD

*B*ecause he hath set his love upon me, therefore I WILL deliver him: I WILL set him on high, because he hath known my name. He shall call upon me, and I WILL answer him: I WILL be with him in trouble; I WILL deliver him and honor him. With long life WILL I satisfy him, and show him my salvation.

Psalm 91:14-16 (KJ)

*S*o don't worry, because I am with you. Don't be afraid, Because I am your God. I WILL make you strong and WILL help you; I WILL support you with my right hand that saves you.

Isaiah 41:10 (NCV)

*N*ot everyone who says to me, Lord, Lord, will enter the kingdom of heaven, but he who does the WILL of My Father Who is in heaven.

Matthew 7:21 (Amplified)

*I*t is not that the Lord is slow in fulfilling he promise, as some suppose, but that he is very patient with you, because it is not his WILL for any to be lost, but for all to come to repentance.

2 Peter 3:9 (NEB)

> *G*ladly I yield in obedience now;
> In all things Thy WILL I'd bow;
> I'll follow where my Saviour led,
> And humbly in His footsteps tread.
>
> Oh, may I count myself to be
> Dead to the sins that wounded Thee,
> Dead to the pleasures of this earth,
> Unworthy of my heavenly birth.
>
> *(Author unknown)*

Adore God because His WILL is perfect.

THE WILL OF GOD

I flee to thee for refuge; teach me to do thy WILL, thou art my God; guide me by thy good Spirit on a straight road.

Psalm 143:9b & 10 (Moffatt)

*C*all to me and I WILL answer you; I WILL tell you great mysteries of which you know nothing.

Jeremiah 33:3 (NJB)

*J*esus replied to them, "My teaching in not really mine but comes from the one who sent me. If anyone wants to do God's WILL, he will know whether my teaching is from God or whether I merely speak on my own authority."

John 7:16 & 17 (Phillips)

I beg of you, therefore, brothers, in view of God's mercies, that you present your bodies a living sacrifice, holy and acceptable to God—your worship with understanding. And do not conform to the present world scheme, but be transformed by a complete renewal of mind, so as to sense for yourselves what is good and acceptable and perfect WILL of God.

Romans 12:1 & 2 (Berkeley)

"*H*e was not WILLING that any should perish;"
Jesus enthroned in the glory above,
Saw our poor fallen world, pitied our sorrows,
Poured out His life for us, wonderful love!

Perishing, perishing! Thronging our pathway,
Hearts break with burdens too heavy to bear:
Jesus would save, but there's no one to tell them,
No one to lift them from sin and despair.

(by Lucy R. Meyer)

Adore God because His WILL is perfect.

THE WILL OF GOD

He WILL not allow your foot to slip or to be moved; He who keeps you WILL not slumber.

Psalm 121:3 (Amplified)

He said to me, "Son of man, stand up on your feet and I WILL speak to you." As he spoke, the Spirit came into me and raised me to my feet, and I heard him speaking to me.

Ezekiel 2:1 & 2 (NIV)

He (Jesus) walked away, perhaps a stone's throw, and knelt down and prayed this prayer: "Father, if you are WILLING, please take this cup of horror from me. But I want your WILL, not mine."

Luke 22:41 & 42 (TLB)

*S*top considering the world precious with the result that you love it, and the things in the world. If anyone as a habit of life is considering the world precious and is therefore loving it, there does not exist the Father's love (i.e. the love possessed by the Father) in him. Because everything which is in the world, the passionate desire of the flesh (the totally depraved nature), and the passionate desire of the eyes, and the insolent and empty assurance which trusts in things that serve the creature life, is not from the Father as a source but is from the world as a source. And the world is being caused to pass away, and its passionate desire. But the one who keeps on habitually doing the WILL of God abides forever.

1 John 2:15-17 (Wuest)

"*He* was not WILLING that any should perish;"
Clothed in our flesh with its sorrow and pain,
Came He to seek the lost, comfort the mourner,
Heal the heart broken by sorrow and shame.

Perishing, Perishing! Harvest is passing,
Reapers are few and night draweth near:
Jesus is calling thee, haste to the reaping,
Thou shalt have souls, precious souls for thy hire.

(by Lucy R. Meyer)

Adore the God who was not WILLING for anyone to perish.

THE WILL OF GOD

And behold, a leper came and worshipped Him, saying, "Lord, if You are WILLING, You can make me clean." Then Jesus put out His hand and touched him, saying, "I am WILLING, be cleansed." And immediately his leprosy was cleansed.

Matthew 8:2 & 3 (NKJ)

Be assured that from the first day we heard of you, we haven't stopped praying for you, asking God to give you wise minds and spirits attuned to his WILL, and so acquire a thorough understanding of the ways in which God works.

Colossians 1:9 (The Message)

First he says, 'Sacrifices and offerings, whole-offerings and sin-offerings, thou didst not desire nor delight in'—although the Law prescribes them—and then he says, 'I have come to do thy WILL.' He thus annuls the former to establish the latter.

Hebrews 10:8 & 9 (NEB)

God has raised from the dead our Lord Jesus, who is the Great Shepherd of the sheep because of his death, by which the eternal covenant is sealed. May he, the God of peace, provide you with every good thing you need in order to do his WILL, and may he, through Jesus Christ, do to us what pleases him. And to Christ be the glory for ever and ever! Amen.

Hebrews 13:20 & 21 (GN)

"*He* was not WILLING that any should perish;"
Am I his follower, and can I live
Longer at ease with a soul going downward,
Lost for the lack of the help I might give?

Perishing, perishing, Thou was not WILLING;
Master forgive, and inspire us anew;
Banish our worldliness, help us to ever
Live with eternity's values in view.

(by Lucy R. Meyer)

Adore God for His perfect WILL.

THE WORD OF GOD

WORD—A single or articulate sound or a combination of articulate sounds or syllables uttered by voice and by custom expressing an idea or ideas. (Webster)

Thy WORD have I hid in mine heart, that I might not sin against thee.

Psalm 119:11 (KJ)

And you shall remember all the way which the Lord your God has led you in the wilderness these forty years, that He might humble you, testing you to know what was in your heart, whether you would keep His commandments or not. And he humbled you and let you be hungry, and fed you with manna which you did not know, nor did your fathers know, that He might make you understand that man does not live by bread alone, but man lives by everything that PROCEEDS OUT OF THE MOUTH of the Lord.

Deuteronomy 8:2 & 3 (NAS)

In the beginning (before all time) was the WORD (Christ) and the WORD was with God, and the WORD was God himself.

John 1:1 (Amplified)

O WORD of God incarnate,
O Wisdom from on high,
O Truth unchanged, unchanging,
O Light of our dark sky;

We praise Thee for the radiance
That from the hallowed page,
A lantern to our footsteps,
Shines on from age to age.

(by William W. How)

Adore THE WORD.

THE WORD OF GOD

WORD, The (Greek, Logos) one of the titles of our Lord, found only in the writings of John. (Today's Dictionary of the Bible)

*H*ow sweet Thy SAYINGS are, sweeter then honey to the taste.

Psalm 119:103 (Moffatt)

*E*very WORD of God proves true. He defends all who come to him for protection.

Proverbs 30:5 (Paraphrased)

*S*o there are three witnesses, (in heaven, the Father, the WORD, and the Holy Spirit, and these three are one, and there are three witnesses on earth,) the Spirit, the water, and the blood, and the three are in unison.

1 John 5:7 (Berkeley)

> *S*ing them over again to me,
> Wonderful WORDS of life;
> Let me more of their beauty see,
> Wonderful WORDS of life
>
> WORDS of life and beauty,
> Teach me faith and duty;
> Beautiful WORDS, wonderful WORDS,
> Wonderful WORDS of life.
>
> *(by Philip P. Bliss)*

Adore The WORD.

November

THE WORD OF GOD

WORD—(Hebrew—Emer, Omer, Imrah, Dabar, Mil Lah) "WORD" is applied to Jesus Christ. (Smith's)

*Y*ou must obey the Lord your God by keeping all his commands and rules that are written in this Book of the Teachings. You must return to the Lord your God with your whole being. This command I give to you today is not to hard for you; it is not beyond what you can do. It is not up in heaven. You do not have to ask, "Who will go up to heaven and get it for us so we can obey it and keep it?" It is not on the other side of the sea. You do not have to ask, "Who will go across the sea and get it?" "Who will tell it to us so we can keep it?" No, the WORD is very near you. It is in your mouth, and in your heart so you may obey it.

Deuteronomy 30:10-14 (NCV)

I tell you most solemnly, whoever keeps my WORD will never see death.

John 8:51 (NJB)

*R*emember what Christ taught and let his WORDS enrich your lives and make you wise; teach them to each other and sing them out in psalms and hymns and spiritual songs, singing to the Lord with thankful hearts.

Colossians 3:16 (Paraphrased)

*C*hrist, the blessed One gives to all,
Wonderful WORDS of life;
Sinner list to the loving call,
Wonderful WORDS of life.

All so freely given,
Wooing us to heaven:
Beautiful WORDS, wonderful WORDS,
Wonderful WORDS of life.

(by Philip P. Bliss)

ADORE The WORD.

THE WORD OF GOD

*R*emember (fervently) the WORD and promise to Your servant, on which You have caused me to hope. This is my comfort and consolation in my affliction, that YOUR WORD has revived me and given me life.

Psalm 119:49 & 50 (Amplified)

*T*he grass withers and the flowers fall, but the WORD of our God stands forever.

Isaiah 40:8 (NIV)

*A*nd the WORD entering a new mode of existence, became flesh, and lived in a tent (His physical body) among us. And we gazed with attentive and careful regard and spiritual perception at His glory, a glory such as that of a uniquely-begotten Son of the Father, full of grace and truth.

John 1:14 (Wuest)

*G*oing through a long line of prophets, God has been addressing our ancestors in different ways for centuries. Recently he spoke to us directly through his Son. by his Son, God created the world in the beginning, and it will all belong to the Son at the end. This Son perfectly mirrors God, and is stamped with God's nature. He holds everything together by what he says—powerful WORDS!

Hebrews 1:1-3 (Message)

*S*weetly echo the gospel call,
Wonderful WORDS of life;
Offer pardon and peace to all,
Wonderful WORDS of Life.

Jesus, only Saviour,
Sanctify forever:
Beautiful WORDS, wonderful WORDS,
Wonderful WORDS of Life.

(by Philip P. Bliss)

Adore the WORD.

THE WORD OF GOD

*Y*our WORD is a lamp to my feet and a light to my path.

Psalm 119:105 (NKJ)

*B*ut I am the Lord thy God, that divided the sea, whose waves roared: The Lord of hosts is my name. And I have put my WORDS in thy mouth, and I have covered thee in the shadow of my hand, that I may plant the heavens, and lay the foundations of the earth, and say unto Zion, Thou art my people.

Isaiah 51:15 & 16 (KJ)

*I*ndeed the Lord has commanded us to do so in the WORDS: "I have set thee for a light for the gentiles, that thou shouldest be for salvation unto the uttermost part of the earth." When the gentiles heard this they were delighted and thanked God for his message. All those who were destined for eternal life believed, and the WORD of the Lord spread over the whole country.

Acts 13:47 & 48 (Phillips)

*F*or the WORD that God speaks is alive and full of power—making it active, operative, energizing and effective; it is sharper than any two edged sword, penetrating to the dividing line of the breath of life (soul) and (the immortal) spirit, and of joints and marrow (that is, of the deepest parts of our nature) exposing and sifting and analyzing and judging the very thoughts and purposes of the heart.

Hebrews 4:12 (Amplified)

> *T*he WORD of God, a river of pleasure,
> The WORD of God, 'Tis food for the mind,
> The WORD God, Its light faileth never,
> The WORD of God, what treasure we find.
> The WORD of God, a message of love,
> The WORD of God, it came from above.

(by Arthur E. Smith)

Adore The WORD.

THE WORD OF GOD

*T*he ways of God are without fault. The Lord's WORDS are pure. He is a shield to those who trust him.

Psalm 18:30 (NCV)

"*B*ut you shall speak My WORDS to them whether they listen or not, for they are rebellious."

Ezekiel 2:7 (NAS)

*D*o all you have to do without complaint or wrangling. Show yourselves guileless and above reproach, faultless children of God in a warped and crooked generation, in which you shine like stars in a dark world and proffer the WORD of life.

Philippians 2:14-16 (NEB)

*N*ow that you have purified yourselves by obeying the truth, and have a sincere love for your fellow believers, love one another earnestly with all your hearts. For through the living and eternal WORD of God you have been born again as children of a parent who is immortal, not mortal.

1 Peter 1:22 & 23 (Good News)

*O*pen Thy WORD of truth,
That I may see
Thy message written clear
And plain for me;

Then in sweet fellowship
Walking with Thee,
Thine image on my life
Engraved will be.

(by Mary A. Lathbury)

Adore the WORD.

THE WORD OF GOD

*M*y son, pay attention to my WORDS, listen carefully to the WORDS I say; do not let them out of your sight, keep them deep in your heart. They are life to those who grasp them, health for the entire body.

Proverbs 4:20-22 (NJB)

I have given them Thy WORD and the world has hated them, for they are not worldly, just as I am not worldly. I do not pray that Thou wilt take them out of the world, but that Thou wilt preserve them from the evil one. As I am not worldly, so they are not worldly. Consecrate them by the truth. Thy WORD is truth.

John 17:14-17 (Berkeley)

*H*e who says, "I know him, but does not obey his commands is a liar and the truth is not in him; but whoever obeys his WORD in him love to God is really complete.

1 John 2:4 & 5 (Moffatt)

*T*hen I saw Heaven open wide—and oh! a white horse and its Rider. The Rider, judges and makes war in pure righteousness. His eyes are a blaze of fire, on his head many crowns. He has a Name inscribed that's known only to himself. He is dressed in a robe soaked with blood, and he is addressed as "WORD of God." The armies of Heaven, mounted on white horses and dressed in dazzling white linen, follow him.

Revelation 19:11-13 (Message)

O God of Light, Thy WORD a lamp unfailing,
Shines through the darkness of our earthly way,
O'er fear and doubt, o'er black despair prevailing,
Guiding our steps to Thine eternal day.

Undimmed by time, the WORD is still revealing
To sinful men Thy justice and Thy grace;
And questing hearts that long for peace and healing
See Thy compassion in the Saviour's face.

(Sarah E. Taylor)

Adore The WORD.

THE WORD OF GOD

*W*hen their rulers are overthrown in stony places, their followers shall hear my WORDS, that they are sweet—pleasant, mild and just.

Psalm 141:6 (Amplified)

*H*eaven and earth will disappear, but my WORDS remain forever.

Matthew 24:35 (Paraphrased)

*T*he Spirit is He who makes alive. The flesh is not of any use at all. The WORDS which I have spoken to you, spirit are they and life.

John 6:63 (Wuest)

*B*ut they deliberately forget that long ago by God's WORD the heavens existed and the earth was formed out of water and with water. by water also the world of that time was deluged and destroyed. by the same WORD the present heavens and earth are reserved for fire, being kept for the day of judgment and destruction of ungodly men.

2 Peter 3:5-7 (NIV)

> *M*aster speak! Thy servant heareth,
> Waiting for Thy gracious WORD;
> Longing for Thy voice That cheereth,
> Master let it now be heard.
> I am listening Lord, for Thee;
> What hast Thou to SAY to me?
>
> *(by Frances R. Havergal)*

Adore The WORD.

THE WORD OF GOD

And He was handed the book of the prophet Isaiah. And when He had opened the book, He found the place where it was written: "The Spirit of the Lord is upon Me, Because He has anointed Me to preach the gospel to the poor. He has sent Me to heal the brokenhearted, to preach deliverance to the captives and recovery of sight to the blind, to set at liberty those who are oppressed, to preach the acceptable year of the Lord." Then He closed the book, and gave it back to the attendant and sat down. And the eyes of all who were in the synagogue were fixed on Him. And He began to say to them, "Today this Scripture is fulfilled in your hearing." So all bore witness to Him, and marveled at the gracious WORDS which proceeded out of His mouth.

Luke 4:18-22 (NKJ)

Jesus asked the twelve followers, "Do you want to leave too?" Simon Peter answered him, "Lord, where would we go?" You have the WORDS of eternal life. We believe and know you are the Holy One from God.

John 6:67 & 68 (NCV)

Then He said to me, "These WORDS are trustworthy and true. The Lord God who inspires the prophets has sent his angel to show his servants what must shortly happen. And remember, I am coming soon."

Revelation 22:6 & 7 (NEB)

Thy WORD is like a garden, Lord,
With flowers bright and fair;
And everyone who seeks may pluck
A lovely cluster there.

Thy WORD is like a deep, deep mine;
And Jewels rich and rare
Are hidden in its mighty depths
For every searcher there.

(by Edwin Hodder)

Adore The WORD.

THE WORK OF GOD

WORK—Exertion of strength, energy or other faculty, physical or mental; effort or activity directed to some purpose or end; toil; labor; employment. (Webster)

Harken unto this, O Job; stand still and consider the wondrous WORKS of God.

Job 37:14 (KJ)

How manifold are thy WORKS, Eternal One, all of them wisely made.

Psalm 104:24 (Moffatt)

After Jesus finished saying this, he looked up to heaven and said; Father, the hour has come. Give glory to your Son, that the Son may give glory to you. For you gave him power over all men, so that he might give eternal life to all those you gave him. And this is eternal life: for men to know you, the only true God, and to know Jesus Christ, whom you sent. I showed your glory on earth; I finished the WORK you gave me to do.

John 17:1-4 (Good News)

> Holy, Holy, Holy! Lord God Almighty!
> Early in the morning our song shall rise to Thee;
> Holy, Holy, Holy! Merciful and Mighty,
> God in three persons, blessed Trinity!
>
> Holy, Holy, Holy! Lord God Almighty!
> All Thy WORKS shall praise Thy name, in earth, and sky and sea,
> Holy, Holy, Holy! Merciful and Mighty!
> God in Three Persons, blessed Trinity!

(by Reginald Heber)

Adore God for His WORKS.

THE WORK OF GOD

■ WORK—synonyms—Labor, toil, drudgery, employment, occupation, action, performance, feat, achievement, composition, book, volume, production. (Webster)

*G*reat are the WORKS of the Lord; They are studied by all who delight in them.

Psalm 111:2 (NAS)

*Y*es, as Yahweh did on mount Perazim, he is going to rise, as he did in the Valley of Gibeon he is going to stir himself to do the deed, his extraordinary deed, to WORK the WORK, his mysterious WORK.

Isaiah 28:21 (NJB)

*J*esus answered, The WORK God wants you to do is this: Believe the One he sent.

John 6:29 (NCV)

> *T*he spacious firmament on high,
> With all the blue, ethereal sky,
> And spangled heavens, a shining frame,
> Their great Original proclaim:
>
> The unwearied sun, from day to day,
> Does his creator's power display,
> And publishes to every land
> The WORK of an almighty hand.
>
> *(by Joseph Addison)*

Adore God for His WORKMANSHIP.

THE WORK OF GOD

*I*saiah also cries out concerning Israel: "Though the number of children of Israel be as the sand of the sea, the remnant will be saved. For He will finish the WORK and cut it short in righteousness, because the Lord will make a short WORK upon the earth.

Romans 9:27-28 (NKJ)

*M*any, O Lord my God, are the wonderful WORKS which You have done, and your thoughts toward us; no one can compare with You! If I should declare and speak of them, they are too many to be numbered.

Psalm 40:50 (Amplified)

*S*o long as daytime lasts we must practice the WORKS of My Sender; a night approaches when no one will be able to WORK

John 9:4 (Berkeley)

*F*or we are his WORKMANSHIP, created in Christ Jesus to do good deeds which God planned for us to do.

Ephesians 2:10 (Phillips)

*N*ow in a song of grateful praise
To Christ, the Lord, our voice will raise;
With all Thy saints we'll join to tell;
Christ Jesus "Hath done all things well!"

All worlds His glorious power confess,
His wisdom all His WORKS express;
But, O His love!— Our tongues would tell;
Christ Jesus "Hath done all things well!"

(by Samuel Medley)

Adore God for the WORKS He has done.

THE WORK OF GOD

*Y*et, O Lord, you are our Father. We are the clay, you are the potter; we are all the WORK of your hand.

Isaiah 64:8 (NIV)

*S*o, then the Lord Jesus, after He had spoken to them, was received up into heaven, and sat on the right hand of God. And those having gone forth, preached everywhere, the Lord WORKING with them, and confirming the Word through the attesting miracles which accompanied them.

Mark 16:19 & 20 (Wuest)

*T*his silenced the entire assembly, and they listened to Barnabas and Paul describing all the signs and wonders God had WORKED through them among the pagans.

Acts 15:12 (NJB)

*W*hen I heard of the solid trust you have in the Master Jesus and your outpouring of love to all the Christians, I couldn't stop thanking God for you—every time I prayed, I'd think of you and give thanks. But I do more than thank. I ask—ask the God of our Master Jesus Christ, the God of glory—to make you intelligent and discerning in knowing him personally, your eyes focused and clear, so that you can see exactly what he is calling you to do, grasp the immensity of this glorious way of life he has for Christians, oh, the utter extravagance of his WORK in us who trust him—endless energy, boundless strength!

Ephesians 1:15-19 (The Message)

> *R*ejoice in Him, again, again.
> The Spirit strikes the word,
> And faith takes up the happy strain;
> Our joy is in the Lord.
>
> Clean every whit; Thou saidst it Lord;
> Shall one suspicion lurk?
> Thine, surely is a faithful word,
> And Thine a finished WORK.
>
> *(by Mary Bowley Peters)*

Adore the God of WORKS.

THE WORK OF GOD

*B*ehold ye among the heathen, and regard, and wonder marvelously: for I will WORK a WORK in your days, which ye will not believe, though it be told you.

Habakkuk 1:5 (KJ)

*B*ut Jesus answered them, My Father has WORKED (even) until now.—He has never ceased WORKING. He is still WORKING—and I too must be at (divine) WORK.

John 5:17 (Amplified)

*W*e are God's WORKERS, WORKING together; you are like God's farm, God's house.

1 Corinthians 3:9 (NCV)

*H*aving been buried with Him in baptism, in which you were also raised up with Him through faith in the WORKING of God, who raised Him from the dead.

Colossians 2:12 (NAS)

*T*he veil is rent: Lo! Jesus stands
Before the throne of grace;
And clouds of incense from His hands
Fill all the glorious place.

His precious blood is sprinkled there,
Before and on the throne;
And His own wounds in heaven declare
The WORK that saves is done.

(by James G. Deck)

Adore the God of finished WORK.

THE WORK OF GOD

*N*ow I, King Nebuchadnezzar, praise and extol and honor the King of Heaven, all of Whose WORKS are faithful and right, and His ways are just; and those who walk in pride He is able to abase and humble.

Daniel 4:37 (Amplified)

*F*or the Father loves the Son and shows him everything he does himself, and he will show him even greater things than these, WORKS that will astonish you.

John 5:20 (NJB)

*M*en have different gifts, but it is the same Spirit who gives them. There are different ways of serving God, but it is the same Lord who is served. God WORKS through different men in different ways, but it is the same God who achieves his purposes through them all.

1 Corinthians 12:4-6 (Phillips)

*T*he one who is habitually committing sin is out of the devil as a source, because from the beginning the devil has been sinning, For this purpose there was manifested the Son of God, in order that HE MIGHT BRING TO NAUGHT the works of the devil.

1 John 1:8 & 9 (Wuest)

*T*hou to heaven hast now ascended,
Entering there by Thine own blood;
All the WORK of suffering ended,
Fully wrought the will of God.

For Thy Church Thou still art caring,
For us pleading in Thy love;
And our place of rest repairing
In the Father's house above.

(Author unknown)

Adore God for the WORK He has done in you.

THE WORK OF GOD

When I consider your heavens, the WORK of your fingers, the moon and the stars, which you have set in place, what is man that you are mindful of him, the son of man that you care for him?

Psalm 8:3 & 4 (NIV)

The Jews gathered around him and said," How long are you going to keep us in suspense? Tell us the plain truth: are you the Messiah?" Jesus answered: "I have already told you, but you would not believe me. The WORKS I do by my Father's authority speak on my behalf.

John 10:24 & 25 (Good News)

Therefore, my beloved, as you have been obedient always and not simply when I was present, so, now I am absent, WORK all the more strenuously at your salvation with reverence and trembling, for it is God who in his goodwill enables you to will this and achieve it.

Philippians 2:12 & 13 (Moffatt)

"Most assuredly, I say to you, he who believes in Me, the WORKS that I do he will do also; and greater WORKS than these he will do, because I go to My Father.

John 14:12 (NKJ)

WORK, for the night is coming,
WORK, through the morning hours;
WORK, while the dew is sparkling;
WORK, mid springing flowers.

WORK, when the day grows brighter,
WORK, in the glowing sun;
WORK, for the night is coming,
When man's WORK is done.

(by Annie L. Coghill)

Adore God for allowing you to be involved in His WORK.

THE GOD WHO MADE
AND WHO LOVES THE WORLD

WORLD—The whole system of created things; the universe, the earth. (Webster)

*H*e lifts the poor from the dust—Yes, from a pile of ashes—and treats them as princes sitting in the seats of honor. For all the earth is the Lord's and he has set the WORLD in order.

1 Samuel 2:8 (Paraphrased)

*T*he Lord reigneth, he is clothed with majesty; the Lord is clothed with strength, wherewith he hath girded himself; the WORLD also is established, that it cannot be moved.

Psalm 93:1 (KJ)

"*G*od loved the WORLD so much that he gave his one and only Son so that whoever believes in him may not be lost, but have eternal life."

John 3:16: (NCV)

> *T*he whole WORLD was lost in the darkness of sin;
> The Light of the WORLD is Jesus;
> Like sunshine at noonday His glories shone in,
> The Light of the WORLD is Jesus.
>
> No darkness have we who in Jesus abide,
> The Light of the WORLD is Jesus;
> We walk in the Light when we follow our Guide,
> The Light of the WORLD is Jesus.
>
> *(by Philip P. Bliss)*

Adore God for His love of the WORLD.

THE GOD WHO MADE
AND WHO LOVES THE WORLD

He has made the EARTH by His power, He has established the WORLD by His wisdom, and has stretched out the HEAVENS by His understanding.

Jeremiah 51:15 (Amplified)

All the ends of the EARTH will remember and turn to the Lord. And all the families of the nations will worship before the Lord.

Psalm 22:27 (NAS)

For we have personally listened, and we know that He is the (Christ, the) Saviour of the WORLD.

John 4:42 (Berkeley)

You are the light of the WORLD—it is impossible to hide a town built on the top of a hill.

Matthew 5:14 (Phillips)

> *Ye* dwellers in darkness with sin blinded eyes,
> The Light of the WORLD is Jesus
> We walk in the Light when we follow our guide
> The Light of the WORLD is Jesus.
>
> No need of the sunlight in heaven we're told.
> The Light of the WORLD is Jesus;
> The Lamb is the Light in the City of Gold.
> The Light of the WORLD is Jesus.
>
> *(by Philip P. Bliss)*

Adore God for being the Light in this WORLD.

THE GOD WHO MADE, LOVES
AND WHO WILL JUDGE THE WORLD

Sing to Yahweh, sing to the music of harps, and to the sound of many instruments; to the sound of trumpet and horn acclaim Yaweh the King! Let the sea thunder and all that it holds, and the WORLD, with all who live in it; let all the rivers clap their hands and the mountains shout for joy, at the presence of Yahweh, for he comes to judge the EARTH, to judge the WORLD with righteousness and the nations with strict justice.

Psalm 98:5-9 (NJB)

"I will punish the WORLD for its evil, and the wicked for their iniquity; I will halt the arrogance of the proud, and will lay low the haughtiness of the terrible.

Isaiah 13:11 (NKJ)

In the WORLD you are having tribulation. But be having courage. I have come off victorious over the WORLD with a permanent victory.

John 16:33 (Wuest)

Known unto God are all his works from the beginning of the WORLD.

Acts 15:18 (KJ)

God loved the WORLD of sinners lost,
And ruined by the fall;
Salvation full, at highest cost,
He offers free to all.

Believing souls, rejoicing go;
There shall to you be given
A glorious foretaste here below,
Of endless life in heaven.

(by Martha Stockton)

Adore God for His plan of salvation even before the WORLD began.

THE GOD WHO MADE, LOVES
AND WILL JUDGE THE WORLD

*B*ut the Eternal is the real God, an everlasting King; who by his power made the EARTH, who by his wisdom founded the WORLD.

Jeremiah 10:10 & 12 (Moffatt)

*L*et all the EARTH fear the Lord; let all the people of the WORLD revere him.

Psalm 33:8 (NIV)

*G*od was in Christ, making peace between the WORLD and himself. In Christ, God did not hold the world guilty of its sins. And he gave us this message of peace.

2 Corinthians 5:19 (NCV)

*G*od's wrath is revealed coming down from heaven upon all the sin and evil of men, whose ways prevent the truth from being known. God punishes them, because what men can know about God is plain to them. God himself made it plain to them. Ever since God made the WORLD, his invisible qualities, both his eternal power and his divine nature, have been clearly seen. Men can perceive them in the things God has made. So they have no excuse at all.

Romans 1:18-20 (Good News)

*I*t was alone that Jesus suffered in Gethsemane,
Alone He drained the bitter cup of deepest woe for me,
Alone He bore the rugged cross on Calvary's darkened hill;
The Saviour came to do the Father's will.

It was alone that Jesus died upon the cruel tree,
Alone He shed His precious blood in cleansing power for me,
Alone He lay in EARTH'S dark prison, silent, cold, and still;
The Saviour died to do the Father's will.

(by Helen Griggs)

Adore God for His plan for the WORLD.

THE GOD WHO MADE, WHO LOVES,
AND WHO WILL JUDGE THE WORLD

The EARTH is the Lords, and the fullness of it, the WORLD and they who dwell in it.

Psalm 24:1 (Amplified)

Then I, the King, shall say to those at my right, 'Come, blessed of my Father, into the Kingdom prepared for you from the founding of the WORLD.'

Matthew 25:34 (Paraphrased)

Every God-begotten person conquers the WORLD'S ways. The conquering power that brings the WORLD'S ways to its knees is our faith. The person who wins out over the WORLD'S ways is simply the one who believes Jesus is the Son of God.

1 John 5:4 (The Message)

The seventh angel blew his trumpet, and voices in heaven were shouting: "The sovereignty of the WORLD has passed to our Lord and his Christ, and he shall reign for ever and ever.

Revelation 11:15 (Wuest)

I serve a risen Saviour, He's in the WORLD today;
I know that He is living, whatever men may say;
I see his hand of mercy, I hear his voice of cheer,
And just the time I need Him, He's always near.

In all the WORLD around me I see His loving care,
And though my heart grows weary, I never will despair;
I know that He is leading through all the stormy blast,
The day of His appearing will come at last.

(by Alfred H. Ackley)

Adore God because He is coming again to rule over this WORLD.

THE GOD TO WORSHIP

▦ WORSHIP—To adore; to pay divine honors to; to reverence with supreme respect and veneration; as, to worship God. (Webster)

*A*scribe to the Lord the glory due His name; Bring an offering, and come before Him; WORSHIP the Lord in holy array.

1 Chronicles 16:29 (NAS)

*P*ay tribute to Yahweh, you sons of God, tribute to Yahweh of glory and power, tribute to Yahweh of the glory of his name, WORSHIP Yahweh in his sacred court.

Psalm 29:1 & 2 (NJB)

"*W*here is the newborn king of the Jews? For we saw his star in the east and we have come to WORSHIP him."

Matthew 2:2 (Berkeley)

O WORSHIP the King, all glorious above,
O gratefully sing His power and His love;
Our shield and Defender, the Ancient of days,
Pavilioned in splendor and girded with praise.

Frail children of dust, and feeble as frail,
In Thee do we trust, nor find Thee to fail;
Thy mercies how tender! how firm to the end!
Our Maker, Defender, Redeemer and Friend.

(by Robert Grant)

Adore and WORSHIP God.

November 21

THE GOD TO WORSHIP

🔲 WORSHIP synonyms—Honor, adore, revere, reverence. (Webster)

*M*ake a joyful shout to God, all the earth! Sing out the honor of His name; Make His praise glorious. Say to God, "How awesome are Your works! Through the greatness of Your power your enemies shall submit themselves to You. All the earth shall WORSHIP You and sing praises to You; They shall sing praises to your name."

Psalm 66:1-4 (NKJ)

*A*nd it shall come to pass, that from one new moon to another, and from one Sabbath to another, shall all flesh come to WORSHIP before me, saith the Lord.

Isaiah 66:23 (KJ)

*J*esus said to the devil, "Go away from me, Satan! It is written in the Scriptures, 'You must WORSHIP the Lord your God and serve only him.'"

Matthew 4:10 (NCV)

*T*hou Son of God, eternal Word,
Who heaven and earth's foundation laid,
Upholding Thy word and power
The universe Thy hands have made.
We WORSHIP Thee, all glorious Lord,
Forever be Thy name adored!

As Lamb of God, Thy path we view,
Thy Father's will Thy whole delight;
To Calvary we trace Thy way,
Each step of Thine, with glories bright;
We WORSHIP Thee, all glorious Lord,
Forever be Thy name adored!

(by Inglis Fleming)

Adore and WORSHIP God.

THE GOD TO WORSHIP

WORSHIP—General Observations. It is as natural to worship as it is to live, The feeling and expression of high adoration, reverence, trust, love, loyalty, and dependence upon a higher power, human or divine, is a necessity to man. To these sentiments, to a greater or lesser degree, to every man something or somebody, real or imaginary appeals. And that something secures worship... which impels them to testify by words and acts of love and gratitude to the Author of life and the Giver of all good. (Unger)

All the nations you have made will come and WORSHIP before you, O Lord; they will bring glory to your name.

Psalm 86:9 (NIV)

The message that came to Jeremiah from the Eternal: Stand at the gate of the Eternal's house and make his proclamation there. "Listen to the Eternal's message, all you Judahites, who enter by these gates to WORSHIP the Eternal; here is what the Lord of hosts, the God of Israel has to say. Amend your life and doings, that I may dwell among you in the temple here."

Jeremiah 7:1-4b (Moffatt)

But the time is coming and is already here, when the real worshipers will WORSHIP the Father in Spirit and in truth. These are the worshipers the Father wants to WORSHIP him. God is Spirit, and those who WORSHIP him must WORSHIP in spirit and truth.

John 4:23 & 24 (GN)

> For us Thine untold sufferings,
> Exalted to the Father's throne,
> For us the darkness and the woe,
> With glory and with honor crowned,
> In love, transcending all compare,
> All at Thy glorious name shall bow,
> Thou, Lord, for us to death did go,
> As Lord of all by each be owned.
> We WORSHIP Thee, all glorious Lord,
> We WORSHIP Thee, all glorious Lord,
> For ever by Thy name adored!
> Forever be Thy name adored!
>
> *(by Inglis Fleming)*

Adore and WORSHIP God.

THE GOD TO WORSHIP

WORSHIP—The acts and postures in WORSHIP are similar in Oriental nations, and have come down to the present from remote antiquity unchanged... Prayer is made standing, with the hand lifted or crossed or folded;...The hands are also stretched forth in supplication... Kneeling is a common mode;... prostration of the body, resting on the knees and arms, the forehead touching the ground, and the whole body lying along, the face being down. (Smith's)

O come, let us WORSHIP and bow down; let us kneel before the Lord our Maker. (in reverent praise and supplication)

Psalm 95:6 (Amplified)

They will receive the wages of their pride, for they have scoffed at the people of the Lord of Hosts. The Lord will do terrible things to them. He will starve out all those gods of foreign powers, and everyone shall WORSHIP Him, each in his own land throughout the world.

Zephaniah 3:10 & 11 (Paraphrased)

*O*ne of them was named Lydia, a dealer in purple fabric from the city of Thyatira, who was a WORSHIPPER of God, was listening, and the Lord opened her heart to respond to what Paul said. She was baptized and her household with her.

Acts 16:14 & 15a (NEB)

*G*racious God, we WORSHIP Thee,
Reverently we bow the knee;
Jesus Christ our only plea:
Father, we adore Thee

Low we bow before Thy face,
A son of God, O wondrous place!
Great the riches of Thy grace:
Father we adore Thee.

(by S. Trevor Francis)

Adore and WORSHIP God

THE GOD TO WORSHIP

WORSHIP—Hebrew—shahah (to bow down) to prostrate one's self before another in order to do him honor and reverence. Greek—proskuneo, properly to kiss the hand to (toward) one, in token of reverence, also by kneeling or prostration to do homage. (Unger's)

*L*et us go into His dwelling place; Let us WORSHIP at His footstool.

Psalm 132:7 (NAS)

*A*ll the sons of Israel, seeing the fire come down and the glory of Yahweh resting on the Temple, bowed down on the pavement with their faces to the earth; they WORSHIPPED and gave praise to Yahweh.

2 Chronicles 7:3 (NJB)

*F*or we (Christians) are the true circumcision, who WORSHIP God in Spirit and by the Spirit of God, and exult and glory and pride ourselves in Jesus Christ, and put no confidence or dependence (on what we are) in the flesh and on outward privileges and physical advantages and external appearances.

Philippians 3:3 (Amplified)

O lead me up to heavens heights,
To see the Lord enthroned in light:
That gazing on His glory there,
I may reflect His image here.

There, too, the Eternal Three in One,
Blest Father, Spirit, and the Son,
Rest undisturbed forever more;
I wonder, WORSHIP and adore.

(by Alfred Mace)

Adore and WORSHIP God.

THE GOD TO WORSHIP

The twenty-four elders fall down before Him who sits on the throne and WORSHIP Him who lives forever and ever, and cast their crowns before Him saying, "You are worthy, O Lord to receive glory and honor and power; For you created all things, and by Your will they exist.

Revelation 4:10 & 11 (NKJ)

Then the twenty-four elders, seated on their thrones before God, fell on their faces and WORSHIPPED God.

Revelation 11:16 (Berkeley)

Fear God at once and at once give Him glory, because the hour of His judgment has come, and WORSHIP Him at once who made the heaven and the earth and the sea and springs of water.

Revelation 14:7 (Wuest)

Then he (Angel) said to me, "Write this down: Happy are those who are invited to the wedding-feast of the Lamb!" Then he added, "These are true words of God." At that I fell at his feet to worship him, but he said to me, "No, I am your fellow servant and fellow-servant with your brothers who are holding fast their witness to Jesus. Give your WORSHIP to God. (This witness to Jesus inspires all prophecy)

Revelation 19:9 & 10 (Phillips)

Father, we WORSHIP Thee,
Through Thy beloved Son;
And, by the Spirit now draw near
Before Thy holy throne.

For what Thou art, we praise
And WORSHIP and adore:
To Father, Son and Holy Spirit
Be glory ever more.

(by Alfred P. Gibbs)

Adore and WORSHIP God.

THE GOD WHO USES WRITING

WRITE—To make known, express, announce, indicate, disclose, or communicate by means of characters formed by a pen, pencil, or the like. (Webster)

The Lord said to Moses, "Chisel out two stones like the first ones, and I will WRITE on them the words that were on the first tablets, which you broke.

Exodus 34:1 (NIV)

Thus speaketh the Lord God of Israel saying, WRITE thee all the words that I have spoken unto thee in a book.

Jeremiah 30:2 (KJ)

So Philip found Nathaniel and told him: "We have found the one whom Moses WROTE in the book of the law, and of whom the prophets also WROTE. He is Jesus, the son of Joseph, from Nazareth."

John 1:45 (Good News)

> Though poor and needy I can trust my Lord,
> Though weak and sinful I believe His WRITTEN WORD;
> Oh glad message! every child of God
> "Hath everlasting life."
>
> Though all unworthy, yet I will not doubt,
> For him that cometh, He will not cast out;
> "He that believeth," oh, the good news shout,
> "Hath everlasting life!"
>
> *(by James McGranaham)*

Adore God for His WRITTEN WORD.

THE GOD WHO USES WRITING

So WRITE this song and teach it to the Israelites, teach them to repeat it, that this song may be a witness for me against the Israelites.

Deuteronomy 30:19 (Moffatt)

My son, keep my words, lay up with you my commandments (for use when needed) and treasure them. Keep my commandments and live, and keep my law and teaching as the apple (the pupil) of your eye. Bind them upon your fingers, WRITE them on the tablet of your heart.

Proverbs 7:1-3 (Amplified)

My friends, I was fully engaged in WRITING to you about our salvation—which is yours no less than ours—when it became urgently necessary to WRITE at once and appeal to you to join the struggle in defense of the faith, the faith which God entrusted to his people once and for all.

Jude 2 & 3 (NEB)

It was the Lord's Day and I was worshipping, when suddenly I heard a loud voice behind me, a voice that sounded like a trumped blast, saying, "I am A and Z, the First and the Last!" And then I heard him say, "WRITE down everything you see, and send your letter to the seven churches in Ephesus, the one in Smyrna, and those in Pergamos, Thyatira, Sardis, Philadelphia, and Laodicea."

Revelation 1:10 & 11 (Paraphrased)

I've a message from the Lord, Hallelujah!
The message unto you I'll give;
"Tis RECORDED in His WORD, Hallelujah!
It is only that you "Look and live."

I've a message full of love, Hallelujah!
A message, O my friend for you;
'Tis a message from above, Hallelujah!
Jesus said it and I know 'tis true.

(by William A. Ogden)

Adore God for His WRITTEN word.

THE GOD WHO USES WRITING

*F*or the Lord has built up Zion; He has appeared in His glory. He has regarded the prayer of the destitute, and has not despised their prayer. This will be WRITTEN for the generation to come; that a people yet to be created may praise the Lord.

Psalm 102:16 & 17 (NAS)

"*T*he sin of Judah is WRITTEN with an iron pen, engraved with a diamond point on the tablet of their heart and on the horns of their altars"

Jeremiah 17:1 (NJB)

*J*ust as it is WRITTEN in the prophet Isaiah: Behold, I send my messenger before Your face, who will make ready Your way;

Mark 1:2 (Amplified)

*A*nd as for us, we are bringing good news to you of the promise which was made to our fathers, that God has completely fulfilled this to our children, having raised up Jesus (as the Messiah), as also in the second Psalm it stands WRITTEN.

Acts 13:33 (Wuest)

*T*rust not in "doing," it cannot avail,
Good resolutions and works can but fail;
"Grace, grace alone" is the saved sinners plea,
"Not of works" the SCRIPTURES say, "Salvation is free."

Trust not in feelings, your heart is depraved,
Trust only Jesus, who now lives to save;
Tears of repentance, though real they may be,
Never can purchase heaven, for "Salvation is free."

(Author unknown)

Adore the God of the WRITTEN word.

THE GOD WHO USES WRITING

*Y*ou saw my bones being formed as I took shape in my mother's body. When I was put together there you saw my body as it was formed. All the days planned for me were WRITTEN in your book before I was one day old.

Psalm 139:15 & 16 (NCV)

*T*hen the fingers of the hand were sent from Him, and this WRITING was WRITTEN. Mene, Mene, Tekel, Upharsen. This is the interpretation of each word. Mene: God has numbered your kingdom, and finished it; Tekel: You have been weighed in the balances, and found wanting; Peres: Your kingdom has been divided, and given to the Medes and Persians."

Daniel 5:24-28 (NKJ)

*H*e then said to them, These are my teachings, which I spoke to you while I was still with you, that everything WRITTEN in the Law of Moses and the Prophets and Psalms about Me must come true. He then opened their minds to understand the SCRIPTURES. He said to them, As it is WRITTEN, that Christ should suffer and rise from the dead on the third day, and that repentance, leading to forgiveness of sin, must be preached in His name to all nations.

Luke 24:44-47 (Berkeley)

*T*hen I looked again and before my eyes the Lamb was standing on Mount Zion, and with him were a hundred and forty-four thousand who had his name and his Father's name WRITTEN upon their foreheads.

Revelation 14:1 (Phillips)

I love to tell the story of unseen things above,
Of Jesus and His glory, Of Jesus and His love.
I love to tell the story, because I know 'tis true.
It satisfies my longings As nothing else can do.

I love to tell the story, 'Tis pleasant to repeat
What seems each time I tell it, more wonderfully sweet.
I love to tell the story, for some have never heard
The message of salvation from God's own HOLY WORD.

(by Catherine Hankey)

Adore God for the WRITTEN word.

THE GOD WHO WAS WOUNDED

WOUND—To inflict harm or injury; literally or figuratively. (Webster)

*B*ut he was WOUNDED for our transgressions, he was BRUISED for our iniquities: the chastisement of our peace was upon him; and with his stripes we are healed.

Isaiah 53:5 (KJ)

*T*hen Pilate took Jesus and had him FLOGGED
The soldiers twisted together a crown of THORNS and put it on his head.
Here (Golgotha) they CRUCIFIED him
One of the soldiers PIERCED Jesus side with a spear.

John 19:1, 2, 18 & 34 (NIV)

*W*OUNDED for me, WOUNDED for me,
There on the cross He was WOUNDED for me;
Gone my transgressions, and now I am free,
All because Jesus was WOUNDED for me.

Dying for me, dying for me,
There on the cross He was dying for me,
Now in His death my redemption I see,
All because Jesus was dying for me.

Rising for me, rising for me,
Up from the grave He has risen for me;
Now evermore from death's sting I am free,
All because Jesus has risen for me.

(by Ovens & Roberts)

Adore God for His willingness to be WOUNDED.

THE GOD WHO WOUNDS
AND WHO HEALS WOUNDS

*D*on't you see that I alone am God? I kill and make alive. I WOUND and I heal—No one delivers from my power.

Deuteronomy 32:39 (Paraphrased)

*T*herefore all who devour you shall be devoured; and all your adversaries, every one of them, shall go into captivity; and those that plunder you shall be for plunder, and all who prey upon you I will give for prey. For I will restore you to health and I will heal you of all your WOUNDS," declares the Lord.

Jeremiah 30:16 & 17a (NAS)

"*B*ehold, happy is the man whom God corrects; Therefore do not despise the chastening of the Almighty. For He bruises, but He binds up; He WOUNDS, but His hands make whole.

Job 5:17 & 18 (NKJ)

*H*e (Jesus) went around the whole of Galilee, teaching in the synagogues, preaching the gospel of the Kingdom, and CURING whatever illness or infirmity there was among the people.

Matthew 4:23 (NEB)

O blessed voice of Jesus, which comes to hearts OPPRESSED,
Come unto me ye weary ones, and I will give you rest.
O loving voice of Jesus, which comes to cheer the night,
Come unto me dear children and I will give you light.

O cheering voice of Jesus; which comes to aid our WOUNDS
Come unto me ye fainting, and I will give you life.
O welcome voice of Jesus, which drives away our doubts,
And whosoever cometh, I will not cast him out.

(by Wm. C. Dix)

Adore God for the WOUNDS He allows and for their healing.

THE WILL OF GOD

🔳 WILL—To determine by an act of choice; to form a distinct volition of; to ordain, to decree; to decide. (Webster)

Then the Lord God said, "It is not good for the man to be alone; I WILL make him a helper suitable for him."

Genesis 2:18 (NAS)

"But I WILL establish My covenant with you; and you shall go into the ark—you, your sons, your wife, and your sons wives with you."

Genesis 6:18 (NKJ)

For after seven days I WILL make it rain on earth for forty days and forty nights, and I WILL blot off the earth every living creature that I ever made."

Genesis 7:4 (Moffatt)

Be not dismayed what-e'er betide,
God WILL take care of you;
Beneath His wings of love abide,
God WILL take care of you.

God WILL take care of you,
Through every day, O'er all the way;
He WILL take care of you,
God WILL take care of you.

(by Civilla D. Martin)

Adore God for His WILL in all matters.

THE WILL OF GOD

*T*hen his (Abraham's) guest said, "I shall visit you again next year without fail, and your wife WILL then have a son.

Genesis 18:10 (NJB)

*I*saac spoke up and said to his father Abraham, "Father?" "Yes, my son?" Abraham replied. "The fire and the wood are here," Isaac said, "but where is the lamb for the burnt offering?" Abraham answered, "God himself WILL provide the lamb for the burnt offering, my son." And the two of them went on together.

Genesis 22:7 & 8 (NIV)

*A*nd the Lord said, (to Moses) I have surely seen the affliction of my people which are in Egypt, and have heard their cry by reason of their taskmasters; for I know their sorrows. Come now therefore, and I WILL send thee unto Pharaoh, that thou mayest bring forth my people the children of Israel out of Egypt.

Exodus 3:7 & 10 (KJ)

> *T*hrough days of toil when heart doth fail,
> God WILL take care of you;
> When dangers fierce your path assail,
> God WILL take care of you.
>
> No matter what may be the test,
> God WILL take care of you;
> Lean weary one, upon His breast,
> God WILL take care of you.
>
> *(by Civilla D. Martin)*

Adore God for His perfect WILL.

THE WILL OF GOD

"*N*ow is the time!" he (Abner) told them, "For the Lord has said, 'It is David by whom I WILL save my people from the Philistines and from all their enemies.'"

2 Samuel 3:18 (Paraphrased)

*A*fter the Lord had said these things to Job, he said to Eliphaz the Temanite, "I am angry with you and your two friends, because you have not said what is right about me, as my servant Job did. Now take seven bulls and seven male sheep, and go to my servant Job, and offer a burnt offering for yourselves. My servant Job will pray for you, and I WILL listen to his prayer."

Job 42:7 & 8 (NCV)

*T*he Lord has heard my supplication; the Lord WILL receive my prayer.

Psalm 6:9 (NKJ)

I, the Lord, WILL instruct you and teach you in the way you should go; I WILL counsel you with My eye upon you.

Psalm 33:8 (Amplified)

*M*y help comes from the Lord, Who made heaven and earth. He WILL not allow your foot to slip; He who keeps you WILL not slumber. The Lord WILL protect you from all evil; He WILL keep your soul. The Lord WILL guard your going out and your coming in from this time forth and forever.

Psalm 121:2 & 3, 7 & 8 (NAS)

*H*e was not WILLING that any should perish;
Jesus enthroned in the glory above,
Saw our poor fallen world, pitied our sorrows,
Poured out His life for us, wonderful love

(by Lucy R. Meyer)

Adore God for His perfect WILL.

THE WILL OF GOD

*T*each me to do THY WILL; for thou art my God; thy spirit is good; lead me into the land of uprightness.

Psalm 143:10 (KJ)

*T*he Lord WILL not let a good man starve to death, nor WILL he let the wicked man's riches continue forever.

Proverbs 10:3 (Paraphrased)

*T*he Lord Yahweh WILL wipe away the tears from every cheek; he WILL take away his people's shame everywhere on earth, for Yahweh has said so.

Isaiah 25:8 (NJB)

*T*hey have gone back to the iniquities of their ancestors, who would not listen to what I said; they have gone after foreign gods, to serve them; the house of Israel and the house of Judah have broken the compact that I made with their fathers. Therefore (the Eternal declares) I am bringing on them disaster that they cannot escape; nor WILL I listen to them, when they cry to me.

Jeremiah 11:10 & 11 (Moffatt)

*B*ut you, Bethlehem Ephrathah, though you are small among the clans of Judah, out of you WILL come for me one who WILL be ruler over Israel, whose origins are from old, from ancient times.

Micah 5:2 (NIV)

*H*e was not WILLING that any should perish:
Clothed in our flesh with its sorrow and pain,
Came He to seek the lost, comfort the mourner,
Heal the heart broken by sorrow and shame.

(by Lucy R. Mayer)

Adore God for His perfect WILL.

THE WILL OF GOD

*O*ur Father in heaven, Thy name be hallowed; Thy kingdom come, Thy WILL be done, On earth as it is in heaven. For if you forgive others the wrongs they have done, your heavenly Father WILL also forgive you.

Matthew 6:9,10,14 (NEB)

He (Jesus) said, See, My mother and My brothers! Whoever does the WILL of God that one is My brother and sister and mother.

Mark 3:35 (Berkeley)

*J*esus left and went, as he usually did, to the Mount of Olives; and the disciples went with him. When he came to the place he said to them, "Pray that you will not fall into temptation." Then he went off from them, about the distance of a stone's throw, and knelt down and prayed. "Father," he said, "if you WILL, take this cup away from me. Not my will, however, but your WILL be done.

Luke 22:39-42 (GN)

*H*owever, I am telling you nothing but the truth when I say, it is profitable— good, expedient, advantageous—for you that I go away. Because if I do not go away, the Comforter (Counselor, Helper, Advocate, Intercessor, Strengthener, Standby) will not come to you—into close fellowship with you. But if I go away, I WILL send Him to you—to be in close fellowship with you.

John 16:7 (Amplified)

> *Th*ere's not a friend like the lowly Jesus,
> No, not one! no, not one!
> None else could heal all our soul's diseases,
> No, not one! no, not one!
>
> Jesus knows all about our struggles,
> He WILL guide till the day is done;
> There's not a friend like the lowly Jesus,
> No, not one! no, not one!
>
> *(by Johnson Oatman)*

Adore God's perfect WILL.

THE WILL OF GOD

And it shall be in the last days, saith God, I WILL pour forth my spirit upon all flesh.

Acts 2:17 (Phillips)

For God, whom I serve in my spirit in the preaching of the gospel of His Son, is my witness as to how unceasingly I make mention of you, always in my prayers making request, if perhaps now at last by the WILL of God I may succeed in coming to you.

Romans 1:9 & 10 (NAS)

Paul, a divinely-summoned and divinely appointed ambassador belonging to Christ Jesus, an ambassador by reason of God's determining WILL.

1 Corinthians 1:1 (Wuest)

We are the temple of the living God. As God said: "I WILL live with them and walk with them. And I WILL be their God, and they WILL be my people." Leave those people and be separate, says the lord. Touch nothing that is unclean, and I WILL accept you. "I WILL be your father, and you WILL be my sons and daughters, says the Almighty."

2 Corinthians 6:16b-18 (NCV)

If I come to Jesus,
He WILL save my soul,
Seal me by His Spirit,
Cleanse, and make me whole.

If I come to Jesus,
Happy I shall be;
He is gently calling
To people like me.

(by Fanny J. Crosby)

Adore God for His perfect WILL.

THE WILL OF GOD

*F*or this is the WILL of God, that you should be consecrated—separated and set apart for pure and holy living: that you should abstain and shrink from all sexual vice; That each one of you should know how to possess (control, manage) his own body (in purity, separated from things profane, and) in consecration and honor.

1 Thessalonians 4:3 & 4 (Amplified)

*C*ome close to God, and he WILL come close to you.

James 4:8 (NEB)

*L*et every listener hear what the spirit says to the churches: To the victorious I WILL give the right to eat from the tree of life which grows in the paradise of God.

Revelation 2:7 (Phillips)

*A*nd I heard a strong voice from the throne say, "Behold God's dwelling place is among men and He WILL dwell with them: they shall be His peoples, and God WILL personally be with them and shall wipe away every tear from their eyes. Death shall be no longer, nor grief, nor crying, nor any further pain, because the first things have passed away.

Revelation 21:3 & 4 (Berkeley)

*I*f I come to Jesus,
If I come to Jesus,
He WILL save my soul,
He WILL take my hand,
Seal me by His Spirit,
He WILL kindly lead me
Cleanse, and make me whole.
To the better land.

There with happy people,
Robed in snowy white,
I shall see my Saviour,
In that world so bright.

(by Fanny J. Crosby)

Adore God for His perfect WILL.

December 9

THE GREAT AMEN

AMEN—This Hebrew word means FIRM, and hence also FAITHFUL. The phrase "God of TRUTH" in Hebrew means "the God of AMEN". (Today's)

*T*hen write this to the angel of the church of Laodicea: These are the words of the AMEN, the FAITHFUL and TRUE witness, the beginning of God's creation.

Revelation 3:14 (Phillips)

*W*hosoever asks to be blessed on earth will ask to be blessed by the GOD of TRUTH, and whoever takes oath on earth will take oath by the GOD of TRUTH.

Isaiah 65:16 (NJB)

*F*or as many promises as are promises of God have become in Him yes and are a yes at present. Wherefore also through Him is the AMEN to the glory of God through us.

2 Corinthians 1:20 (Wuest)

> *A*ll praise to Him who reigns above,
> In majesty supreme,
> Who gave His Son for man to die,
> That He might man redeem.
>
> Blessed be the name,
> Blessed be the name,
> Blessed be the name of the Lord.
> AMEN!
>
> *(by Clark & Hudson)*

Adore the great AMEN.

THE GREAT AMEN

AMEN—1. A term in Scripture to denote Christ. 2. So be it. 3. An expression of hearty assent, or confession of faith. (Webster)

*B*lessed be the Lord God of Israel from everlasting, and to everlasting. AMEN, and AMEN.

Psalm 41:13 (KJ)

*P*raise be to the Lord God, the God of Israel, who alone does marvelous deeds. Praise be to his glorious name forever; may the whole earth be filled with his glory. AMEN and AMEN.

Psalm 72:18 & 19 (NIV)

*P*eace be to the brethren, and love joined with faith, from God the Father and the Lord Jesus Christ, the Messiah, the Anointed one. Grace (God's undeserved favor) be with all who love our Lord Jesus Christ with undying and incorruptible [love]. AMEN—so let it be.

Ephesians 6:23 & 24 (Amplified)

> *G*lory be to the Father,
> And to the Son,
> And to the Holy Ghost;
> As it was in the beginning,
> Is now and ever shall be,
> World without end.
> AMEN, AMEN.
>
> *(Author unknown)*

Adore God for being the final Word, our AMEN.

THE GREAT AMEN

AMEN—used at the beginning of a sentence it emphasizes what is about to be said. It is frequently employed by our Lord and Translated "VERILY". (Unger's)

Newer versions say "TRULY"

*V*ERILY I say unto you, All sins shall be forgiven unto the sons of men, and blasphemies wherewith so ever they shall blaspheme.

Mark 3:28 (KJ)

*A*nd he said, TRULY, I say to you, unless you repent (change, turn about) and become like little children (trusting, lowly, loving, forgiving) you can never enter the kingdom of heaven at all.

Matthew 18:3 (Amplified)

*J*esus answered him, TRULY, I assure you, unless a person is born from above he cannot see the kingdom of God.

John 3:3 (Berkeley)

> *O*h, what a Saviour, that He died for me!
> From condemnation He hath made me free;
> "He that believeth on the Son," saith He,
> "Hath everlasting life.
>
> "VERILY, VERILY, I say unto you,"
> "VERILY, VERILY", message ever new;
> "He that believeth on the Son," 'tis true.
> "Hath everlasting life."
>
> *(by James McGransham)*

Adore the Great AMEN.

THE GREAT AMEN

AMEN—It is used as a word of confirmation, binding a saying, or an oath, and as a response or closing to a prayer. (Smith's)

"The curse of God be upon anyone who makes and worships an idol, even in secret, whether carved of wood or made from molten metal—for those handmade gods are hated by the Lord." And all the people shall reply, "AMEN."

Cursed is anyone who despises his father or mother. And all the people shall say, "AMEN"

Cursed is he who moves the boundary marker between his land and his neighbor's. And all the people shall say, "AMEN."

Cursed is he who takes advantage of a blind man. And all the people shall say, "AMEN".

Cursed is he who is unjust to the foreigner, the orphan, and the widow. And etc. "AMEN"

Cursed is he who commits adultery   "AMEN"
Cursed is he who has sexual intercourse with an animal   "AMEN"
Cursed is he who in secret slays another   "AMEN"
Cursed is he who accepts a bribe to kill   "AMEN"
Cursed is anyone who does not obey these laws   "AMEN"

Deuteronomy 27:15-26 (Paraphrased)

Blessed be Yahweh the God of Israel, from all eternity and for ever! Here, all the people are to say, "Amen".

Psalm 106:48 (NJB)

Come, almighty to deliver,
Let us all Thy life receive;
Suddenly return, and never,
Never more Thy temples leave.

Thee we would be always blessing,
Serve Thee as Thy hosts above,
Pray and praise Thee without ceasing,
Glory in Thy perfect love.
AMEN.

(Author unknown)

Adore the great AMEN.

THE GREAT AMEN

Praise the Lord forever! AMEN and AMEN.

Psalm 89:52 (NJB)

The prophet Jeremiah spoke in the presence of the priests and in the presence of all the people who were standing in the house of the Lord, and the prophet Jeremiah said, "AMEN! May the Lord do so; may the Lord confirm your words which you have prophesied to bring back the vessels of the Lord's house and all the exiles from Babylon to this place."

Jeremiah 28:5 & 6 (NAS)

Don't bring us into temptation, but deliver us from the evil one. AMEN.

Matthew 6:13 (Paraphrased)

May God, who rules over all, be forever praised! AMEN

Romans 9:3b (GN)

> The Lord's my shepherd, I'll not want;
> He makes me down to lie In pastures green;
> He leadeth me the quiet waters by.
>
> Yea, though I walk through death's dark vale,
> Yet will I fear no ill; For Thou art with me
> And Thy rod and staff me comfort still.
>
> Goodness and mercy all my life
> Shall surely follow me; And in God's house
> Forever more My dwelling place shall be.
> AMEN.

(by William Whittingham)

Adore the great AMEN.

THE GREAT AMEN

The grace of our Lord Jesus Christ be with you. My love be with you all in Christ Jesus. AMEN.

1 Corinthians 16:23 & 24 (NKJ)

Grace and peace to you from God our Father and the Lord Jesus Christ who gave himself for our sins to rescue us from the present evil world—by the will of our God and Father, to whom be glory for ever and ever. AMEN.

Galatians 1:3-5 (Moffatt)

And the God of all grace, who called you into eternal glory in Christ, will himself, after your brief suffering, restore, establish, and strengthen you on a firm foundation. He holds dominion for ever and ever. AMEN.

1 Peter 5:10 & 11 (NEV)

AMEN! (So be it) they cried. Blessing and glory and majesty and splendor and wisdom and thanks and honor and power and might (be ascribed) to our God to the ages and ages—forever and ever, throughout the eternity's of the eternity's! AMEN! (So be it)

Revelation 7:12 (Amplified)

Majestic sweetness sits enthroned
Upon the Saviour's brow;
His head with radiant glories crowned,
His lips with grace over-flow.

Since from His bounty I receive
Such proofs of love divine,
Had I a thousand hearts to give,
Lord, they should all be thine.
AMEN.

(by Samuel Stennett)

Adore the great AMEN.

OUR GOD OF WONDERS

■ WONDERS—That which excites surprise; a strange thing; a cause of astonishment or admiration; a prodigy or miracle. (Webster)

*F*or unto us a child is born, unto us a son is given, and the government shall be upon his shoulders, And he will be called WONDERFUL Counselor, Mighty God, Everlasting Father, Prince of Peace.

Isaiah 9:6 (NIV)

*M*any, O Lord my God, are the WONDERFUL works which thou hast done, and thy thoughts which are to us-ward: they cannot be reckoned up in order unto thee: if I would declare and speak of them they are more than can be numbered.

Psalm 40:5 (KJ)

*A*nd I will show WONDERS in the sky above and signs on the earth beneath, blood and fire and smoking vapor; The sun shall be turned into darkness and the moon into blood, before the obvious day of the Lord comes, that great and notable and conspicuous and renowned (day).

Acts 2:19 & 20 (Amplified)

*W*ONDERFUL story of love;
Tell it to me again;
WONDERFUL story of love;
Wake the immortal strain!

Angels with rapture announce it,
Shepherds with WONDER receive it,
Sinner, O won't you believe it?
WONDERFUL story of love.

(by J.M. Driver)

Adore our God of WONDERS.

OUR GOD OF WONDERS

WONDERS synonyms—Admiration, appreciation, astonishment, reverence, surprise, amazement, marvelous. (Webster)

Your rules are WONDERFUL. That is why I keep them.

Psalm 119:129 (NCV)

You will eat to your hearts content, will eat your fill, and praise the name of Yahweh your God who has treated you so WONDERFULLY. (My people will not be disappointed any more.)

Joel 2:26 (NJB)

The chief priests and doctors of the law saw the WONDERFUL things he did, and heard the boys in the temple shouting, "Hosanna to the Son of David."

Matthew 21:15 (NEB)

WONDERFUL story of love;
Jesus provides a rest;
WONDERFUL story of love;
For all the pure and blest,

Rest in the mansions above us,
With those who've gone on before us,
Singing the rapturous chorus,
WONDERFUL story of love.

(by J. M. Driver)

Adore our God of WONDERS.

OUR GOD OF WONDERS

I will confess and praise You, for you are fearfully WONDERFUL, and for the awful WONDER of my birth! WONDERFUL are Your WORKS, and that my inner self knows right well.

Psalm 139:14 (Amplified)

'*Tis* the Eternal who this love supplies, so great a guide, so WONDERFULLY wise.

Isaiah 28:29 (Moffatt)

Stretch out your hand to heal, and grant that WONDERS and miracles may be performed through the name of your holy Servant Jesus.

Acts 4:30 (GN)

So then they remained for a considerable time, speaking freely with reliance on the Lord, who witnessed to the message of His grace by granting signs and WONDERS to occur through them.

Acts 14:3 (Berkeley)

> *Would* you be free from the burden of sin?
> There's power in the blood, power in the blood;
> Would you o'er evil a victory win?
> There's WONDERFUL power in the blood.
>
> Would you do service for Jesus you King?
> There's power in the blood, power in the blood;
> Would you live daily His praises to sing?
> There's WONDERFUL power in the blood.
>
> *(by Lewis E. Jones)*

Adore our God of WONDERS.

OUR GOD OF WONDERS

I will (earnestly) recall the deeds of the Lord; yes, I will (earnestly) remember the WONDERS (You performed for our fathers) of old.

Psalm 77:11 (Amplified)

I (King Darius) make a decree, That in every dominion of my kingdom men tremble and fear before the God of Daniel: for he is the living God, and steadfast forever, and his kingdom that which shall not be destroyed, and his dominion shall be even unto the end. He delivereth and rescueth, and he worketh signs and WONDERS in heaven and in earth, who hath delivered Daniel from the power of the lions.

Daniel 6:26 & 27 (KJ)

These words produced absolute silence, and they listened to Barnabas and Paul while they gave detailed account of the signs and WONDERS which God had worked through them among the Gentiles.

Acts 15:12 (Phillips)

"*Mighty* your acts and MARVELOUS, O God, the Sovereign-Strong! Righteous your ways and true, King of the nations! Who can fail to fear you, God, give glory to your name? Because you and you only are holy, all nations will come and worship you, because they see your judgments are right."

Revelation 15:3 (Message)

*W*ONDERFUL, WONDERFUL Jesus!
Who can compare with Thee!
WONDERFUL, WONDERFUL Jesus!
Fairer than all art Thou to me.

WONDERFUL, WONDERFUL Jesus!
Oh, how my soul loves Thee!
Fairer than all the fairest,
Jesus, art Thou to me!

(by Benjamin A. Baur)

Adore our God of WONDERS.

THE GOD OF YESTERDAY, TODAY AND FOREVER

YESTERDAY—The day last past; the day next before the present. (Webster)

*L*ord, you have been our refuge age after age. Before the mountains were born, before the earth or the world came into birth you were God from all eternity and for ever. To you, a thousand years are a single day, a YESTERDAY now over, an hour of the night.

Psalm 90:1,2 & 4 (NJB)

*I*t is in the power of my hand to do you hurt; but the God of your fathers spake unto me YESTERNIGHT, saying, Take thou heed that thou speak not to Jacob either good or bad.

Genesis 31:29 (KJ)

*J*esus Christ is the same YESTERDAY, TODAY and FOREVER. So do not be swept off your course by all sorts of outlandish teachings; it is good that our souls should gain their strength from the grace of God.

Hebrews 13:7 & 8a (NEB)

> *O* how sweet the glorious message
> Simple faith may claim:
> YESTERDAY, TODAY, FOREVER
> Jesus is the same!
>
> Still He loves to save the sinful,
> Heal the sick and lame,
> Cheer the mourner, calm the tempest
> Glory to His name.
>
> *(by Albert B. Simpson)*

Adore the God of YESTERDAY.

THE GOD OF YESTERDAY, TODAY AND FOREVER

TODAY—This present day. (Webster)

*T*HIS IS THE DAY which the Lord has made: we will rejoice and be glad in it.

Psalm 118:24 (NKJ)

*P*ray along these lines: 'Our Father in heaven, we honor your holy name. We ask that your kingdom will come now. May your will be done here on earth, just as it is in heaven. Give us our food again TODAY, as usual, and forgive our sins, just as we have forgiven those who have sinned against us. Don't bring us into temptation, but deliver us from the Evil One. Amen

Matthew 6:9-13 (Paraphrased)

*H*e made a solemn promise to our ancestor Abraham, and vowed he would rescue us from our enemies, and allow us to serve him without fear, to be holy and righteous before him, all the DAYS of our life.

Luke 1:73-75 (GN)

*H*e who pardoned erring Peter He who let the loved disciple
Never needest thou fear, On His bosom rest
He who came to faithless Thomas Bids thee still, with love as tender,
All thy doubts will clear; Lean upon His breast.

Luke 1:73-75 (GN)

*Y*ESTERDAY, TODAY, FOREVER,
Jesus is the same;
All may change, but Jesus never
Glory to His name.

(by Albert B. Simpson)

Adore the God of THIS PRESENT DAY.

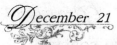

December 21

THE GOD OF YESTERDAY, TODAY AND FOREVER

FOREVER—Throughout eternity; endlessly; for ever. (Webster)

The Eternal reigns FOR EVERMORE!

Exodus 15:18 (Moffatt)

The Lord is King FOR EVER AND EVER;

Psalms 10:16a (NAS)

The people came back at Him, "We have learned in the Law that the Christ remains FOREVER.

John 12:34a (Berkeley)

Now to Him Who is able to strengthen you in the faith which is in accordance with my Gospel and the preaching of (concerning) Jesus Christ the Messiah, according to the revelation—the unveiling—of the mystery of the plan of redemption which was kept in silence and secret for long ages, but is now disclosed and through the prophetic Scriptures is made known to all nations, according to the command of the eternal God, (to win them) to obedience to the faith, to (the) only wise God be glory FOR EVERMORE through Jesus Christ, the Anointed One! Amen—so be it.

Romans 16:25-27 (Amplified)

> Love of the Sovereign King
> Blest in this love we sing;
> To God our praises bring;
> All sins forgiven.
>
> Jesus, our Lord,
> To Thee Honor and majesty,
> Now, and FOREVER be,
> Here, and in Heaven
>
> *(by Thomas Kelly)*

Adore the God who will reign FOREVER.

THE GOD OF YESTERDAY, TODAY AND FOREVER

FOREVER synonyms—Perpetually, eternally, endlessly. (Webster)

God said to Moses, I am who I am, This is what you are to say to the Israelites: 'I AM has sent me to you.'" God also said to Moses, "Say to the Israelites, "The Lord, the God of your fathers—the God of Abraham, the God of Isaac and the God of Jacob—has sent me to you. This is my name FOREVER, the name by which I am to be remembered from generation to generation."

Exodus 3:14 & 15 (NIV)

The Lord is King FOR EVER and EVER; the nations are perished out of His land.

Psalm 10:16 (Amplified)

For God so loved the world that he gave his only begotten Son, that whosoever believeth in him shall not perish, but have EVERLASTING life.

John 3:16 (KJ)

Those who believe in the Son have ETERNAL life, but those who do not obey the Son will never have life. God's anger stays on them.

John 3:36 (NCV)

Oh, what a Saviour, that He died for me!
From condemnation He hath made me free;
"He that believeth on the Son," saith He,
"Hath EVERLASTING life."

All my iniquities on Him were laid,
All my indebtedness by Him was paid;
All who believe on Him, the Lord hath said,
"Hath EVERLASTING LIFE."

(by James McGranaham)

Adore the God of YESTERDAY, TODAY AND FOREVER.

THE GOD OF YESTERDAY, TODAY AND FOREVER

The dead cannot sing praises to Jehovah here on earth, but we can! We praise him FOREVER! Hallelujah! Praise the Lord!

Psalm 115:17 & 18 (Paraphrased)

And I saw another angel flying in mid-heaven, having a message of good news ETERNAL in its character to proclaim as glad tidings to those who live upon the earth, and to every nation and tribe and language and people, saying with a great voice, Fear God at once and at once give Him glory, because the hour of His judgment has come, and worship Him at once who made the heaven and the earth and sea and springs of water.

Revelation 14:6 & 7 (Wuest)

All who were standing around the Throne—Angels, Elders, Animals—fell on their faces before the Throne and worshipped God saying: "Oh, Yes! The blessing and glory and wisdom and thanksgiving, the honor and power and strength, To our God FOR EVER and EVER! Oh, Yes!

Revelation 7:12 (Message)

There will be no more night. They will not need the light of a lamp or the light of the sun, for the Lord will give them light. And they will reign FOR EVER and EVER.

Revelation 22:5 (NIV)

Though all unworthy, yet I will not doubt,
For him that cometh, He will not cast out;
He that believeth, oh, the good news shout,
"Hath EVERLASTING life!"

Verily, verily, I say unto you,
Verily, verily, message ever new;
"He that believeth on the Son," tis true,
"Hath EVERLASTING life."

(by James McGransham)

Adore the God of YESTERDAY, TODAY and FOREVER.

THE GOD WHO CREATED ANGELS

ANGEL—literally, a messenger; one employed to communicate news or information to another at a distance. A Spirit, or a spiritual being, employed by God, to communicate His will to man. (Webster)

*N*ow the ANGEL found her by a spring of water in the wilderness, by the spring on the way to Shur. And he said, Hagar, Sarai's maid, where have you come from and where are you going?" And she said, "I am fleeing from the presence of my mistress Sarai." Then the angel of the Lord said to her. "Return to your mistress, and submit yourself to their authority. "Moreover the ANGEL of the Lord said to her, "I will greatly multiply your descendants so that they shall be too many to count."

Genesis 16:7-10 (NAS)

*N*ow I am sending an ANGEL in front of you, to guard you as you go and to guide you to the place I have prepared.

Exodus 23:20 (Moffatt)

*N*ow the birth of Jesus took place under these circumstances: When His mother Mary had been promised in marriage to Joseph, before they came together she was found to be pregnant (through the power) of the Holy Spirit. And her (promised) husband Joseph, being a just and upright man and not willing to expose her publicly and shame and disgrace her, decided to repudiate and dismiss (divorce) her quietly and secretly. But as he was thinking this over, behold, an ANGEL appeared to him in a dream, saying, Joseph, descendant of David, do not be afraid to take Mary (as) your wife, for that which is conceived in her is of (from, out of) the Holy Spirit.

Matthew 1:19 & 20 (Amplified)

O Come, all ye faithful, joyful and triumphant,
O come ye, O come ye to Bethlehem;
Come and behold Him born the King of ANGELS
O Come, let us adore Him, Christ, the Lord

Sing, choirs of ANGELS, Sing in exultation,
O sing, all ye bright hosts of heaven above.
Glory to God, all glory in the highest;
O come, let us adore Him, Christ the Lord.

(by Frederick Oakley)

Begin your prayer time adoring the God of ANGELS.

THE GOD WHO CREATED ANGELS

▦ ANGEL—In its most common use in Scripture the word designates certain spiritual and superhuman beings, who are there introduced to us as messengers of God. (Unger)

*T*hen Gideon understood he had been talking to the ANGEL of the Lord. So Gideon cried out, "Lord, God! I have seen the ANGEL of the Lord face to face! But the Lord said to Gideon, "Calm down! Don't be afraid! You will not die!" So Gideon built an altar there to worship the Lord and named it The Lord Is Peace.

Judges 6:22-24 (NCV)

*W*hen the Sabbath was over, just as the first day of the week was dawning, Mary from Magdala and the other Mary went to look at the tomb. At that moment there was a great earthquake, for an ANGEL of the Lord came down from Heaven, went forward and rolled back the stone and took his seat upon it.

Matthew 28:1 & 2 (Phillips)

*T*he High Priest and all his companions, members of the local party of the Sadducees, became extremely jealous of the apostles; so they decided to take action. They arrested the apostles and placed them in the public jail. But that night an ANGEL of the Lord opened the prison gates, led the apostles out, and said to them, "Go and stand in the Temple, and tell the people all about this new life."

Acts 5:17-20 (GN)

> *W*hile shepherds watched their flocks by night,
> All seated on the ground,
> The ANGEL of the Lord came down,
> And glory shone around
>
> "Fear not!" said he, for mighty dread
> Had seized their troubled mind,
> "Glad tidings of great joy I bring
> To you and all mankind"
>
> *(by Nahum Tate)*

Begin you prayer time adoring the God of ANGELS.

THE GOD WHO CREATED ANGELS

A certain man of Zorah, named Manoah, from the clan of the Danites, had a wife who was sterile and remained childless. The ANGEL of the Lord appeared to her and said, "You are sterile and childless, but you are going to conceive and have a son. Now see to it that you drink no wine or other fermented drink and that you do not eat anything unclean, because you will conceive and give birth to a son. No razor may be used on his head, because the boy is a Nazirite, set apart to God from birth, and he will begin the deliverance of Israel from the hand of the Philistines."

Judges 13:2-5 (NIV)

*S*o, on an appointed day, attired in his royal robes and seated on a rostrum, Herod harangued them; and the populace shouted back, "it is a god speaking, not a man!" Instantly an ANGEL of the Lord struck him down, because he had usurped the honor due to God; he was eaten up with worms and died.

Acts 12:21-23 (NEB)

*A*nd I saw upon the right hand of One seated on the throne a scroll which was inscribed on both sides and sealed shut with seven seals. And I saw an ANGEL, a strong one, proclaiming with a great voice, Who is worthy to open the scroll and to break its seals?

Revelation 5:1 & 2 (Wuest)

*A*NGELS, from the realms of glory,
Wing your flight over all the earth;
Ye who sang creations story,
Now proclaim Messiah's birth

Come and worship, come and worship,
Worship Christ the Newborn King

(by James Montgomery)

Begin your prayer time adoring the God who created ANGELS.

THE GOD WHO CREATED ANGELS

*T*hen Nebuchadnezzar said, "Blessed be the God of Shadrach, Meshach and Abednego, for he sent an ANGEL to deliver his trusting servants when they defied the king's commandment, and were willing to die rather than serve or worship any god except their own.

Daniel 3:28 (Paraphrased)

*F*or what advantage shall a man have if he acquires the whole world and forfeits his own life, or what shall a man offer in exchange for his life? For the Son of Man is about to come in the glory of the Father with His ANGELS, and He shall reward each according to his behavior.

Matthew 16:26 & 27 (Berkeley)

I, Jesus, have sent My ANGEL to testify to you these things in the churches. I am the Root, and the Offspring of David, the Bright and Morning Star.

Revelation 22:16 (NKJ)

*I*t came upon the midnight clear, That glorious song of old,
From ANGELS bending near the earth To touch their harps of gold:
"Peace on the earth, good-will to men, From heavens all-gracious King":
The world in solemn stillness lay to hear the ANGELS sing.

Still through the cloven skies they come, With peaceful wings unfurled,
And still their heavenly music floats O'er all the weary world:
Above its sad and lowly plains They bend on hovering wing:
And ever o'er its Babel sounds The blessed ANGELS sing.

(by Edmond Sears)

Begin your prayer time adoring the God who created ANGELS.

THE ZEAL OF THE LORD

ZEAL—Passionate ardor for any person or cause; intense and eager pursuit or endeavor; an eagerness of desire to attain or accomplish some object, which may be manifested either in favor of or in opposition to any person or thing. (Webster)

For out of Jerusalem shall go forth a remnant, and they shall escape out of Mount Zion: the ZEAL of the Lord of hosts shall do this.

2 Kings 19:31 (KJ)

The Lord will march out like a mighty man, like a warrior he will stir up his ZEAL; with a shout he will raise the battle cry and will triumph over his enemies.

Isaiah 42:13 (NIV)

And His disciples remembered that it is written (in the Holy Scriptures), The ZEAL, the fervor of love for Your house will eat Me up. I will be consumed with jealousy for the honor of Your house.

John 2:17 (Amplified)

Rock of Ages, cleft for me,
Let me hide myself in Thee;
Let the water and the blood,
From Thy riven side which flowed,
Be of sin the double cure,
Cleanse me from its guilt and power.

Not the labors of my hands
Can fulfill Thy laws demands;
Could my ZEAL no respite know,
Could my tears forever flow,
All for sin could not atone,
Thou must save and Thou alone.

(by Augustus M. Toplady)

Adore God for the ZEAL of His love.

THE ZEAL OF THE LORD

⊞ ZEAL synonyms—Ardor, fervor, enthusiasm, fervency, earnestness, animation, eagerness, vehemence. (Webster)

"*For* out of Jerusalem shall go forth a remnant, and out of Mount Zion survivors. The ZEAL of the Lord of hosts shall perform this."

Isaiah 37:32 (NAS)

Thus shall My anger be spent, and I will cause my fury to rest upon them, and I will be avenged; and they shall know that I, the Lord, have spoken it in my ZEAL, when I have spent my fury upon them.

Ezekiel 5:13 (NKJ)

In great anguish he prayed even more FERVENTLY; his sweat was like drops of blood falling to the ground.

Luke 22:44 (GN)

> *S*oftly and tenderly Jesus is calling,
> Calling for you and for me;
> See, on the portals He's waiting and watching,
> Watching for you and for me.
>
> Come home, come home,
> Ye who are weary, come ;
> EARNESTLY, tenderly, Jesus is calling,
> Calling, "O sinner, come home."

(by Will L. Thompson)

Adore God for His ZEAL.

THE ZEAL OF GOD

*L*ook down from Heaven and see from the dwelling place of Your holiness and Your glory. Where are Your ZEAL and Your jealousy, and Your mighty acts (which you formerly did for Your people)? Your yearning pity and the (multitude of) compassions of Your heart are restrained and withheld from me.

Isaiah 63:15 (Amplified)

*B*rethren, the consuming desire of my heart and my supplication to God on behalf of them is with a view to their salvation. For I bear testimony to them that a ZEAL for God they have, but not according to a full and accurate knowledge.

Romans 10:1 & 2 (Wuest)

*E*paphras, who is one of you, a servant of Christ, saluteth you, always laboring FERVENTLY for you in prayers, that ye may stand perfect and complete in all the will of God.

Colossians 4:12 & 13 (KJ)

I continually discipline and punish everyone I love; so I must punish you, unless you turn from your indifference and become ENTHUSIASTIC about things of God.

Revelation 3:19 (Paraphrased)

*Y*e Christian heralds, go proclaim
God shield you with a wall of fire,
Salvation through Emmanuel's name
With flaming ZEAL your hearts inspire,

To distant climes the tidings bear,
Bid raging winds their fury cease,
And plant the Rose of Sharon there.
And hush the tempests into peace.

And when our labors all are over,
Then we shall meet to part no more;
Meet with the blood-bought throng to fall,
And crown our Jesus Lord of all

(by Bourne H. Draper)

Adore God for His ZEAL.

THE ZEAL OF GOD

*L*ook down from Heaven and see from the dwelling place of Your Holiness and Your glory. Where are Your ZEAL and Your jealousy, and your mighty acts (which your formerly did for your people)? Your yearning pity and the (multitude of) compassions of your heart are restrained and with held from me.

Isaiah 63:15 (Amplified)

*B*rethren, the consuming desire of my heart and my supplication to God on behalf of them is with a view to their salvation. For I bear testimony to them that a ZEAL for God they have, but not according to a full and accurate knowledge.

Romans 10:1 & 2 (Wuest)

*E*paphras, who is one of you, a servant of Christ, saluteth you, always laboring FERVENTLY for you in prayers, that ye may stand perfect and complete in all the will of God.

Colossians 4:12 (KJ)

I continually discipline and punish everyone I love; so I must punish you, unless you turn from your indifference and become ENTHUSIASTIC about things of God.

Revelation 3:19 (Paraphrased)

*Y*e Christian heralds, go proclaim
God shield you with a wall of fire,
Salvation through Emmanuel's name
With flaming ZEAL your hearts inspire,
To distant climes the tidings bear,
Bid raging winds their fury cease,
And plant the Rose of Sharon there.
And hush the tempests into peace.

And when our labors all are over,
Then we shall meet to part no more;
Meet with the blood-bought throng to fall,
And crown our Jesus Lord of all.

(by Bourne H. Draper)

Adore God for His ZEAL.

BIBLIOGRAPHY

King James Version .... KJ
New Century Version .... NCV
New International Version .... NIV
The Living Bible .... TLB or Paraphrased
The Amplified Old Testament .... Amplified
The Bible .... Moffatt
The Message .... Message
The New American Standard .... NAS
The New English Bible .... NEB
The Jerusalem Bible .... TJB
The New King James .... NKJ
The Amplified New Testament .... Amplified
The New Testament .... Berkeley
The New Testament .... Good News or GN
The New Testament .... Wuest

Hymns of Truth and Praise
The Hymnal for Worship and Celebration
Choice Sacred Songs

Notes

Notes

TO ORDER BOOKS

in Canada

Centre for World Mission
Box 2436
Abbotsford, B.C. V2T 4X3

in the United States

Dick Renich
ACW Press Distribution
5501 N. 7th Ave. #502
Phoenix, AZ 85013 - 1755

or

Faith Works / NBN
15200 Faith Works / NBN Way
Blue Ridge Summit, PA 19214

Dr. June M. Temple

O Come, Let Us Adore Him!

Художник *С. Журий*
Компьютерная верстка *Л. Даниловцевой*

ЛР № 01234 от 17.03.2000
Подписано в печать 27.06.2003. Формат 60x88 $^1/_{16}$.
Бумага офсетная. Гарнитура Гарамонд.
Печать офсетная. Физ. печ. л. 25
Тираж 1000 экз. Заказ 941

Миссия евангельских христиан «Шандал»
197198, Россия, Санкт-Петербург, а/я 614
E-mail: mission@shandal.ru
www.shandal.ru

Отпечатано с готовых диапозитивов
в Академической типографии «Наука» РАН
199034, Санкт-Петербург, 9 линия, 12